Romance Writing

Published

Roger Luckhurst, Science Fiction
Lynne Pearce, Romance Writing
Charles Rzepka, Detective Fiction
Jason Scott-Warren, Early Modern English Literature
Andrew J. Webber, The European Avant-garde
Tim Whitmarsh, Ancient Greek Literature

Romance Writing

LYNNE PEARCE

polity

First published in 2007 by Polity Press

Polity Press
65 Bridge Street
Cambridge CB2 1UR, UK

Polity Press
350 Main Street
Malden, MA 02148, USA

ISBN-10: 0-7456-3004-9
ISBN-13: 978-07456-3004-5
ISBN-10: 0-7456-3005-7 (pb)
ISBN-13: 978-07456-3005-2 (pb)

A catalogue record for this book is available from the British Library.

Typeset in 11.25 on 13 pt Dante
by SNP Best-set Typesetter Ltd, Hong Kong
Printed and bound in Great Britain by MPG Books Ltd, Bodmin, Cornwall

The publisher has used its best endeavours to ensure that the URLs for external websites referred to in this book are correct and active at the time of going to press. However, the publisher has no responsibility for the websites and can make no guarantee that a site will remain live or that the content is or will remain appropriate.

Every effort has been made to trace all copyright holders, but if any have been inadvertently overlooked the publishers will be pleased to include any necessary credits in any subsequent reprint or edition.

For further information on Polity, visit our website: www.polity.co.uk

To the musician and writer
NICK CAVE

Jan van Eyck, *The Marriage of Giovanni Arnolfini and Giovanna Cenami* (1434)

Contents

Acknowledgements

Although this book has been written largely during the past twelve months, the ideas informing it have been at least ten years in the making, and many friends and colleagues have contributed to their evolution in different ways. My first acknowledgement, however, must be to the institutions and agencies that have sponsored me, namely: the Arts and Humanities Research Council (AHRC) for granting me the research leave to complete the writing; the University of Lancaster – and in particular the Department of English & Creative Writing – for the period of sabbatical leave that was attached to this; and Polity Press for commissioning the project. My two editors at Polity, Sally-Ann Spencer and Andrea Drugan, are amongst the best I have worked with: thank you for your enthusiasm, guidance and (prompt) practical support. Thanks also to Catherine Clay for helping me with the index, and to Justin Dyer, who has been an outstanding copy-editor.

The project has also benefited greatly from the publication, in 2004, of the Blackwell *Companion to Romance*, and I would like to offer special thanks to its editor, Corinne Saunders (Durham University), for her personal interest in my work and for organizing the panel at the 2002 European Society for Studies in English (ESSE) conference (Strasbourg) which first alerted me to the significance of 'spectacle' across the romance genre. More recently, the comments of my anonymous readers have also been very helpful; in particular, the lead to the work of Jean-Luc Nancy.

Several colleagues from Lancaster read versions of the book in draft form, and I am indebted to their collective insight and direction. My first acknowledgement in this regard must be to Hilary Hinds for her invaluable scrutiny of four of the chapters and, in particular, the restraining hand she laid on my 'treatment' of Jane Austen. I fear that not *all* my polemic has been excised in that regard, but the book as a whole has certainly benefited from her judicious advice. Many thanks, too, to Arthur Bradley, Catherine Clay, Lee Horsley and Jackie Stacey, who commented on individual chapters, and to Fred Botting and Scott Wilson for their contributions *vis-à-vis* the Gothic and Lacan, respectively. Robert Appelbaum, Tess Cosslett, Catherine Spooner and Jayne Steel also made helpful suggestions for further reading in terms of historical contextualization.

On a more personal note, I should like to thank everyone in 'The Robin's Nest' tearoom in Taynuilt for keeping me company during my writerly retreat: in particular, Mairead and Murray Sim (for supplying the coffee and scones), and Anne and Roy Bowers for their sound advice on what not to do (and when) with my computer. Viv Tabner, meanwhile, has sustained me with her good humour and optimism throughout, as well as a never-ending supply of new music.

My final thanks, on this occasion, go to the musician and writer Nick Cave, to whom this book is dedicated. For me, Cave's love songs are a spectacular – and unflinching – monument to romantic love in all its beauty and terror.

The frontispiece, Jan van Eyck's *The Marriage of Giovanni Arnolfini and Giovanna Cenami* (1434), is reproduced by kind permission of the Trustees of the National Gallery, London/CORBIS. Lyrics from Nick Cave's 'The Train Song' are reproduced by kind permission of Mute Song and Penguin Books.

Preface

The cover illustration to this volume depicts a pair of star-crossed lovers, Paolo and Francesca, floating entwined – and for ever – amidst the fires of hell. Their story, which is told in Book V of Dante's *Inferno* (1984 [c. 1308–14]), may be read as a warning against not only adultery (Paolo is Francesca's brother-in-law) but also the all-consuming nature of romantic love in general; their wish – 'never to be parted' – was, after all, innocent enough in prospect; their 'crime' merely their failure to heed its consequence. Although the story of Paolo and Francesca has its origins way back in the early Middle Ages, its tragic trajectory arcs across the centuries. Indeed, for Denis de Rougemont (1983 [1940]), it is the fate of another pair of adulterous lovers – Tristan and Iseult – that has *defined* 'love in the Western world' (the title of his book) over the past seven centuries; social and cultural context may change, but the architectonics of this – necessarily tragic – love story lies behind all subsequent re-scriptings.

Whilst de Rougemont's universalizing of romantic love is tied to a persuasive psychoanalytic thesis, the gauntlet it throws down to a project such as this – with a remit to chart *change* rather than continuity across the centuries – is considerable. Indeed, it is a challenge that goes to the heart of the paradox I have been forced to grapple with in the writing of this book: namely, the fact that romantic love is a discourse that *proclaims* itself universal and inescapable, yet is anything but. As several theorists and commentators cited in this book propose, there are other – safer, saner – ways of 'doing' love than to do it 'romantically'; yet what too many of us know, and what the literature surveyed in the pages which follow will surely attest, is that the adventure, thrill, abandonment and spectacle associated with romantic love in its unreconstructed form is a drug that is hard to quit. In writing about this discourse, I have therefore found myself treading the awkward tightrope of wanting to acknowledge its claims to universality at an experiential level (however illusory that universalism may be), at the same time as never letting slip its status as an ideology: a course that Roland Barthes negotiated with such canniness in *A Lover's Discourse* (1990 [1977]).

Another – not unrelated – tightrope is the one that connects – yet simultaneously divides – the discourse of love from the discourse of the erotic and, indeed, psycho-sexual explanations of interpersonal relations. Although it is impossible to write about writings on love without also writing about 'desire', they trade in different values and tell different stories. Thus, while several of the textual readings I perform here draw upon psychoanalysis, others don't, and my rationale has been to respond to, and evaluate, the texts concerned on their own intellectual and discursive terms.

A word more needs to be said about my textual rationale generally. First, there is no escaping the fact that this is a cultural history of romantic love and its associated literary genre centred firmly on Britain and Europe (the cultural-historical territory that was first staked out so brilliantly by Denis de Rougemont). The literary history I survey in the first part of each chapter is, for the most part, mainstream and canonical, whilst the texts I subject to a close reading in the second section have been chosen largely because they are works I know well and, through them, I can pursue to best effect the theory and methodology I set up in Chapter 1. This means that they are indicative, rather than representative, with the intention that readers may subsequently bring my hypothesis to bear on their own reading. It will also be noted that all the texts upon which I perform these close readings are by women; a happenstance that I *could* defend ideologically with the long-accepted argument that romance is, after all, a 'woman's genre', but which is – once again – more to do with my familiarity with these particular authors. Male authors *do* feature elsewhere in the chapters, and to mitigate any perceived bias it might help if I declare that – in the realm of contemporary fiction – I find much more with which to identify and to admire in the writing of Nick Hornby than in that of Helen Fielding. Indeed (as will be seen as early as Chapter 2), the gendering of romance – and its readers – was never a simple matter. A further, very visible bias will be the book's whiteness and, once again, I would prefer to declare my hand rather than make excuses. Whilst Chapters 6 and 7 do deal with a fair selection of texts by black and postcolonial authors, there is no question that a further book is waiting to be written on the complex relationship that exists between different races and cultures and romantic love in its white, Western specificity. In addition – and as de Rougemont himself acknowledged in 1940 – there are also books to be written which draw on other histories and cultures in order to make visible different kinds of *non-romantic* interpersonal love (and hence put into perspective the specificity of the one we are dealing with here). It should also be noted that the purpose of the third section of each chapter is to introduce readers to a selection of texts which provide a point of contrast to that considered in the close reading, and to extend the literary-historical overview begun in the first.

This brings us to the question of how, faced with the challenging remit of being asked to write a cultural history of romance in 90,000 words, I conceived a way of producing something other than a very superficial, very inadequate, survey. Although this is something I discuss at some length at the end of Chapter 1, here I would simply advise readers that my task was helped considerably by the realization – quite early on in the project – that although romance *as a genre* is reasonably well represented in literary history, the role and representation of romantic love (the emotion, the discourse, the dynamic) *within* the genre – outwith Mills & Boon-type popular romance – has been surprisingly underplayed. Keeping my eye firmly fixed on the discourse-within-the-genre has thus helped me focus my analysis enormously, and readers should therefore be advised that when I use the terms 'romantic love' (meaning the discourse) and 'romance' (meaning the romance *genre*) I do so advisedly; they articulate with one another, yes, but they are not interchangeable. The focus of my project has also been helped by the fact that, from the start, I set myself a very clear research question: namely, how, and to what extent, has romantic love (in the Western world) changed over the past five centuries, and how have these changes been registered and (re)produced by literary romance? The means – indeed, the 'method' – I came up with to answer this question is the subject of Chapter 1, but I don't think I shall give too much away if I observe that probably the *only* way a conceit that aspires to transhistorical universality can be meaningfully linked to its cultural–historical moment is through its 'supplementary benefits': what else it gives the lover *besides* love, in other words.

Thus having sampled – in the preceding paragraph – something of the philosophical and political challenge we face when thinking, and reading, about love, readers will be pleased to learn that – in the history of *literature* – the complexity is more often than not packaged as a story. 'Romance' and 'narrative' have, indeed, always gone hand-in-hand, and something else that became obvious to me as soon as I began working in the field was the fact that what romantic love (the emotion, the discourse) seeks to conceal, romance (the genre) *reveals* through its wonderful and spectacular stories. 'Spectacle', indeed – like 'adventure', 'surprise' and 'obstacle' –, is a conceit so intrinsic to romance writing from the Middle Ages onwards that, in the pages that follow, it serves as a constant reminder for why romance and literature need each other so much. Whatever pain and suffering romantic love may cause us to endure as the subjects of its ideology, there is, at least, the glorious consolation of its manufacture into art: the stories that, by some miracle, convince us of its beauty.

Historical Context: Suggestions for Further Reading

On the suggestion of one of my readers, I list below some texts that those unfamiliar with the earlier historical periods covered by this book may find useful:

- Barry Coward 1994: *The Stuart Age 1603–1714*. 2nd edn. London: Longman.
- Christopher Hill 2001 [1961]: *The Century of Revolution 1603–1714*. London and New York: Routledge.
- Anne Laurence 1994: *Women in England 1500–1700: A Social History*. London: Weidenfeld and Nicolson.
- Roy Porter 2001: *Enlightenment: Britain and the Creation of the Modern World*. London: Penguin.
- Matthew Sweet 2002: *Inventing the Victorians*. London: Faber and Faber.
- Keith Wrightson 1982: *English Society 1580–1680*. London: Hutchinson.

Scholarly texts dealing specifically with love, marriage and the family across the centuries are cited in the relevant chapters.

Lynne Pearce
June 2006

1

Introduction

The Alchemy of Love

In the interest of getting this book off to a suitably impassioned start, I begin with the proposition that romantic love is the most singular, and most singularly devastating, emotion visited upon humankind. 'Losing our heart' to another is, indeed, the (traumatic) experience that most defines us: that eradicates, in an instant, the subjects we once were and reincarnates us in another guise.[1] From that fateful moment on, who we are is defined in part by the being we love, even though s/he is no longer what s/he was either. The first access of desire transforms the beloved even as it transforms us in the manner of the following equation: $x + y \rightarrow x' + y'$. This, at least, is one hypothesis.

The fact that, in the course of my reading for this project, I was seduced into devising my own model of romantic love tells us everything about the discourse *as a discourse*. Because, for most of us, romantic love is the most ecstatic *and* traumatic event we are likely to suffer, it is hardly surprising that we should seek an explanation; more, that we should desire this explanation to be *the* explanation. Just witness the obsessive, even biblical, fervour of so many of the texts/authors that have taken on the subject.[2] Western civilization, in particular, has been apparently hell-bent on discovering a universal explanation for this most lawless of emotions;[3] and this, in turn, has resulted in the widely held belief that romantic love is the same everywhere: transhistorical, transcultural and terrifyingly omnipotent. Such a view has certainly been prevalent in the literatures and philosophies of the Western world since the time of Shakespeare, and the coupling of love with *desire* post-Freud has provided the contemporary world with further universalist models to account for the most involuntary and/or irrational of human impulses.

A moment's reflection should, however, cause even then the most evangelical amongst us to accept that there is room for more than one theory of romantic love; more, that the different theories must, themselves, be seen to correspond to cultural–historical discourses that in turn create, recreate and sustain different experiences of romantic love. This is why philosophy, literature and the arts in general play such a vital role in the (re)production of love. However unique and earth-shattering the condition of falling in love continues to be for the individual concerned, common-sense thus also tells us that it is not. The touch-papers that light the fuse that *causes x* to combust when s/he first meets y lie scattered all about us. It is just that for the individual concerned they remain, necessarily, invisible.

'Spectacular Spectacular'[4]

The invisible, occluded or darkly hidden nature of romantic love is, indeed, one of its most defining characteristics.[5] As an emotion that is probably best understood as a heady cocktail of psychic drives, cultural discourses and social constraints, it is experienced by its subjects as a traumatic 'impossibility' that is worse than irrational. Sexual desire, as psychoanalysis has shown us, positions individuals at the centre of a host of competing drives – some 'permitted' by the ego, some not – whilst the (various) cultural and social conventions which inform the emotion at the level of discourse add to the confusion.

Yet the fact that the conditions of 'falling in love' and 'being in love' are, by definition, so confused, contradictory and perverse as to render them inchoate and invisible to their subject is hardly borne out in our literature and culture. Indeed, the texts and discourses that have produced, and reproduced, our most popular versions of romantic love in the West over the last nine centuries have rendered the phenomenon not only visible but visibly *spectacular*: spectacular in its joy, spectacular in its grief, spectacular in its challenges and ordeals, spectacular in its transformative effect (on both the amorous subject *and* his/her world). Linked to this making visible of the 'great unspeakable' is, of course, romance's recourse to narrative. As I discuss below, taming love by turning it into a story is the oldest of the 'deep structures' used to make (artificial) sense of its complexity, not least in accounting for the apparently irrational behaviour of the beloved (such as hostility, faithlessness, disappearance). For the historical period covered by this book, at least – that is, the seventeenth century to the present –, we (as historical subjects) have been understandably reluctant to regard the hurtful behaviour of our beloveds as an indication that we, for whatever reason, are no longer the primary object of their affection/attention and have invented no end of stories to account for it. Indeed, interludes of misunderstanding, separation and enforced absence have been *endemic* to romance narrative ever since the texts of Arthurian legend. The traumatic, invisible moment of rejection experienced by most lovers at some point in their relationships is thus converted into a spectacular adventure with a happy ending. Indeed, so intrinsic is this resolution to romance-as-we-know-it that Denis de Rougemont (1983 [1940]) elected to turn the formula on its head and search for theories that explain romantic love as *a quest for* (spectacular) *obstacles*. The resulting (and equally spectacular) *love story* is certainly what has most commonly come to be understood by the term 'romance'.

What thus emerges from this opening discussion is a manifestation of what I consider to be one of the most crucial points of distinction for a book attempting a 'cultural history' of romance: namely, the distinction between *romantic love, the discourse* and emotion, and *romance, the genre*. Indeed, what the condition of being in love *conceals*, romance – I would contend – *reveals*. And the fact that what it reveals is not the messy 'truth' of the condition but its spectacular, fantastical 'other' is the reason it provides us – as readers and as subjects – with such limitless pleasure; why it inclines us, moreover, to 'fall in love' ourselves and to produce stories every bit as spectacular, fantastical and pleasurable to account for the traumatic moment that has seemingly redefined us.

The Deep Structures of Romance

Apart from clarifying the distinction between the human condition and the genre when speaking about romance, we need also to attend to the major tension that exists between texts/theories that proclaim love a truly universal (transhistorical, transcultural) phenomenon and those that argue for its specificity. As someone deeply persuaded by many of the structuralist, poststructuralist and psychoanalytic accounts of romantic love, I found the remit to write its 'cultural history' a severe personal challenge. Notwithstanding the fact that I could, if I chose, interpret the brief simply as an invitation to write a straightforward 'literary history', I still had grave doubts about my ability to make the romance texts of the eighteenth century look very different to those from the twentieth century. Later in this chapter I shall explain the hypothesis, and methodology, I eventually devised to solve this problem, but turn first to an overview and interrogation of some of the deep structures themselves. As will be seen, all three groups of thinkers are driven by a desire to understand the causes, patterns and mechanisms of romantic love, and all strive for a definitive solution. This, as I implied in my opening remarks, is hardly surprising. Because love hails, and seizes, each individual in such a defining way, it somehow deserves a defining explanation.

The Philosophical Tradition

In terms of the history of *Western* thought, the first great battles over the meaning, and mechanisms, of love were fought out by classical and church philosophers: in particular, Plato, Aristotle, Capellanus, St Paul and St Augustine. During, and after, the Enlightenment, Descartes, Hegel, Hume, Rousseau and Nietzsche all pitched into the debates, whilst in the twentieth century a wide spectrum of philosophers continued to investigate the condition within the terms of their own discipline. Within the Anglo-American tradition these included Bayley (*The Character of Love*, 1963), Fromm (*The Art of Loving*, 1974), Singer (*The Nature of Love*, 1984–7) and Soble (*The Structure of Love*, 1990); whilst continental philosophy, often in more open dialogue with psychoanalysis, has featured significant contributions from Sartre (*Being and Nothingness*, 1956 [1943]), Barthes (*A Lover's Discourse*, 1990 [1977]), Levinas (*Totality and Infinity*, 1969 [1961]), Foucault (*The Care of the Self*, 1988 [1984]) and Nancy (*The Inoperative Community*, 1991). Despite the desire to achieve a single, universal definition of love, it is striking how many of these texts describe the perverse, contradictory and seemingly irrational nature of romantic love *before* attempting to reduce it to an equation or bend it to a rule of logic. Long before the days of psychonalysis, Henri de Montherlant, for example, observed: 'We like someone *because* . . . we love someone *although*' (in Soble 1990: 163). Indeed, the problem with romantic love is that it is an emotion that is not causally engendered in any obvious way: not only is it difficult to explain 'why' we fell in love with *x* and not with *y*, but also why we continue to love them when (for example) they treat us badly.

At the heart of classical, and subsequent, debates over the meaning and mechanism of love is the distinction between Eros and Agape. These models have been seized upon by different philosophers in the pursuit of very different arguments, but some of the most frequently invoked dualisms are shown in Table 1.1. As with all dualist thinking, there are huge philosophical problems with this set of oppositions. The pairings I have produced here are derived from a number of philosophical texts which invoke Eros and Agape in their quest for a definition of love, but it is very striking that all depend upon the promotion of some pairs and the suppression of others. This is because the contradictions are intense. A philosopher (like Alan Soble) focusing on the question of whether love is 'property-based' or not pursues a very materialist analysis of erosic love,[6] whilst Denis de Rougemont, whose hypothesis understands romantic love as a sublimated death-drive, focuses on its transcendent, 'heaven-bound'

Table 1.1 *The dualistic model of erosic/agapic love*

Eros	Agape
Love of individual	Love of God/neighbour(s)
Based on personal properties	Involuntary/unconditional
Object-centred	Subject-centred
Repeatable	Non-repeatable
Definite	Infinite
Rational	Irrational
Bodily	Spiritual
Heaven-bound	Heaven-present

intentions. Inasmuch as most subsequent discourses of romantic love would seem to mix and appropriate aspects of both Eros and Agape, there is also a good deal of philosophical gripe about 'misappropriation'. Soble, for example, berates Stendhal, Barthes and Singer for conceiving of romantic love agapically and hence fudging the importance of personal properties in causing individuals to fall in love with one another. My own solution to the Eros–Agape problem is encapsulated in the equation with which I opened this chapter ($x + y \rightarrow x' + y'$). Although deliberately tongue-in-cheek (how *can* love possibly be reduced to a single equation?), it allows for the possibility of romantic love *beginning* erosically (x is arrested/seized by some attractive quality in y) and then *becoming* agapic (x now loves y in the involuntary/unconditional way in which one might love God). Although Soble considers this possibility briefly at the beginning of his book ('Personal love, some have argued, can succeed (or be genuine) only if it is "agapized"' (Soble 1990: 5)), it is only to contest it: 'Much of the book defends the eros tradition (or "erosic" love) and argues that the agape tradition may succumb to similar tangles and objections when it is used to characterize personal love' (5). What Soble should possibly have clarified at this point, however, is the difference between his objective (a definition of '*personal* love') and that of many of those he argues against (including de Rougemont and Barthes) who are focused specifically on '*romantic* love'. As he himself concedes a little later, the *discourse* of romantic love is very obviously inscribed by both traditions (even if that is a mixing based on philosophical error and/or confusion):

> Romantic love is a special case. Because romantic love is often seen as a
> historical development of courtly love, it may fall within the eros tradition
> and have the features of the first view of personal love: powerful passion

for the object is generated by an accurate perception of its goodness or beauty, and the lover realizes that these properties are responsible for the passion. But romantic love may also exhibit features of the second view: it arises (and disappears) mysteriously, incomprehensibly; the lover is not always expected to have reasons for his or her passion; and the lover is only under an illusion that the beloved has attractive properties. (Soble 1990: 15–16)

Soble's philosophical resolution to the question of whether romantic love is more properly thought of as erosic or agapic depends upon 'the relationship between the illusion and x's loving': 'If x's loving y leads x to the illusion that y has P, the romantic love is agapic; but if x has the illusion that y has P and, on the basis of this falsely attributed property, x loves y, then it is erosic' (Soble 1990: 16). What this formula does not allow for is the possibility of *x* being precipitated into love by *y*'s properties and *then* succumbing to the illusion. This last remains my own preferred model: not only because I fail to see the necessity of defining romantic love purely in terms of its first cause, but – even more importantly – because the *movement* from Eros to Agape endorses the notion that it is a profoundly *transformative* experience.[7] As I proposed at the beginning of the chapter, love transforms both the lover and the beloved through a complex relay of desire, illusion and (to invoke Freud) hallucination. Thus whilst philosophers can – and probably will – continue to debate whether *personal* love is erosic or agapic, it seems infinitely more suggestive to conceive of *romantic* love as a hybrid; moreover, to allow that its tendency towards Eros or Agape will shift from author to author, discourse to discourse, century to century *and* in response to official and oppositional ideologies. The romantic love endorsed by the Christian church (and the institution of marriage) may, for example, be seen to tend towards the erosic pole whilst the discourses of Courtly Love and Romantic Friendship are instinctively agapic.

Leaving aside the problem of 'first causes', the defining characteristics of love unleashed in the Eros/Agape debate deserve further discussion – not least because we shall encounter them repeatedly in the chapters that follow. Table 1.2 lists some of the 'first principles' of love that recur in the works of the philosophers.

Placed alongside the dualistic model of erosic and agapic love presented earlier, readers should have little trouble working out which of the two poles these 'first principles' more naturally adhere to; they will also be familiar with a number of these conceits via the clichés and sayings associated with romantic love that have circulated for centuries: for example, 'Love is for ever'/'No love lasts for ever'; 'You and no other'; 'I love you

Table 1.2 *The first principles of love*

- Love is inspired by beauty or other admirable qualities
- All loved creatures are beautiful
- Love is constant
- Love is exclusive
- Love is reciprocal
- Love entails concern for the other (possibly above concern for oneself)
- Love entails sacrifice for the other
- Love bestows value on the beloved without calculation
- Love is non-repeatable
- Love seeks the reunion of the separated
- Love is consequent upon the satisfaction of desire
- Love is unsatisfied desire
- Love is irrational
- Love is unconditional
- Love is mutual
- Love is a universal/existential condition

---

not for what you are, but in spite of what you are'; 'Beauty lies in the eye of the beholder'; 'You and me against the world'; 'Better to have loved and lost than never to have loved at all'. Indeed, the fact that such pronouncements have survived so long would seem to attest to their experiential truth-value. Pursuing the deeper philosophical implications of some of these principles also offers an invaluable insight into how love has been *made* to 'mean differently' across history, however; how, in particular, it has been possible for 'first principles' to become 'last principles' in the interests of ideology and politics. The two that I have chosen to elaborate here (for reason of their relevance to the textual analyses that follow) are: 'concern for the other' and 'exclusivity'.

Concern for the other

For most philosophers, the value/esteem/well-being of the beloved presents itself as a key feature of love, though there is no consensus that it should be considered a *defining* characteristic. In the case of romantic love, in particular, it can easily be argued that (sexual) desire to possess the beloved necessarily outweighs any concern for his or her well-being. Some commentators would, however, counter this with the argument that such 'selfish' desire is more properly thought of as lust, not love; moreover, that the *desire* of 'authentic' romantic love is a desire *to give* as well as *to take*. In the Courtly Love tradition, indeed, the desire is *predominantly* one of giving and not taking.

In the course of this volume we will necessarily encounter texts which feature both types of lover: those whose love is defined primarily by their desire to possess, and those who 'love-to-give'. Moreover, although there are fairly obvious social and cultural factors at work here (for example, male lovers are traditionally the takers, females the givers), the dominant ideological model of romance operating at any given time will have a significant bearing, too. For example, the Victorian era – renowned for its potent mixing of the Gothic and Courtly Love traditions – may be seen to favour a version of love which turns (passionately, even hysterically) upon devotion to the other, whilst the consumerist, self-interested cultures and discourses of the twentieth century may be seen to re-fashion it in terms of solipsistic desire and satisfaction (see Chapter 7). Indeed, the psychologist Eric Fromm has argued that the (erosic) 'property-based' model of personal love chimes perfectly – if depressingly – with contemporary consumerist behaviour in general (Soble 1990: 102). The difficulty, of course (as will be debated *vis-à-vis* the concept of 'the Gift' below), is how to distinguish whether concern for the other and/or a desire to benefit the other is *ever* truly free of self-interest.

Leaving temporarily aside the issue of motive, however, I would argue strongly that romantic love *is* frequently characterized by a profound need/desire to benefit the other. From the period of Courtly Love on, romantic love discourse conceives of the emotion as a *passionate outpouring* wherein the lover fervently desires to sacrifice him- or herself to the service and well-being of the other. Psychoanalytic theory can easily interpret this as the subject's need/desire to dissolve/transcend his or her own ego, of course, but the impulse is experienced by both the lover and his/her beloved as an *outward motion*. Indeed, this sense of love as a *movement* from *x* to *y* is implicit in Descartes's definition: 'Love is an emotion of the soul caused by a movement of the spirit, which impels the soul to join itself willingly to objects that appear agreeable to it' (in Soble 1990: 1); and it is also central to Nancy's (1991) account of the 'shattering' of the self in love, as we shall see below.

However the idea may be undermined by philosophy and psychology, then, the notion that love – including romantic love – is impelled, and defined, in part by a desire to put the needs/interests of the beloved first remains a powerful one. Yet whether it is any more defining than the notionally selfish demand-satisfaction model cited above remains a moot point. As Soble reminds us, 'nasty' (jealous, selfish) lovers are also lovers (Soble 1990: 100); indeed, in the history of Western literature, they are some of the best-remembered ones.

Exclusivity

As noted above, 'you and no other' is a cry that reverberates through the centuries as one of the most passionately held 'first principles' of romantic love. It is, of course, also a vow that is habitually broken when relationships fail and erstwhile lovers discover that they *can* love again. Even Barthes, whose *Lover's Discourse* plumbs the depths of exclusive passion, concedes this eventual possibility ('I begin again without repeating' (Barthes 1990: 198)). The *literature* of romance most often stops short of this tawdry recycling, however, and prefers (as in popular fiction) to limit its narrative to the moment of (first) consummation or to have its lovers die (spectacularly) before their vow can be put to the test. No common-sense prognosis will, however, prevent lovers feeling – and believing in – the exclusivity and non-repeatability of their love when they first succumb to it. Indeed, it is precisely this irrational valuing of the beloved over all others on the grounds of his/her uniqueness that distinguishes romantic love from other models of personal love. It is also a view that has been endorsed by philosophers like Brown who cite the death/loss of the beloved as the consummate 'test' of love ('The test of genuine love [is] that it continues after all possible use of the object merely as a means . . . ceases' (Brown, *Analysing Love*, 1987, in Soble 1990: 207)) and, of course, by Freud, who (from a psycho-sexual perspective) observes that 'people never willingly abandon a libidinal position, not even, indeed, when a substitute is already beckoning to them' (Freud 1984b [1915]: 253). Moreover, inasmuch as romantic love discourse is so inextricably entwined with the discourses of Christianity, the notion of romantic love being anything less than 'infinite' is implicitly shameful. In this regard, indeed, romantic love joins Christian love as essentially an act of *faith*, and the assured permanence/non-repeatability of love becomes a measurable *benefit* in the context of the manifestly unstable life of any relationship.

As will be noted in the discussion of Courtly Love which follows (see Chapter 2), this will-to-exclusivity may also be seen to work best when the love between *x* and *y* is unequal. This is not to say that devotion is conditional upon resistance (indeed, as I note below, most romantic love requires *some* degree of reciprocity), but the aloofness of one lover certainly facilitates the devotion of the other. One notable exception to this is, of course, the mutual passion/devotion of so-called 'Platonic lovers', whose love is explained as the recovery of their missing 'other half'. This is certainly another well-worn, and compelling, fantasy within Western romantic love discourse – and one that has been open to all manner of psychoanalytic interpretation – being distinguished, in particular, by the emphasis it places on *sameness* or *complementarity*.[8] In most popular (and some would say incorrect) readings of the Aristophanes story, what the lover is seeking is similarity rather than difference (Soble 1990: 78). This model will be especially important in explaining same-sex models of romantic love (see Chapters 5 and 6), but for the moment I wish simply to register the very real challenge involved in sustaining desire for an 'other' that continually threatens to be assimilated into the self. As I have argued elsewhere, intimacy depends, paradoxically, upon the *unfamiliarity* of the other, and this may be seen to explain why their 'uniqueness' is frequently conceived as strange, hostile or uncanny (Pearce 2006). What we desire to love exclusively, and for ever, is an other who shall ever remain distinct from – and hence desirable to – ourselves.

A contemporary French philosopher whose work on ethics and community also makes a major contribution to our understanding of romantic love is Jean-Luc Nancy. First published as part of the collection *The Inoperative Community* (1991), his essay 'Shattered Love' resonates strongly with my own conceptualization of love as radically, even irreversibly, transformative of the individuals concerned. Starting from the assertion that 'love is the extreme movement, beyond the self, of a being reaching completion' (Nancy 1991: 86), he details seven philosophical formulations of love that confer increasing power on 'the other' (y) in the process of this completion and which, in manifestations 6 and 7, entail the notional loss of the self *to the place of the other*:

> The fifth meaning would be that philosophy thinks the suppression of the self in love, and the correlative suppression of the self of love, as its ultimate truth and its final effectivity: thus, love infinitely restitutes itself beyond itself (in the final analysis, death and transfiguration . . .). The sixth meaning would be that this 'beyond the self' in which, in a very general manner, love has taken place is necessarily *the place of the other*, or of an alterity without which neither love nor completion would be possible. But the seventh meaning would nevertheless be that this 'beyond' is the place of the same, where love fulfils itself, the place of the same in the other, if love consists, in Hegel's terms, of 'having in another the moment of one's subsistence'. (Nancy 1991: 86–7)

The sixth formulation here, with its insistence on both alterity and the reformulation of the subject, corresponds closely to the terms implicit in my own $x + y \rightarrow x' + y'$ equation. Later in the essay, moreover, Nancy challenges the logic that such a movement ultimately ends in a solipsistic 'return to the self' (the seventh formulation here) by re-thinking the nature of the 'transcendence' involved. This, indeed, is where he introduces his figure of the 'broken heart' and the (liberating) 'shattering' of the self through love; through the 'event' of love, the subject is so transformed that s/he can no longer return to the self s/he was:

> ... I do not return to myself *from* love ... I do not return from it, and consequently, something of *I* is definitively lost or dissociated in its act of loving. That is undoubtedly why *I* return ... but *I* return broken: I come back to myself, or I come out of it, broken. The 'return' does not annul the break; it neither repairs it nor sublates it, for the return in fact takes place across the break itself, keeping it open. Love re-presents *I* to itself broken ... (Nancy 1991: 96)

A little later, Nancy reiterates the radical consequences of this break not only for the subject-in-love but for the subject *per se*:

> For the break is a break in his self-possession as a subject; it is, essentially, an interruption in the process of relating oneself to oneself outside of oneself. From then on, *I* is *constituted broken*. As soon as there is love, the slightest act of love, the slightest spark, there is the ontological fissure that cuts across and disconnects the elements of the subject-proper – the fibers of its heart. (Nancy 1991: 96)

Whilst, for Nancy, this observation on the fatal shattering of the self through love is only the first step in an even more ambitious refiguring of the self in relation to the community (he invokes Heidegger to argue that the condition of *Mitsein* must always precede *Dasein* (Nancy 1991: 103)), it is of particular relevance to my own inquiry into the dynamics of specifically romantic love. Indeed, his move from interpersonal to communal love-relations also touches, indirectly, upon my own investigations into the 're-direction' of love from self to world through mutual 'work'/productivity ($x + y \rightarrow x' + y' = z$) in Chapters 5 and 7. Despite its superficially negative connotations, Nancy's 'shattered heart' has extraordinarily redemptive possibilities.

The Narrative Logic of Romance

Ever since Vladimir Propp's ground-breaking work on the folktale in the 1920s it has been clear that one of the most compelling, and enduring, deep structures of romance is its narrative archetype. The film/TV mediation of romantic discourse in the twentieth century means that today, especially, love is known and experienced primarily *as a story*. In this section I present a brief overview of those theorists whose work on romance adheres to this principle, as well as suggesting why recent 'trauma theory' is useful in helping to unpack what 'the love story' conceals. Needless to say, narratives – and especially *adventure narratives* – are one of the principal means by which the 'unseen' is rendered spectacular within the history of the genre (see Chapter 2).

For all structuralist – and indeed poststructuralist – attempts to uncover the deep structures of romance, Vladimir Propp's *Morphology of the Folktale* (1986 [1928]) is the quintessential Ur-text. Through his extensive survey of hundreds of classic folk tales, Propp discovered a remarkable uniformity with respect to both character and event. This was as a result of realizing that, despite superficial variables, *all* the characters in the tales could be allocated to one of seven 'spheres of action', namely:

1. The villain
2. The donor (provider)
3. The helper
4. The princess (or sought-for object)
5. The dispatcher
6. The hero
7. The false hero (Hawkes 1977: 69)

Similarly, all the key events could be reduced to thirty-one 'functions', defined by Propp as 'an act of a character defined from the point of view of its significance from the point of view of the action' (Propp 1968: 21; Hawkes 1977: 68). These might include events such as the hero being sent on a mission, encountering a range of obstacles, doing battle with the 'villain', and securing the hand of the 'princess' in marriage. The remarkable, and fascinating, discovery at the heart of Propp's research was the fact that the number of functions in fairy tales could be limited to a specific number and that 'the *sequence* of functions is always identical' (Hawkes 1977: 69). Even more remarkable, perhaps, has been the recognition that these elements constitute the deep structure – the DNA, if you like – of most subsequent narrative fiction in the Western world. This is certainly the case with regard to the romance genre, whose 'classic' and 'popular' variants may both be seen to follow Propp's functions very closely indeed.

The first theorist to give full recognition to this fact was Janice Radway in her celebrated 1984 study, *Reading the Romance*. In this ground-breaking ethnographic study of (female) popular romance readers, Radway adapted Propp's model into her own, which she presented as 'The Narrative Logic of Romance':

1. The heroine's social identity is destroyed
2. The heroine reacts antagonistically to an aristocratic male
3. The aristocratic male responds ambiguously to the heroine
4. The heroine interprets the hero's behaviour as evidence of a purely sexual interest in her
5. The heroine responds to the hero's behaviour with anger or coldness
6. The hero retaliates by punishing the heroine
7. The hero and heroine are physically and/or emotionally separated
8. The hero treats the heroine tenderly
9. The heroine responds warmly to the hero's act of tenderness
10. The heroine re-interprets the hero's ambiguous behaviour as the result of a previous hurt
11. The hero proposes/openly declares his love for/demonstrates his unwavering commitment to the heroine with a supreme act of tenderness
12. The heroine responds sexually and emotionally
13. The heroine's identity is restored (Radway 1984: 134, 150)

For Radway, this adaptation of Propp's model tells the story of the heroine's 'transformation from an isolated, asexual, insecure adolescent who is unsure of her own identity, into a mature, sensual and very married woman who has realized her full potential and identity as the partner of a man and as an implied mother of a child' (Radway 1984: 134). The feminist implications of this narrative will be dealt with presently, but for the moment I would invite readers simply to pause and consider how *true* this template remains for popular representations of romance today. Indeed, I would contend that there are very few Hollywood romances that depart significantly from either Radway's list of functions or its associated 'spheres of action' (hero/false hero or 'foil'; heroine/ false heroine or 'foil'; 'true villain') (Radway 1984: 130–3). Although, as I have argued elsewhere, more sophisticated romances (both 'traditional' and contemporary) may *appear* to disrupt these deep structures by adding moral/emotional complexity to the characters (who, exactly, is the 'hero' and who the 'villain'?), it is usually the narrative itself that answers the question: that is, the 'hero' will always be the person who assumes *the hero's narrative function* and not simply 'the nice guy' (see Pearce 1995: 26; Pearce 1998: 14–18). It is an exemplary case of actions speaking louder than words.

The larger question I wish to consider here, however, is what these 'Ur' romance narratives conceal/reveal about romantic love itself. Why is love experienced 'as a story', and why do we need to keep telling it? I consider, briefly, three possible explanations.

Concealing male dependence

First, there is the feminist response. For Janice Radway and her followers (see also Paizis 1998 and Dixon 1999, both discussed in Chapter 6), the 'narrative logic of the romance' provides female subjects with an explanation/ consolation for the bad behaviour of their men. The fact that the crux of each love story turns upon the hero's unkind/aggressive behaviour being converted (often *without a* very convincing excuse) into love and tenderness is, according to Radway, quite reason enough why women should wish to keep hearing/reading the same story over and over again. Indeed, for Radway it is the very fact that the hero's 'bad behaviour' towards the heroine is *not* explicitly linked to his subsequent act of tenderness that accounts, paradoxically, for the stories' appeal: women/wives are supposedly consoled by the suggestion that this apparently *illogical behaviour* is in some way typical, and that they may have to wait a long time (possibly for ever) to discover what caused the cruelty:

> Although the hero's punishment of the heroine results in his separation from her, the separation is never connected explicitly *at this point in the story* with his ensuing act of kindness. Because the hero does not indicate overtly either in his thoughts or in his conversation that this separation causes him to recognize his dependence upon the heroine, function 7 [see list above] is not presented as an effective agent in the transformation of function 8. The separation simply occurs and then the hero demonstrates miraculously that he can be tender to the heroine. (Radway 1984: 148)

According to Radway, the prime ideological interest in hiding the real reasons for the hero's behaviour in this way is to avoid 'the contradiction between admission of dependency and relationality [that is, the hero was frightened by the prospect of needing/losing the heroine] and the usual definition of masculinity as total autonomy' (Radway 1984: 148). Inasmuch as Radway is working in the context of Chodorow's analysis of male–female relationships, this is a very convincing argument.[9] I would argue, however, that it is still *more of an explanation* for what is happening in these stories than is strictly necessary. Indeed, as I go on to suggest in the 'Trauma Stories' section below, it is the fact that both the hero's *and* heroine's behaviour is often so *wantonly* illogical that tells us most about why romance needs its stories.

Concealing the death-drive

For Denis de Rougemont, the concealed object of all love stories (or, at least, those stemming from the mythical stories of Tristan and Iseult) is

death. This thesis, which also takes as its starting point the mystic reconfiguration of love within the Courtly Love tradition, makes its case via a
grand sweep of Western literature and culture. It also concludes with
bold – and, for the time in which it was first published (1940), hugely
controversial – sociological claims about how the enduring popularity of
the Tristan myth may be used to explain: (a) the demise of modern marriage; and (b) humankind's predilection for war. De Rougemont writes:

> The myth that has been agitating us for eight hundred years as spell, terror,
> or ideal, is at one and the same time a passion sprung from dark nature,
> an energy excited by the mind, and a pre-established potentiality in search
> of the coercion that shall intensify it. In having shed its original guise, it
> has merely become more dangerous. (de Rougemont 1983: 23)

The notion that romantic love is a 'potentiality in search of the coercion
that shall intensify it' is certainly borne out in de Rougemont's analysis of
the Tristan myth as one in which a series of spectacular *obstacles* both 'make
the story' *and* conceal/reveal the ultimate object of the lovers' passion:

> The events narrated are but images or projections of a longing and of
> whatever runs counter to this longing, excites it, or merely protracts it.
> . . . Objectively, not one of the barriers to the fulfilment of their [i.e.,
> Tristan and Iseult's] love is insuperable, and yet each time they give up. It
> is not too much to say they never miss a chance of getting parted. When
> there is no obstruction, they invent one, as in the case of the drawn sword
> and of Tristan's marriage [to 'the other Iseult']. (de Rougemont 1983: 37)

The obstacle of Iseult's married status (she is the wife of King Mark) is, of
course, present even before Tristan makes his 'loveless' (and, according to
several versions of the myth, unconsummated) marriage to 'the other
Iseult' (often referred to as 'Iseult of the White Hand'). Indeed, it is this
insuperable social and ideological constraint that places the Tristan myth
firmly in the Courtly Love tradition.[10] Tristan and Iseult's love is defined
by its very *impossibility* in the 'real'/social world, and, as de Rougemont
observes, the story itself (Tristan's challenges and quests; the lovers' frequent partings and separations) ensures that it remains that way.

De Rougemont's explanation for the denial of satisfaction associated not
only with *Tristan* but with the whole Courtly Love tradition may be taken
in two stages: first, it is a fairly obvious means of 'converting' mortal love
into spiritual love through the experience of bodily transcendence; second,
it enables the lovers to realize (by means of their own *will*) a perfect death.
Dying for love (inasmuch as the increasing seriousness of the 'obstacles'
ends in the death of one of the lovers, or both of them) brings death back
within the subject's control and renders it beautiful: 'Passion has thus only

played the part of a purifying ordeal, it might almost be said of a penance, in the service of transfiguring death. Here we are in sight of the ultimate secret' (de Rougemont 1983: 45–6).

As well as revealing the sublimation of love-in-death, what the Tristan myth does supremely is render love *visible*. Without this almighty series of obstacles not only would there be no sublimation of love, but there would be nothing we could recognize *as love*. And this is why the literary-historical origins of romance are so profoundly bound up with the *adventure* narrative (see Chapter 2). It is not only its covert drive towards death, but *all* aspects of love that need revealing; and it is in the extravagant, often fantastical, events and landscapes of these early romances that we find the origins of so many of the images, symbols and motifs that are still the backdrop of romance today. Indeed, it is my belief that the survival of these key elements – especially the exotic (that is, stereotypically 'romantic') *locations* of romantic fiction – should be afforded far more positive significance than this (Pearce 2004: 531–4). Romantic love *needs* its stories not only in order to impose some logic on illogical desires, but also on account of their associated iconography.

The other dimension to de Rougemont's thesis that deserves brief mention is the (highly controversial) link he made between the origins of the Courtly Love tradition and heretical religions, in particular, Catharism and Tantrism. Both, in their different ways, encouraged the love of an idealized female other as a type of mystical exercise that would facilitate the lover's 'transport' from the mortal ('fallen') world to heaven. A similar principle is also at work in Platonism, where all human love (conceived under the figure of 'Eros') is seen as a stepping-stone to divine love. For Catharism and Tantrism, however, a particular emphasis is placed on self-imposed chastity. The lover, in other words, is bound both to desire his beloved and to forsake her, producing a tension that is, itself, mystical and fulfilling. Tantrism is, of course, known today primarily for its associated sexual exercises aimed at prolonging, and hence increasing the pleasure of, the sexual act, but Tantric *chastity* is fully mystical in intention: 'Tantric "chastity" thus consisted of making love without actually making it, of seeking mystical exaltation and beatitude through a *She*, who had to be "served" in a humiliating posture' (de Rougemont 1983: 117). What links de Rougemont's theory of romantic love as an expression of the death-drive with the origins of Courtly Love in these mystical religions is, therefore, a conceit that the *objective* of such love is the opposite of sexual fulfilment. Romantic love requires sex in order to prompt desire, but as soon as the desire is formed it is directed *beyond* the object of desire.

Such a rationale is certainly useful in helping to understand the mechanisms at work in many of the literary texts dealt with in the course of the book. The fact that so much (textual) romance stops short of sexual fulfilment – *for whatever reason* – is vital in helping us understand exactly *what* the lovers concerned are giving to, and receiving from, one another. Whilst I would thus hesitate to fully endorse de Rougemont's totalitarian vision (that is, *all* lovers are in pursuit of (ideal) death), it is clear that love is truly more often a means than an end. *Vis-à-vis* my own model of love's alchemy, however ($x + y \rightarrow x' + y'$), this 'transport' beyond the personal/sexual is recognized in the *transfiguration* of x and y, who are now bound to one another on account of what they have gifted one another alongside their love. For some pairs of lovers this may well be the means to a 'perfect death' (see Chapter 4), but for others – at different cultural–historical moments – it may be a more social and/or political commodity (for example, a change of status/identity; self-actualization; social liberation). This hypothesis, central to my own attempt to historicize romantic love, is developed in the subsection 'The Gift of Love' below.

Trauma stories

As I have discussed elsewhere, many fascinating connections can be made between romantic love and trauma: in particular, the use of story-telling in the treatment of trauma (Pearce 2004: 525–31). As the following discussion of the 'deep structures' of psychoanalysis will confirm, there is nothing new in thinking about love as an inherently traumatic experience, but the link between this observation and the genre's compulsion to narrative has not (as far as I am aware) been properly explored.

My hypothesis is a simple one: namely that, in the manner of trauma therapy, we turn to narrative to make first *visible* (indeed, spectacular) and then *causal* all that is essentially irrational, contradictory and *cause-less* about romantic love. In other words, the will-to-narrative in romance is first and foremost a means of putting into some sort of order the wilfully irrational psychic and sexual drives that subtend the condition, helped, it must be said, by the social and cultural forces and conventions that fundamentally distinguish *love* from *desire*.

As I noted in my earlier essay, the rhetoric(s) of trauma and romance are strikingly similar, especially *vis-à-vis* the moment of falling in love, or (in Barthes's terminology) *ravissement*. Compare, for example, these two extracts:

> Love at first sight is a hypnosis: I am fascinated by an image: at first shaken, electrified, stunned, 'paralyzed' as Menon was by Socrates, the model of

loved objects, of captivating images, or again converted by an apparition, nothing distinguishing the path of enamoration from the Road to Damascus; subsequently ensnared, held fast, immobilized, nose stuck to the image (the mirror). (Barthes 1990: 189)

While the trauma uncannily returns in actual life, its reality continues to elude the subject who lives in its grip and unwittingly undergoes its cease-less repetitions and re-enactments. The traumatic event, although real, took place outside the parameters of 'normal reality', such as causality, sequence, place and time. The trauma is thus an event that has no begin-ning, no ending, no before, no after. This absence of categories that define it, lends a quality of 'otherness', a salience, a timelessness and a ubiquity that puts it outside the range of comprehension, or recounting, and of mastery. Trauma survivors live not with memories of the past, but with an event that could not, and did not, proceed through to completion, has no ending, achieved no closure, and therefore, as far as the survivors are concerned, continues into the present and is current in every respect. (Felman and Laub 1992: 68–9)

Placed alongside one another, the traumatic nature of the first moment of falling in love becomes strikingly obvious: it is, indeed, a moment that takes place 'outside the parameters of "normal reality"', and is supremely without causality, sequence, beginning or end. The condition persists, moreover, for as long as the lover remains in the condition of first ravish-ment (some would say, for as long as s/he remains 'in love'), rendering each new meeting, and each new separation, a visceral repetition of the first trauma which is always perpetually unscrolling itself in the subject's mind. The moment of *ravissement*, then, may be seen not only as outside of time but also as outside of 'story time'. Without these temporal sign-posts, the moment of falling in love simply does not make narrative sense – and yet this is precisely what the *discourse of romance*, and the *romance genre*, attempt to bring off by making the moment of falling in love into the first episode of a story: that is, the archetypal *love story*.

Barthes himself notes this fantasy of temporal rationalization a little later in the 'Ravissement' entry:

There is a deception in amorous time (this deception is called: the love story). I believe (along with everyone else) that the amorous phenomenon is an 'episode' endowed with a beginning (love at first sight) and an end (suicide, abandonment, disaffection, withdrawal, monastery, travel, etc.). Yet the initial scene during which I was ravished is merely reconstituted: it is *after the fact*. I reconstruct a traumatic image which I experience in the present and yet which I conjugate (which I speak) in the past. (Barthes 1990:193)

Along with Barthes, then, I believe and propose that 'the love story' is an essentially artificial attempt to impose causality, temporality and coherence on an emotional event which has none of those things. For as long as the subject remains 'in love' (with all the self-abandonment and suspended animation that this necessarily entails), there is no 'story'. This is not to say, however, that we (as lovers, and as romance readers) will not conspire to create one in order to impose some causality and explanation on emotions and behaviours that are – terrifyingly – without those things (for example, the fact that s/he leaves me despite the fact s/he loves me; the fact that s/he's cruel to me despite the fact s/he loves me; the fact that s/he desires me *and* someone else (Pearce 2004: 529)). For although all such eventualities may, and do, occur in the traumatic present of love, the coincidence is felt by most subjects as an impossible contradiction. Hence our recourse to order, sequence and story: the willed illusion that these 'ob/scene' (Johnson 2007) distractions to love are merely a 'phase' with a beginning and, mercifully, an end. Indeed, it could be argued that the longevity of any romantic attachment precisely depends upon the lovers' ability to write a script that will keep the troubling demons at bay.

The Psychoanalytic Depths

It would, I think, be fair to say that psychoanalysis tells us both everything and nothing about romantic love. Inasmuch as the work of Freud and his followers (most notably, Lacan) made visible the (often perverse) function of the psycho-sexual drives, it has enabled a radical new understanding of desire; but inasmuch as (sexual) desire is only *one* element in the production/consumption of romantic love, it has its limits. Working with the assumption that romantic love is experienced by the subject as a complex interaction of psychic drives, cultural discourses and social constraints, we must acknowledge that even if psychoanalysis goes a long way to explaining why we desire who we do, when we do and how we do, this will still not account for the full complexity of the experience. Many of the 'first principles' of love discussed above are not easily accounted for by psychoanalysis, for example; and the social/cultural face of love – its sexual politics, its institutions, its spiritual aspirations – means that it must always be distinguished from the operations of desire *per se*. Indeed, as we have already seen, many of the most popular discourses of romantic love enjoy an extremely complex, often contradictory, relationship to sexual desire (or, at least, its consummation).

Yet desire as it has been construed by psychoanalysis is, itself, one of the most perverse and contradictory conditions known to humankind. For Freud, its perversity lay primarily in the discovery that all individuals are destined to re-enact the needs and frustrations of their early childhood relationships (the Oedipus and Electra complexes) and only with considerable effort (and the successful operation of the superego) move on to successful 'mature' relationships with members of the opposite sex (Freud 1986 [1905–33]: 269–411). Freud was also the first theorist to realize the crucial importance of *idealization* and, indeed, *narcissism* in the creation of the love-object and thus begin to explain both the compulsive nature and ultimate 'impossibility' of romantic love (Freud 1984a [1914]). This idealization, moreover, requires the imposition of *obstacles* to enhance its desirability: 'An obstacle is required in order to heighten the libido and where natural resistances to satisfaction have not been sufficient, men [*sic*] have at all times erected conventional ones so as to be able to enjoy love' (Freud 1977b [1912]: 256–7).

As Stacey and Pearce note in the introduction to *Romance Revisited*, this requirement points to close interconnection between the psycho-sexual drive and the 'cultural production of romance' *vis-à-vis* the *narrative* construction of barriers: 'This process of "erecting" obstacles (to ensure delayed gratification) makes the other person special, unattainable, or "ideal", in so far as their status grows proportionally to the difficulty of attainment. A central characteristic of romantic love, then, is *idealisation*: the overvaluation of the love object (as in the phrase "love blinds")' (Stacey and Pearce 1995: 29). Stacey and Pearce also observe that, 'despite the cultural association of romance with femininity . . . Freudian psychoanalysis highlights the tendency for *men* to idealize their love objects' (Stacey and Pearce 1995: 29). There is certainly plenty of evidence of this bias in the literary-historical productions of romantic love (de Rougemont himself concedes that the history of Courtly Love has been written almost entirely from the point of view of male experience). Feminist psychoanalytic theorists (see Juliet Mitchell (1974), Rose (1986), Wright (1984)) have, however, found the deep structures of Freud's analysis of love and desire to be germane to both men and women, not least because both sexes may be seen to be on an impossible quest to replace their 'original' – and now lost – 'object of desire' ('an endless series of substitute objects none of which, however, brings full satisfaction' (Freud 1977b: 258)). However, in advance of the discussions that ensue, it is worth noting that whilst Freud's analysis offers an explanation of why x may initially fall in love with y (that is, correspondence to an overt/covert parental template), it does not account for the way in which the template is transfigured through the other person to become its own unique (and irreplaceable) 'ideal object'. As I have already signalled, replacing this hybridized image-repertoire is notionally harder than replacing the original, lost love-object.

Freud's insights into the fundamental insatiability (and hence impossibility) of desire are taken even further in Lacan's work. Apart from the additional layers of complexity afforded by Lacan's focus on the role of language in the constitution of the subject, his identification of narcissism as fundamental to subject formation (through the operation of the Imaginary) proposes that the 'lost' object of desire is effectively an irrevocable 'fantasy' version of the self (Lacan 1988 [1975], cited in Wright 1992: 272).[11] Moreover, many feminist readings of Lacan have noted how this 'lost object' is subsequently 'symbolized by woman, who can never be represented in patriarchal language as anything other than "lack"' (Stacey and Pearce 1995: 30; Belsey 1994: 57–8). This formula also neatly accounts for the role of the female subject in the Courtly Love tradition. As Jacqueline Rose has observed: '[Courtly Love is] the elevation of the woman into the place where her absence or inaccessibility stands in for male lack' (Rose 1986: 72; Belsey 1994: 98–101).

Apart from accounting for some of the more perverse reflexes of sexual desire, however, Lacan's theory is also instrumental in helping us understand why its endless deferral/non-satisfaction is nevertheless experienced as *pleasure*. At the heart of his theory is the message that desire, for all its constituent insatiability, is a fundamentally 'good' and healthy thing; it is, on the contrary, *the repression of desire that makes us sick*.[12] Acceptance of this point is, I would suggest, crucial to a positive reception not only of Lacan's theories but also of many of the discourses and scenarios considered in this book. Inasmuch as it clearly *is* the product of (psychic) fantasy and ideology, romantic love will, for many, continue to be regarded as a harmful 'illusion' that is visited upon its unfortunate subjects as a kind of madness (see Langford 2002). What psychoanalysis has taught us is that love – or, at least, desire – is nevertheless a madness that we cannot live without: an ego without an 'ideal object' is liable to entropy and, unless it can narcissistically discover a version of the self who will fulfil that role, or successfully replace it with a material fetish, or with God, it is doomed to much unhappiness. Whatever desire is or is not, it is clearly a *relational* function: a conclusion that concurs with Descartes's conception of love as an 'outward motion' (Soble 1990: 1) and with Nancy's as 'an incessant coming-and-going' (Nancy 1991: 98). Without that outward motion of the self, or soul, towards another, the ego's relation to *everything* outside itself is liable to fail.

More recently, Queer theorists such as Judith Butler (1990, 1993) and Eve Kosofsky Sedgwick (1985, 1993) have worked both with, and against, psychoanalysis in their assault on the orthodoxies that shore up more normative accounts of sex, sexuality and gender. The extent to which the radical re-thinking of the latter in terms of performance, imitation, repetition and masquerade has also impacted upon the figuring of romantic love *per se* is, however, more difficult to ascertain (see Pearce and Wisker 1998). Whilst both Butler and Sedgwick perform several memorable queer readings of texts which are also love stories – for example, Sedgwick's reading of James's *The Wings of the Dove* in *Tendencies* (Sedgwick 1993) and Butler's of Cather's 'Tommy the Sentimental' (Butler 1993) –, their deconstructions are focused on gender, sexuality and sexual identity rather than the condition of being in love. Indeed, as I have noted in my analysis of Butler's reading of Cather (see Pearce 2004: 189), what is inevitably lost in the queering of a canonical text – and this is not intended as a criticism – is its humanist rationale; and this, for better or worse, is where its love-interest will most commonly reside. Thus, whilst Butler's explanation of Tommy's perverse, final rejection of Jessica (whom she clearly adores) is fully persuasive in terms of her conflicted sexuality, it fails to account for the excess of unresolved *emotion* with which the story ends. With its focus on the *unconscious* desires that shape sexuality both personally and institutionally, much Queer theory will – inevitably – ride rough-shod over an ideology as *consciously* scripted as romantic love. Ideally, however, readers and critics need to find ways of tackling the pervasiveness of the one within the other. As will be seen in Chapter 7, many of our most successful postmodernist writers who are also branded 'queer' – such as Jeanette Winterson and Hanif Kureishi – produce fiction which deconstructs sexuality at the same time that it clings to romantic love in its most unreconstructed forms. This is not to deny that a writer like Kureishi creates scenarios in which romantic love begins to 'mean' differently (see again Chapter 7), but this re-scripting is only loosely articulated with the queering of sexual and racial identity also performed by his novels. In the case of *The Buddha of Suburbia* (1990), for example, Karim can rightly be seen to occupy a very queer *subject* position (Oswell 1998: 161), and yet his *love* (for Charlie, Eleanor and, indeed, his family) is ultimately very conventional indeed. The question of whether romantic love may, itself, be queered thus constitutes a challenge for writer and critic alike. Whilst it could be argued that there are no limits to the permutations of perverse *desire*, love – as this book will attest – endures on account of principles and boundaries that can be pushed but never broken. As has been shown by

Foucault's work on homosexual love in *The Care of the Self* (1988), the ancient binaries that distinguished 'fine and just love from that which is not' (Foucault 1988: 191–2) were only mapped onto heterosexual marriage and homosexual relationships gradually, and by default; what distinguishes love from not-love is ultimately less to do with subject positionings and sexual practices than with the *values* that we have already seen listed amongst the 'first principles' of love: 'virtue, friendship, modesty, candor, stability' (Foucault 1988: 191), and, latterly, chastity, purity and reciprocity. Romantic love, then, is so emphatically a discourse born of Humanism and Christianity that it is hard to imagine any radical queering that would not also signal its demise.

The Gift of Love

As I have already observed, the task of reconciling the 'deep structures' of romantic love (as an apparently a-historical universal condition) with a cultural history of the genre is a severe conceptual challenge. Although one way around this is to focus simply on the *literary history per se* (see Part I of Chapter 2), my own interest has always been in the relationship between the genre and discourse of love as it is experienced more widely. My challenge, then, was to produce a hypothesis, and a methodology, that would enable me to explore the relationship between text and discourse at different historical/cultural moments and thus assess how love does, indeed, come to 'mean differently' over time.

De Rougemont's classic *Love in the Western World* (1940) was one of the first texts to insist upon the cultural–historical specificity of romantic love. Although, as we have seen, his book is deeply bound up with the deep structures of romance (and makes a major contribution to those debates), he nevertheless insists that the Tristan myth/Courtly Love tradition represents but *one*, partial account of love:

> 'Everything changes except the human heart,' say the old sages, but they are wrong. Metaphorically speaking, the human heart is strangely sensitive to variations in time and place. What we call 'passionate love' is unknown in India and China. They have no words to render the concept. A Hindi [*sic*] once said to a friend of mine: 'When we experience something that the western novels describe, all we say is "It's a romance!"' (de Rougemont 1983: 5)[13]

And he also observes – in a coda absolutely central to the argument that has been pursued here – that the 'West is distinct from other cultures not only by its invention of passionate love in the twelfth century and the secular elaboration of conjugal love, but by its *confusion* of the notions of eros, agape, sexuality, passion' (de Rougemont 1983: 5). The acknowledgement of 'confusion' at the level of discourse/ideology here is, I believe, vital if we are to account for the experiential complexity of romantic love and to avoid getting trapped in the sort of dualistic bind (romantic love is *either* erosic or agapic) that we have witnessed amongst the philosophers. To admit, on the contrary, that 'modern love' is the product of many contradictory principles and beliefs also helps to explain why lovers are doomed to so much suffering and why (for example) the institution of marriage has struggled so hard to accommodate it.

Rather less helpful to the remit of this volume is the fact that de Rougemont's notion of 'historical and cultural' specificity extends across nine hundred years! Whilst acknowledging that both Courtly Love and the Tristan myth are, indeed, paradigms that have endured, it is my quest to discover *what else* – besides spiritual enlightenment and/or the 'will-to-death' – romantic love has come to 'mean' across the centuries. Jean-Paul Sartre cites de Rougemont in a pronouncement that 'passionate love' is 'always the expression of a certain lifestyle and world view common to a whole class or period' (*Situations II* [1946] cited in de Rougemont 1983: 367–8). Our challenge is thus to discover a means of identifying *how* 'lifestyles' and 'world-views' connect with feelings and desires; to reveal what, *besides love*, romance is seen to offer its lovers; what, indeed, is *love's gift?*

The method I have developed for answering this question derives, in part, from semiology: in particular, Judith Williamson's ground-breaking work on how advertisements work (Williamson 1978). At the heart of Williamson's theory is the assumption that most contemporary ads 'sell' their products by linking them with a desirable concept/'value' that will, effectively, be purchased along with the product. Car advertisements remain the paradigmatic example here, since we are all familiar with the way in which values such as power, speed, prestige, machismo, novelty, are frequently given more emphasis in the ads than is the product itself. This 'supplementary value' has traditionally been represented in the ads by something that denotes it (for example, a cheetah might be featured in a car ad to signify speed). As readers will also be aware, however, modern advertising has become increasingly obscure in its use of these supplementary signifiers, and Williamson and her followers have proposed that the cerebral *challenge* this represents to consumers is a crucial element in their interpretation and significantly enhances the desirability of the product.

My proposal, then, is that, in a similar way, we attempt to read off the supplementary value(s) associated with romantic love in any given cultural–historical moment. What does love offer its subjects *besides* the notional transformation/completion of the self ([′] in my base-line function $x + y \rightarrow x' + y'$)? What supplementary/excess value (z) (if any) is produced through the *transformation* of the lovers as a consequence of the act of love? What does this *gift* (if there is one) tell us about what is most prized, most sought-after, in the different eras?

The notion of romantic love producing, or providing access to, something beyond itself is, as we have already observed, centrally present in de Rougemont's formulation. Death (or should that be 'a beautiful death'?) is what the courtly lover is gifted in lieu of having his love requited or his sexual desires fulfilled. What emerges strikingly in this formulation, and is of consequence for the notion of the gift that I shall, myself, be working with, is that it is not the lovers themselves who are doing the giving but rather the special *conditions* of their love. De Rougemont touches upon this in his chapter 'The Love of Love' when he says of Tristan and Iseult: '[L]ike all great lovers, they imagine they have been ravished "beyond good and evil" into a kind of transcendental state outside ordinary experience, into an ineffable absolute irreconcilable with the world, but that they feel to be *more real than the world*' (de Rougemont 1983: 39). The fact that their love is directed not to each other but to 'love itself' also explains the lovers' constant need for partings and separation: they are ever in pursuit of 'that hidden flame which absence rekindles' (de Rougemont 1983: 42). Many of the texts that I consider in Chapter 4 feature pairs of lovers who readily fit de Rougemont's description here. Indeed, the Gothic tradition from the eighteenth century to the present leaves us in little doubt that romantic love is never more than a means to a (sublime and fantastical) end for the participants concerned.

For the purposes of this book more generally, however, I am proposing that romantic love can 'gift' its subjects a wide range of supplementary benefits. Sometimes these are reflections of the dominant ideologies and institutions of the day (for example, the way in which love could be said to provide women with the gift of a 'name' through marriage: see Chapter 2), but very often they may be seen to stand in opposition to social/institutional orthodoxies. As we have already seen, this certainly applies to the Courtly Love/Gothic traditions, which court death, with de Rougemont arguing strongly that the former is in large part defined by its structural and ideological *opposition* to marriage and all that it represents: 'The Romance misses no opportunity of disparaging the social institution of marriage and of humiliating husbands . . . as well as glorifying the virtue of men and women who love outside, and in despite of, marriage' (de Rougemont 1983: 34). It is also important, moreover, to recognize that opposition and resistance can take many forms; as I shall consider in Chapter 3, the *companionship* enjoyed by the 'sensible' protagonists of Jane Austen's courtship fiction may be seen to defy the corruption of the marriage market in a rather more subtle, but no less effective, way. Indeed, one may argue that it is often the way in which the 'official' and 'unofficial' ideology are held in tension in love's gift that reveals most about the social and cultural values circulating at any given cultural moment. In this respect, the historical present – that is, the early years of the twenty-first century – is proving a fascinating new limit-point, with romantic love being annexed by the cult(ure) of 'Lifestyle', on the one hand, and to those consigned to the margins of society, on the other (see Chapter 7).

Imagining the 'gift of love' as something produced through the *process* of 'falling in love' – rather than as something consciously gifted from one lover to another – has the notional advantage of removing it from the vexed debate of 'giving in order to get' (Soble 1990: 96–9). From Mauss's seminal anthropological essay *The Gift* (1990 [1950]) through to Derrida's more recent, and highly provocative, writings on giving (Derrida 1992, 1995), the whole issue of whether it is truly possible to give something that proclaims itself a gift but which does not expect/require 'return' has become a (rather despairing) moral and philosophical conundrum. Whilst this is too big a debate to get embroiled in here, Derrida's intention is clearly to play (profitable) havoc with Mauss's insistence that gifts *ought* to entail reciprocity ('Refusing requital puts the act of giving outside any mutual ties . . . A gift that does nothing to enhance solidarity is a contradiction' (Mauss 1990: vii)). The vocabulary used in the preceding quote (Mary Douglas's gloss on Mauss, in fact) inadvertently invokes the fine distinction between 'requital' and 'reciprocity' that, for many philosophers, has been critical in this inquiry. For many thinkers, indeed, the concept of reciprocity requires only a *minimal* element of 'exchange' and thus permits x to have a meaningful relationship with y even if what is returned is no more/less than 'the permission to be adored' (Soble 1990: 91–100); the notion that the two parties are obliged to exchange like for like (that is, a full requital) is nonsense in this context. For Derrida, however, the challenge was clearly to think the unthinkable – the 'giftless gift' – and explore what new forms of relationship (both for individuals and nations) this might entail (see also Nancy 2001). At the heart of these disputes concerning the intention of the gift there is, not surprisingly, a rather bad-tempered subtextual agenda about the extent to which subjects are in *conscious* control of their giving (and, indeed, what is 'gifted'). In most of the texts/scenarios I deal with in this volume, the (partial) equivalence of gift with a *supplement* that is more often than not ideological calls into question the extent to which either, or *any*, party can be its donor; these are giftless gifts not by virtue of the careful self-positioning of *x* or *y*, but rather as a consequence of a fantastic, ideological feint of hand that – in true fairy-tale fashion – attaches to the condition of love the chimera of *all* that we most desire. This proposition echoes Derrida's reasoning in *The Gift of Death* (1995), which concludes, quite sensibly, that death is perhaps the *only* gift that escapes the bind of reciprocity: partly because the dead cannot give, and partly because the donor is 'inaccessible' and/or unknown (Derrida 1995: 40). This, in turn, renders the gift an 'event' rather than a 'thing', and – as will be seen in the chapters that follow – this is a distinction that may be usefully invoked to help understand the elusive 'gift of love'.

The conceit of romantic love as the catalyst for a utopian vision of the world that is entirely in excess of the benefits of the relationship itself is also present in the writings of Ernst Bloch. The sections of *The Principle of Hope* (1986 [1959]) which deal with daydreams and what he has dubbed 'anticipatory consciousness' resonate suggestively with the transformative potential of love that I have been presenting here. In this text, Bloch makes a powerful move against the 'repressive burden' associated with Freud's model of the unconscious (Bloch 1986: dustjacket) by arguing for the concomitant presence of a 'Not-Yet-Conscious' in every human subject. Rather than seeing all consciousness and unconsciousness as the product of what has gone before, Bloch identifies a counter-tendency to think, or dream, that which has not yet happened, thereby eschewing the notion that our desires – sexual or otherwise – are always necessarily bound up in the past. By distinguishing between 'filled' emotions (for example, envy, greed, admiration) and 'unfilled' emotions (for example, anxiety, fear, hope, belief), he argues that subjects are capable of responding to 'drive-objects' that *do not yet exist*, as well as ones that lie buried deep in the psyche (Bloch 1986: 74). This is, of course, in profound contrast to the popular reading of Freud and Lacan, for whom desire is always an attempt to restore a former 'lost object' or 'lack'. Whilst this hypothesis clearly requires its own 'leap of faith', its insistence that subjects can conceive of, or create, feelings that are 'new' certainly corresponds to my own focus on love as radically transformative of the subject(s) concerned; moreover, the perceived newness of the 'drive-object' and its associated emotions also helps to account for its aura of *excess* beneficence. In the context of Bloch's work as a whole, the utopian 'window' onto the world that ensues from romantic love may be perceived to translate into a *political vision* that reaches far beyond the individual. The condition of being in love provides the subject with a vision of the world not as it is, but as it might be, and may, as a consequence, become the catalyst for revolution and/or social change. Literature, certainly, is full of instances where the gift of love manifests itself as a desire to 'change the world'; where the heat/energy produced in the transformation of x into x' is realized in events (z) of extraordinary productivity (see Chapters 5 and 7).

This portrait of love, and love's gift, as a wholly positive – and facilitating – fantasy is clearly only one side of the story, however. Even as the excess of feeling may translate into a radical and empowering force, so may it also collude with a repressive orthodoxy. This contrast will be demonstrated very strikingly in Chapters 5 and 6 when we witness texts from the twentieth century annex romantic love very differently. *Why* a subject (x) should respond to one sort of gift-event and not another will, as I propose below, depend upon his or her existing social/cultural positioning and the way in which s/he has been transformed ($x \rightarrow x'$) by love.

As should by now be becoming clear, the historicization of romantic love is a severely challenging remit. This is not to say that the task is impossible, however, especially if we elect to understand history not in terms of decades and centuries, but as a sequence of historical-cultural moments in which a particular range of *discourses* and *literary genres* hold sway. Although many of the gifts discussed in these pages appear, at first glance, profoundly a-historical – for example, 'the gift of immortality' (Chapter 4); 'the gift of selfhood' (Chapter 6) –, they can all be seen to result from the fusion of the transformed self with the fashionable – and, themselves, 'desirable' – discourses of the day: this, indeed, is what I am presenting as love's claim to alchemy. Moreover, as will quickly become clear in Chapter 2, these discourses are themselves mediated by a literary history steeped in codes and conventions that have evolved, little by little, over time. Why one subject (x) will experience love's gift as one thing, and another (y) as something else, will depend upon both his/her existing subject positioning (in terms of class, gender, education, and so on) and – most importantly – on what s/he has *read*. Given the wide range of cultural discourses/values circulating in any one society at any given time, moreover, it is clear that love's supplement *may* translate into any number of things; yet what this cultural history of romance reveals is that, for every given period, a certain set of 'desirables' will tend to dominate. We now begin the story way back in the Middle Ages, when, for the heroes of the earliest metrical and prose romances, the *adventure* engaged in the quest for love and honour was clearly a greater gift than the Princess herself.

2

Romance before the Eighteenth Century

The Gift of a Name

I

I begin with two quotations:

> Neither did I intend this piece for to delight, but to divulge; not to please the fancy, but to tell the truth. Lest after ages should mistake, in not knowing I was daughter to one Master Lucas of St. John's, near Colchester in Essex, second wife to the Lord Marquis of Newcastle; for my Lord having had two wives, I might easily have been mistaken, especially should I die and my Lord marry again.
>
> Margaret Cavendish, Duchess of Newcastle (1989 [1656]: 99)

> Can there bee a more Romance Story then ours would make if the conclusion should prove happy?
>
> Dorothy Osborne to William Temple (1654) (Osborne 1928: 130)

During the period in which Margaret Cavendish and Dorothy Osborne were writing – that is, the mid-seventeenth century – romantic love was informed by very different laws and ideologies than the ones that dominate the discourse today. They were still also a century away from the moment when the birth of the novel and the Romantics' 'discovery' of the Imagination transformed the love story into the psychological thriller that has been synonymous with the genre ever since. Love, for these upper-class English women, was strictly circumscribed by their need to marry, and the most important 'gift' that such a match would confer upon them was that of a 'name'.

The value – total yet precarious – attached to a woman's re-naming after marriage is poignantly expressed in the first of these quotations. The lines, which comprise the final statement in Margaret Cavendish's autobiography, *The True Relation of My Birth, Breeding and Life* (1656), demonstrate just how insecure even a wealthy celebrity remained in terms of her legal, and hence inheritable, identity. No matter how much a 'name' Cavendish might make for herself as a writer and member of the society 'A' list, it would, she realized, count for nothing unless she continued to be distinguished from the Marquis of Newcastle's 'other wives'.[1] Her marriage to the Marquis (described in her autobiography) conferred upon her the ultimate gift of a name/title that would ensure her right to an official identity, but it was not one to which she could attach her personal attributes with any sense of permanence. Whilst the latter pages of the autobiography catalogue her likes, dislikes and temperament in some detail, there is still no guarantee that her unique personhood will survive.

For Dorothy Osborne, likewise, whose love letters to her forbidden suitor, William Temple, form the focus of Part II of this chapter, marriage – or its prospect – was defining of identity. In this extraordinary series of letters, however, the huge value attached to 'the name' is seen as an obstacle rather than a gift inasmuch as both lovers' families wish them to marry people of greater wealth and higher status. Temple's name is not seen as an adequate gift for Osborne, and vice versa. What is fascinating – and, of course, supremely romantic – about these writings, then, is the fact that they explore romantic love and desire without the certainty that it will ever be brought under the aegis of marriage. Osborne is consequently obliged to discover other gifts.

The prime means by which Dorothy Osborne would appear to conceptualize romantic love outside what was, for her, the forbidden objective of marriage was through her reading of literary romance. In this regard, indeed, her letters constitute a unique and invaluable insight into the way a woman of her social class and historical moment reconciled the *genre* of romance with lived experience. What emerges is the portrait of a woman who appears to have been as seduced, and entranced, by her romance reading as any present-day devotee of Mills & Boon. For all the seventeenth-century law and ideology that sought to contain amorous love within the duties of marriage, it is clear that there were discourses still thriving that had enshrined it in chivalry, adventure and sublimated sexual desire from the thirteenth century. Whilst a name might be the official gift of love, educated women like Osborne clearly had other bonuses in mind. In the first part of this chapter, then, I attempt a brief overview of the history of romance genre from the thirteenth to the seventeenth century, paying particular attention to the evolution of romantic love within that genre. This research is then brought to bear upon my analysis of Osborne's writings in Part II and the discussion of cognate seventeenth-century texts (including Margaret Cavendish's autobiography) in Part III.

By way of introduction, I should, however, like to invoke one further text: the Flemish painter Jan van Eyck's iconic *Marriage of Giovanni Arnolfini and Giovanna Cenami* (1434) (see frontispiece). Although painted two centuries before Margaret Cavendish and Dorothy Osborne were given to contemplate the less than transparent relationship between 'love' and 'marriage', the complex mixture of tenderness and solemnity in this representation of a betrothal speaks, similarly, to a clash of discourses. Whilst the merchant's gentle grasp of his future wife's hand at the same time as he signals his 'vow' may be read a metaphor of his gift to her (that is, his name), her open palm signals something far more ambiguous and unknown. And whilst a pessimistic reading might see the emptiness and vulnerability of the open palm as a sign of her inherent *dis*possession (as she passes from man to man she, herself, has nothing much to give), we may figure the gesture more positively in terms of openness or frankness. What is it that these two lovers can gift each other besides dowry and name? The small dog at the feet of the couple is, of course, often seen as supplying one answer to this question (that is, the gift of 'fidelity'), but the history of literary romance offers many more fascinating possibilities. Even in those centuries, then, when romantic love was most heavily circumscribed by the articles of matrimonial law, other values – and expectations – prevailed.

The Progress of Romance: The Evolution of the Genre from the Thirteenth to the Seventeenth Centuries

Ever since Northrop Frye's *A Secular Scripture* (1976), there has been long debate about whether romance is more properly thought of as a *genre* or a *mode*. Even supposing that we settle for the latter, however – and with it the assumption that its key signatures of 'aristocratic society, love interest, chivalry, the monstrous and the supernatural' (King 2004: 140) have inhabited *many* genres – it is clear that there is a fascinating story of genesis, evolution and mutation to be told. Whether figured as mode or genre, romance – as it is practised in the Western world – has an identifiable, if complex, literary history. In this section I attempt to steer my way through that vast archive, focusing, in particular, on what King refers to as 'the love interest'. For, as has already been observed, 'romance' (mode *or* genre) and 'romantic love' (the discourse) are manifestly not the same thing, though the way the former has informed the latter is the chief point of fascination for a book such as this.

Whilst acknowledging that Denis de Rougemont's *Love in the Western World* (1983 [1940]) remains probably the finest – and certainly the boldest – attempt to uncover a causal trajectory in the romance literatures of Western Europe, his identification of the legend of Tristan and Iseult as the single 'Ur' text clearly raises questions about how we classify all those texts which resist its tragic denouement in death. Although exceedingly persuasive as a rationale for explaining the seemingly perverse detours of romantic love *per se*, the focus does tend to marginalize the many thousands of love stories whose *raison d'être* is a happy ending. This, indeed, is a binarism that persists throughout the long history of the genre; romance has always possessed two faces: comic and tragic. Having already given considerable space to de Rougemont's tragic trajectory, it is therefore necessary that I attempt to balance the books by reviewing the origins of romance as a mode defined, in part, by its 'happy ever after'. This was, after all, Dorothy Osborne's own expectation as voiced in the second of the quotations cited at the beginning of this chapter: theirs would make a great 'Romance Story' – *but only* 'if the conclusion should prove happy'.

For Frye, the happy endings of romance were integral to its idealizing *mythos*. Saunders summarizes his conclusions thus:

> Frye observes that the ritual aspects of romance are characterized by: an emphasis on the great cycles of life and death, by the opposition of the ideal to its converse, and by patterns of 'ascent' and 'descent' to 'other worlds', which are linked to the shaping of identity and the process of self-realization. As the mythos of summer, romance leads from a state of order through darkness, winter and death to rebirth, new order and maturity. Adventure is central to romance, as is the quest form: the hero moves through conflict and death struggle to self-realization. (Saunders 2004a: 3)

Whilst it is of course possible to argue, *like* de Rougemont, that, in tragic romance, 'self-realization' and 're-birth' are experienced as the *fulfilment* of the death-wish and not as its (necessarily fantastical) body-swerve, the mythic structure that Frye describes here does, indeed, figure in much early Western European romance. It would certainly seem to apply, for example, to the English metrical romances produced between c. 1250 and the early sixteenth century that continued to peddle both the same motifs (for example, the chivalric qualities of 'valour, honour, piety and the active life' and 'various wicked kings, traitors, giants and dragons' (Brewer 2004: 45)) and a penchant for happy endings. Deeming the early metrical romance to be characterized, above all, by 'repetition with variation' (Brewer 2004: 57), Brewer thus concludes:

> Giants and dragons are the ever-present enemy, the Saracen, quest and
> desire are their base. They are secular but unfailingly pious . . . they have
> a fundamental optimism. Like so many fairy tales, their underlying sym-
> bolic drive is often the process of maturation variously achieved by male
> or female protagonists against various opponents, unless it is of suffering
> bravely endured and ending in success. (Brewer 2004: 62)

What is most significant in Brewer's summary *vis-à-vis* the concerns of this
volume is, of course, the fact that the happiness of these texts' endings is
not expressed in terms of a successful love-match or marriage. Whilst most
of the stories, as we have already established, do include a love-interest
which sees hero and heroine ultimately rewarded with each other as a kind
of prize, their 'fundamental optimism' is located rather in the sur-
vival/maturation of the characters. This subtle shift of objective (whereby
romantic love becomes a means rather than an end) is, of course, consistent with my own figuration of 'love-as-gift', but what Brewer's analysis
reminds us of most explicitly is the fundamental interdependence of
romance and *Bildungsroman*. Common to both genres is the vision of life
as a series of quests, tests and challenges for which the brave are duly
rewarded.

Many literary scholars working in the early modern period acknowledge
that by far the most important set of stories informing the development
of romantic discourse in Western Europe are the Arthurian legends.
Whilst many of these have their origins in France – for example, Chrétien
de Troyes's celebrated *Yvain* – they soon began to be retold in Britain, both
in the metrical romances discussed above and in texts such as Layamon's
Brut (c. 1190–1300) and *Gawain and the Green Knight* (later fourteenth
century). Whilst the latter, whose origins – according to Barron (2004) –
date back to Geoffrey of Monmouth's *Historia Regum Britanniae* (1138),
often have a clear nationalist agenda, it is significant that they share the
same ritual optimism as their metrical cousins. Their heroes – epitomized
by Arthur as 'national champion' (Barron 2004: 72) – are thoroughly 'idealized' and to be distinguished from those belonging to more mimetic traditions by their often supernatural powers (Barron 2004: 68).[2] This is a
sentiment echoed by Brewer, who, with references to the metrical
romances, places particular emphasis on the audience's wish to be uplifted
and inspired:

> All is heightened, the good people are better, the enemies more evil, the
> festivals grander, knights stronger, ladies more beautiful, than in everyday
> life. The implied audience does not want to hear of peasants, nor of
> kitchen-sink realism. Life is harsh and dull enough. What is wanted is what

is brighter, more exciting, more luxurious, a fantasy upper class. (Brewer 2004: 46)

Notwithstanding the heroism and utopianism that gild these early texts, it is, of course, the misdemeanours in Arthur's court – in particular, the liaisons of Tristan and Iseult, Lancelot and Guinevere – that cast the first serious shadow over the genre. Yet whilst these stories are included in the early metrical romances (for example, the Auchinleck MS of *Tristram* (Brewer 2004: 60–1)), it is not until Malory's celebrated prose romance the *Morte d'Arthur* (1485) that they acquire a fully tragic status. According to Brewer, indeed, it is likely that these tales of adultery were shunned by the early romancers because they were fundamentally incompatible with the spirit of the genre ('Adultery is more usually the subject of derisive jesting, as in fabliaux by Chaucer and in French' (Brewer 2004: 61)). This observation serves as a useful check on de Rougemont's identification of the Tristram story as the *definitive* origin of Western romance; it is rather, as I posited earlier, more properly the origin of the *tragic* strand.

But what Malory does with the stories of Arthur and his court is much more than tackle the vexed question of adultery. As Saunders observes, it is the rendition of the stories into expanded – and expansive – *prose fiction* that has made the *Morte d'Arthur* the single most important point of origin for all the millions of romantic novels that have followed (Saunders 2004a: 5). Helen Cooper also points to the explicit formal link between Malory and the development of the novel in the eighteenth and nineteenth centuries, observing that 'the installment method of publication also meant the revival of the interlaced structure pioneered in the prose romances, where a series of simultaneous adventures happening to different characters can be pursued in parallel' (Cooper 2004: 105). It is, Cooper suggests, the 'almost infinite capacity for deferral or closure' (105) of the prose romance that first developed the reader's taste for desultory, picaresque story-telling.

De Rougemont, it will be remembered, focuses on the 'endless deferral' of consummation in the Tristan story to support his hypothesis that the force driving romance in the Western world is a sublimated death-wish. For many scholars, however, the stories of Tristan and Iseult, Lancelot and Guinevere, are seen as expositions of far more than romantic love; the deceptions and betrayals precipitate 'the fall' of the golden age of British history, as mythologized by Arthur and his court (see Cooper 2004: 110). Yet another way of understanding Malory's departure from earlier texts is to see the focus on adultery and dishonour as indicative of a new *psychological realism* being brought to bear upon the genre. Inasmuch as the love interest of the early metrical and prose romances is figured mainly in terms of the narrative surface of the texts concerned – consummation/marriage is the lovers' reward for surviving their many ordeals –, it is not surprising that it was these tales shorn of a happy ending that should prompt a deeper exploration of the condition of being in love.[3] Malory was not, however, the first medieval writer to place the psychology of romantic love at the centre of his romance. In her essay on Chaucer's romances, Corinne Saunders presents *Troilus and Criseyde* (c. 1385) as ground-breaking in its treatment of the hero's 'love-sickness': 'Troilus embodies the experience of *fin'amours*: suddenly struck by the God of Love's arrow, he is wounded through the eyes that lead to the heart, to manifest all the physical symptoms of the malady of love' (Saunders 2004b: 97–8). What Saunders's commentary also hints at here is that in Chaucer's text – as in Malory's *Morte d'Arthur* – the trials and adventures that constitute a test of *chivalry* in early romance are refigured here as the psychological challenges of romantic love itself. Love, at last, becomes the true *object* of the romance genre, and the fantastical 'external' challenges facing earlier knights now re-shape themselves as the doubts and demons of the lover's interior consciousness:

> Dragons and enchantments are there none, yet the all-possessing nature of the experience in love [*sic*] of Troilus makes that experience for him a kind of inward equivalent of *aventure*, just as the new strangeness of love, and that force of idealization which he brings to that experience, give it the momentum of a quest and the quality of a marvel, the marvellous inward adventure of love. (Saunders 2004b: 96)

The psychological depth and realism achieved by medieval writers like Chaucer and Malory in their treatment of romantic love is clearly crucial to the genesis, and evolution, of the 'tragic' trajectory of the romance genre. If we now move on a century or two to consider the types of romance Dorothy Osborne was reading in the mid-seventeenth century, it is to discover that the high seriousness of such texts had been subjected to lighter, brighter packaging.

The Gendering of Prose Romance

It is, perhaps, no coincidence – in sexual-political terms – that the 'lightening up' of romance that characterized the shift from medieval to modern coincided with the increased identification of women with the genre. Although Lori Newcomb shows how hard it is to discover documentary evidence for this supposed 'feminine turn', there is certainly a widely held assumption amongst literary historians that 'romance became a "woman's genre" during the Renaissance period' (Newcomb 2004: 121). One of the first critics to propound this hypothesis was Louis B. Wright, declaring that 'romance in strange opera lands and love stories with happy endings found favour with the Elizabethans even as with feminine readers today' (*Middle-Class Culture in Elizabethan England* (1935), in Newcomb 2004: 121). As Newcomb observes, Wright's evidence seems to have been based on the many Renaissance texts which themselves refer to women reading prose romances (generally in derogatory terms) without considering that this characterization might have more to do with the stereotyping of a certain class of women than with reading practices themselves.

What *is* supported by circumstantial evidence, however, is the fact that – during the Renaissance and into the seventeenth century – women increasingly took the title roles in prose romance. This is explained in part by Elizabeth I's powerful influence on the literary culture of Britain: 'By the middle of Elizabeth's reign, several romances had been titled after a female protagonist alone, including Robert Greene's *Mamillia* (1585) and *Penelope's Web* (1587), and Thomas Lodge's *Rosalynde* (1590)' (Newcomb 2004: 123). In addition, and quite apart from the texts which were dedicated to the Queen, increasing numbers of prose romances were framed by epistles to 'gentlewomen readers' (Newcomb 2004: 124), including Sir Philip Sidney's invocation of his sister in the full title of the *Arcadia*: *The Countess of Pembroke's Arcadia* (1590). The implication here, then, is that such framing signalled the suitability of the genre for a female audience despite the fact that a great many of the texts (for example, Robert Greene's) are slyly insulting of purported female characteristics – such as a tendency to 'prattle' and 'gossip' – whilst ostensibly celebrating female virtue. What all this suggests is that Renaissance and post-Renaissance prose romance was effectively double-voiced (in a Bakhtinian sense), appealing to male readers in a conspiratorial, 'laddish' way (by showing women making fools of themselves) and to women by means of flattering popular sentiment.[4] In this last regard, Newcomb also invokes the widely held seventeenth-century belief that 'women read for sexualized pleasure' (Newcomb 2004: 129), much as is assumed *vis-à-vis* Mills & Boon-type romance today.

In terms of the generic mutation that romance may be seen to undergo as it passes from Malory to Sidney, meanwhile, it is clear that whilst the same motifs and 'romance moments' (Saunders 2004a: 1) survive – e.g. knights, adventures, tests, quests and due rewards – they are now overlaid with irony. As Andrew King observes, writing about Sidney and Spenser, these texts 'invoke and exploit romance conventions to ironic or otherwise complex rhetorical effect' (King 2004: 140). Saunders hence refers to Sidney's *Arcadia* as a 'mixed mode' (Saunders 2004a: 5): a text that is half-serious, and half not, about the world of romance and chivalry and the values they represent. Such ambiguity is hardy surprising in texts whose 'adventures' are thinly veiled commentaries on the history and politics of the age and its fantastical, egotisical Queen (King 2004: 147). With Elizabeth I as the faintly disguised 'super-heroine' of Spenser's epic, the love-interest also bears a political symbolism that necessarily prevents the psychological complexity (and moral 'deviance') that we discovered in Malory. Love and marriage in *The Faerie Queene* (1590–6) labour under the burden of Elizabeth's own longed-for, but endlessly deferred, ideal match. As King has observed, Merlin's prophecy that 'Britomart will marry Artegall and found a noble dynasty' is neither romantic nor surprising (King 2004: 147).

Although the codes and conventions of romance survive in these two great sixteenth-century romances, then, it could be argued that romantic love itself is displaced from the centre stage and, overdetermined by the royal prerogative, is necessarily stripped of psychological drama and complexity. The exploration of tragic – and adulterous – love begun by Malory is reserved for texts (for example, Shakespearean and Jacobean tragedy) whose protagonists are very clearly *not* representatives of the contemporary royal household and in sonnet sequences such as *Astrophil and Stella* (Sidney 1973 [1591]). Following through the hypothesis that links women readers with the romance genre, it is therefore significant that whilst Dorothy Osborne never mentions Shakespeare or other Renaissance/post-Renaissance dramatists, she presents herself as an avid reader of the contemporary 'prose romance' (most of them translated from the French). As we shall see in the next section of this chapter, her consumption of these multi-volumed tomes is, by modern standards, positively heroic, and in the course of her correspondence with William Temple, she candidly reveals what pleases her; and what does not. Whilst the length of the texts never appeared to daunt her, too great an emphasis on politics – at the expense of 'pleasing fiction' – did (Newcomb 2004: 134). The fact that several of the romances she refers to were, indeed, 'political romances' is rarely commented upon and the sections of texts that she directs her lover towards are – more often than not – the stories of the heroes and heroines she finds most attractive and appealing.

Love and Marriage in the Seventeenth Century

Although it is necessary to begin any discussion of love and marriage in the seventeenth century with the caveat that what applied to the propertied classes did not necessarily extend to the lower orders, there is no question that (in Althusserian terms) the 'State Apparatus' and the 'Ideological State Apparatus' were in powerful collusion.[5] The social and economic instability caused by the English Civil War (1642–9) and its aftermath meant that families like the Osbornes and the Temples were obliged to manage their marriage contracts as astutely as possible, and 'marriage for love' was necessarily regarded as an unthinkable luxury – at least by the patriarchs of such families. This was also a century in which the laws of church and state increasingly fed off one another in their claim to authority, and marriage – in particular – was understood in terms of a an absolute hierarchy that stretched from God to man (and, ultimately, woman). As the editors of *Her Own Life* (1989) observe:

> Relationships between men and women in the seventeenth century could be defined by reference to a whole complex of interlocking and interdependent ideas, definitions, conventions and statutes, whether concerning law, religion, society, philosophy, or nature. Ideas from each category were seen to reflect and reinforce the others, for all were based on notions of order or hierarchy, and all were concerned to ascribe men and women to their rightful places within these hierarchies. (Graham *et al.* 1989: 6–7)

The extent to which secular law is seen to follow divine law *vis-à-vis* marriage is illustrated via an extraordinarily powerful set of metaphors in a document from 1632 entitled *The Lawes Resolution of Womens Rights*:

> [I]n this consolidation which we call wedlock is a locking together. It is true, that man and wife are one person, but understand in what manner.
>
> When a small brook or little river incorporateth with Rhodanus, Humber or the Thames, the poor rivulet loseth her name; it is carried and recarried with the new associate; it beareth no sway; it possesseth nothing during coverture. A woman as soon as she is married is called 'covert'; in Latin 'nupta', that is, 'veiled'; as it were clouded and overshadowed; she hath lost her stream. I may more truly, far away, say to a married woman, her new self is her superior, her companion, her master . . . .
>
> All [women] are understood either married, or to be married, and their desires are subject to their husbands; I know no remedy, yet some can shift it well enough. The common law here shaketh hand with divinity. (in Graham *et al.* 1989: 7)

As Graham *et al.* further observe, this text leaves no doubt that, through the awesome conjunction of divine and natural law, women are seen to have no identity of their own and that such a state of affairs fully endorses Margaret Cavendish's fear of being 'effaced from history if she should die and her husband re-marry' (Graham *et al.*: 7). The 'gift of a name' that a woman achieves through marriage is certainly not hers in perpetuity.

At the level of ideology and discourse it is, however, important to mitigate this supremely phallogocentric view of 'wedlock' with some of the more positive representations that circulated in the seventeenth century. As has been noted by some commentators (e.g. Belsey 1988; Davies 1996), John Milton's work *may* be read in a more progressive light in this regard, even if many feminist critics have regarded *Paradise Lost* as one of the most patriarchal texts of all time (see Gilbert and Gubar 2000 [1979]). In anticipation of the reading of Osborne's letters that follows, it is thus useful to see how another seventeenth-century Englishwoman, Alice Thornton, describes her feelings upon the death of her husband. What we see here is a fascinating blend of rhetorical / social convention and what appears to be authentic personal experience. By the same token, marriage itself clearly *is* inscribed by servitude – but also by genuine companionship:

> Now am I left destituted of head-guide, help or support in this world . . .
> Great are my calamities, my case is full of complaints, bereft of a most
> dear and tenderly loving husband that took part with me in all sorrows,
> comforted me in sadnesses. We walked together as dear friends. His love
> was mine, in his sickness I was afflicted. Now I am left of him who was
> my earthly delight, he being gone to his heavenly father and left me to
> lament his loss from me and my poor fatherless children, weak in body,
> afflicted in spirit, low in my estate. (Thornton 1989 [1668]: 162)

Although this text is a fascinating instance of female subordination at a stylistic level – inasmuch as Thornton consistently presents herself as the passive subject of her late husband's active departure ('Now that I am left of him . . .') –, the assertion 'we walked together as dear friends' is a clear pronouncement of the discourse of 'companionate marriage' that emerged during the course of this century. Such sentiment, as we shall see, is central to Dorothy Osborne's dream of conjugal bliss as she attempts to reconcile the aspirations of her French romances with the lived reality of what she sees about her; and it becomes increasingly important to the next generation of writers – such as Jane Austen –, who were looking for a means of redeeming unions devoid of reciprocal sexual desire (see Chapter 3).

II

Dorothy Osborne's Love Letters

> Wee have lived hitherto upon hopes soe Aïrye that I have often wonderd
> how they could support the weight of our misfortunes; but passion gives
> a Strength above Nature, wee see it in mad People, (and not to fflatter our
> selves) ours is but a refined degree of madnesse; what can it bee else, to

be lost to all things in the world but that single Object that takes up on's ffancy, to loose all the quiet and repose of on's life in hunting after it, when there is soe litle likely-hood of ever gaineing it, and soe many more probable, accidents, that will inffallibly make us misse of it. (Osborne 1928: 116)

It is arguable that Dorothy Osborne is the most truly romantic of all the writers to be considered in this volume. This is because, despite the over-whelming pressure of the social and cultural forces telling her that (for a female aristocrat) 'love' was not a meaningful category, she continued to believe in it. Her own personal 'Romance Story' (Osborne 1928: 130) thus constitutes a triumph of literature over law, of desire over destiny; under continual pressure to relieve her family's financial burdens by the best pos-sible marriage, she remains true not only to William Temple but also to a dream of conjugality that actively combines the tenets of Courtly Love – devotion, exclusivity, spiritual transport – with sexual desire and platonic companionship *as well as* a decent fortune and the gift of a (suitably pres-tigious) 'name'. For while this is a woman who remains acutely sensitive to notions of breeding and birthright, there is little question that it was the discourse of romantic love – as promulgated by her multi-volume French romances – that enabled both her and Temple to 'imagine' their story.

Before we turn to a close examination of the letters themselves, it is, however, important to establish some biographical facts about their context. The first of these is that – despite the lovers' recourse to various fairy-tale scenarios – Dorothy Osborne was no Cinderella, and William Temple no lowly shepherd and/or disinherited prince. Both were from high-ranking, noble families with inherited titles and – were it not for Sir Peter Osborne's loss of fortune during the Civil War – they would have been pretty equally matched. In this regard, G. C. Moore Smith's intro-duction to the 1928 Clarendon edition of the *Letters* is a fascinating docu-ment, endorsing, as it does, the gentility and education of both families. Indeed, Moore Smith's biography opens with the wonderfully class-prejudiced observation that 'Dorothy Osborne might with reason feel the pride of race' (Osborne 1928: ix), mirrored – some pages later – by the reassurance that 'Temple, too, could be proud of his family history' (xviii). For Moore Smith, as presumably for the Osbornes and Temples them-selves, 'good breeding' appears to have been a tight mixture of title, edu-cation (via prestigious public schools and certain Cambridge colleges), service and loyalty to the King/Nation, and a rather more ambiguously defined 'honourable' behaviour. Under such conditions, one's 'name' of course became everything and was effectively the *only* means by which women could share in a family's reputation. It is worth noting, however, that education seems to have been of especial importance to both these families, with Osborne taking an occasional swipe at the more 'barbarous' factions of the aristocracy who lacked the intellectual refinements she and Temple so abundantly shared.

For the Osbornes, the Civil War appears to have been the first serious impediment to many centuries' worth of steadily increasing family fortune. Back in Edward VI's reign Dorothy Osborne's great grandfather, Peter Osborne, was appointed 'Keeper of the Privy Purse and Treasurer's Remembrancer in the Exchequer', whilst her own father – also Sir Peter – was knighted on 7 January 1611 and made 'Lieutenant-Governor of Guernsey, Alderney and Sark' (Osborne 1928: xi). The latter appears to have been – at first – a virtual sinecure, although some residence at Castle Court (Guernsey) was required. This pleasant situation changed radically as a result of the war, however, when Sir Peter was prevailed upon by the King for money and then fined by the parliamentarians for bearing arms in the first war against parliament. As a consequence, Sir Peter's annual income dropped from £4000 to £400 and the family moved back to the family home at Chicksands (whence Osborne wrote most of her letters). Osborne's mother died in 1651, and her father in 1654 (towards the end of her pre-marital correspondence with Temple). Indeed, it is her father's death that clears the way for the official announcement of her engagement. Temple's family, meanwhile, appear to have suffered rather less as the result of the war, although they – like the Osbornes – were originally staunch royalists. One of the fascinating historical legacies of Osborne's letters is the insight they offer into the nation's shifting political allegiances, however, with individual members of both families becoming parliamentarians.

Osborne and Temple first met on the Isle of Wight in 1648, after which they travelled, with Dorothy's brother, to St Malo, where Sir Peter Osborne (having resigned the Lieutenantship of Guernsey in 1646) was temporarily resident. It appears that Temple's father soon discovered the extent of his son's interest in Osborne, however, and sent him off on an extended tour of Europe instead. He only returned to his father's house in London in the winter of 1650/1 before beginning a series of visits to Ireland. This meant that there were long periods of time – this first lasting almost two years – when Osborne and Temple did not see each other. It was after William's return to London in the winter of 1650/1 that their correspondence began in earnest, however, and was not dropped until after their eventual marriage on Christmas Day 1654. It is worth noting that, whilst folk tales and ballads frequently have their lovers separated for multiples of seven years, such a long – not to mention clandestine – courtship was not common amongst the materially minded aristocrats of the seventeenth century.

One further item of biographical information needs to be shared before I move on to an analysis of the letters themselves: namely, that William Temple was himself a collector, translator and 'improver' of French romances. During his three years in France, Temple – like Osborne – learned to read and speak French to a high standard and eventually gathered his 'translations' of the romances together into a single volume, which he entitled *A True Romance, or The disastrous chances of love and fortune*. Moore Smith notes that only five of these 'seem to be preserved', and is evidently uncertain of their whereabouts (Osborne 1928: xliv–xlv). What has been preserved, however – and what is surely one of the most revealing supplementary documents cited by Moore Smith –, is the epistolary dedication that Temple attached to his volume. Addressed simply 'To my Lady', there is little doubt that the letter was intended for Osborne and is thus of crucial importance in ascertaining the dynamics of their epistolary relationship. For whilst Temple appears to have preserved most of his letters from Osborne, very few of his are understood to have survived.[6] What this text confirms is that, besides their mutual love of romances, Osborne and Temple shared a distinctive rhetorical intimacy; despite the gender difference, and Osborne's volubility, the tone and expression of their address is remarkably similar. A particular instance of this is found in the section of the epistle in which Temple refers, playfully, to the fact that his dedicatee cannot mistake her identity since she already knows his thoughts 'in any disguise' (Osborne 1928: xxviii). This echoes several of Osborne's own closing sentiments and hints at the way in which the correspondence itself becomes a sort of code; by the end of their courtship, Osborne and Temple can count on the other knowing what they think about almost anything.

On the central importance of literary romance to their own 'Romance Story', Temple's dedication is profound. Not only – as I have already hinted – does it extinguish the myth that it was only women who bought into the sentiment of such texts, but it also highlights the ways in which the sufferings of these literary heroes and heroines provide comfort, and example, for lovers in the material world. Thus Temple writes:

> I found it to no purpose to fly from my thoughts and that the best way was to deceive them with the likeness of objects and by representing others misfortunes to them instead of my owne. Those books became pleasant

> to me wch would have been painfull to a better humor, and whilst I pittyed others I sometimes forgott how much I deservd it my self. (Osborne 1928: xxvii)

And again: 'Besides in the expressing of their severall passions I found a vent for my owne, wch if kept in had sure burst mee before now . . .' (Osborne 1928: xxviii). What these comments would also seem to confirm is that, for Temple as well as Osborne, these romances were read primarily for their love interest rather than for their more general excitement and adventure, and that the relationships they described must have been depicted with a fair degree of psychological realism.

Moving on to Osborne's letters themselves, we should note that reports of her book-reading constitute a frequent – and substantive – occurrence in the correspondence as a whole. Not only does she (repeatedly) urge Temple either to read what she has read, or to send her further volumes of what she is presently engaged in, but she also participates in critical evaluation. Take, for instance, this appraisal of Mme de Scudery's *Grand Cyrus* (1653):

> I sent you a Part of Cyrus last week where you will meet wth one Doralize in the Story of Abradate and Pantheé, the whole Story is very good but her humor makes the best part of it. I am of her opinion in most things that she say's, in her Character of L'honnest home that she is in search of, and her resolution of receiveing noe heart that had bin offerd to any body else. pray tell me how you like her, and what fault you finde in my Lady Car[lisle]. (Osborne 1928: 109)

What we have here, and in her other 'readings', it seems to me, is an early example of what feminist theorists in the 1970s referred to as 'authentic realist criticism': that is, the reading of literary texts with the express purpose of discovering positive role models who may also be 'authenticated' by comparison with the reader's own life-experience (see Mills and Pearce 1996 [1989]: 56–90). It is clear that Osborne found many characters with whom to identify in her French romances (despite their often fantastical story-lines), and that she was also fond of using these (flattering) similarities as a means of further seducing her lover. (By asking Temple to tell her what he thinks about Doralize, she is evidently looking for yet more feedback on what he thinks of her!)

Taking the correspondence as a whole, I think there is little doubt that Osborne was a frustrated – and potentially talented – writer of romance herself, and that her long, sprawling letters were her means of venting that frustration as well as seducing and entertaining her lover. There are certainly many instances, such as here, in Letter 24, when she cannot resist the literary flourish:

> You aske mee how I passe my time heer. . . . About sixe or seven a Clock, I walke out into a Common that lyes hard by the house where a great many young wenches keep Sheep and Cow's and sitt in the shade singing of Ballads; I goe to them and compare their voyces and Beauty's to some Ancient Shepherdesses that I have read of and finde a vaste difference there, but trust mee I think these are as innocent as those could bee. (Osborne 1928: 51)

It may be assumed, then, that as well as being a voracious reader of romances, Dorothy Osborne would secretly have liked to have been the author of them. As it is, the textual staging of her own great 'Romance Story' had to suffice.

As well as playing with many of the conventions of the romance genre – as, for example, her interpolation of the pastoral motif quoted above –, Osborne closely observed the conventions of letter-writing. Recognition of this is important not only in our appreciation of the correspondence as an historical document, but also *vis-à-vis* our analysis of the nature of her love for Temple. Contemporary editors (including Moore Smith) have, for instance, been inclined to advise readers that the letters will not necessarily seem very intimate or affectionate by modern standards. This, I feel, is something of an overstatement of the case. Although key terms in the correspondence – for example, 'friend', 'kind', 'servant' – signify rather differently within a courtship vocabulary than they do today, the letters are certainly not lacking in endearments; more importantly, however, their ambiguity is played with persistently in order that Osborne may both speak her love/desire and preserve her dignity. Here is an example – from the conclusion of the remarkable Letter 17:

> My Ey's grow a little dim though for all the Ale and I beleeve if I should see it this is most strangely scribled. sure I shall not finde fault with you writeing in hast for anything but the shortnesse of your letter, and twould bee very unjust in mee to tye you to a Ceremony that I doe not observe my self, noe, for god sake, let there bee noe such thing between us. a reall kindnesse is so farr beyond all Complement that it never apear's more then when there is least of t'other mingled with it, if then you would have mee beleeve yours to be perfect confirme it to mee by a kinde freedom, tell me if there be anything I can serve you in, imploy mee as you could doe that sister that you say you love soe well, chide mee when I doe any thing that is not well, but then make hast to tell me that you have forgiven mee, and that you are what I shall Ever bee a
>
> faithfull freind (Osborne 1928: 37–8)

That Osborne's repeated use of terms such as 'friend' and 'kindenesse' at the end of this mammoth letter were understood as particularly warm endearments by Temple is confirmed in her next letter, in which (in response to him) she acknowledges:

> I doe not now remember what it was I writt, but it seem's it was very kinde, and possibly you owe the discovery on't to my being asleep, but I do not repent it, for I should not love you if I did not think you discreet enough to bee trusted with the knowledge of all my kindnesse. (Osborne 1928: 38)

Such candour seems, to me, to endorse the view that these letters are formal only because they are written in the language of their time. In granting Temple her 'kindnesse' and requesting his in return, Osborne has effectively laid herself as emotionally open as if – in modern parlance – she had declared 'I love you and will do anything for you'. Here, as is still the case today, intimacy proceeds via its own inimitable blend of the said and the unsaid. The vocabulary may have changed, but the dynamics most certainly have not.

The way in which Osborne is wont to play with the ambiguity implicit in key terms of endearment relates to another conventionalized, and rather more period-specific, feature of her letters: namely, their *raillerie* ('banter'). This term is used by the author herself at the beginning of the letter (Letter 47) in which she proposes to Temple that they break off their informal engagement: 'but I intended this a sober letter, and therefore (sans Raillerie)' (Osborne 1928: 114). Although thus invoked – and rejected – at a truly critical moment in the relationship, '*raillerie*' may, indeed, be considered *the* dominant rhetorical mode of the correspondence as a whole. From Letter 1, in which she archly and ironically responds to Temple's enquiry about whether or not she is still 'free' *vis-à-vis* the figure of a wager ('But for the ten pounde hee Claimes it is not yett due' (Osborne 1928: 3)), through her endless chiding on the subject of his short 'bitts of letters' (Osborne 1928: 36), to the frequent suggestions that he drop her and marry X, Y or Z, Osborne's preference is to spar. This is not to suggest that the letters are short of softer intimacy (we have already noted one example, and there are more to follow), but that *raillerie* is her most characteristic *modus operandi*. Bearing in mind the emphasis that was placed on 'wit' in intellectual circles, together with the notion that successful courtship demanded a skilful display of it, it is possibly the feature of Osborne's writing that is *most* typical of her age and, of course, looks forward to the ironic playfulness of Austen's characters. She certainly recognizes the importance of elegant coquetry in the letters of her contemporaries (for example, Lady Carlisle) and possibly equates it with literary and social sophistication. It is in her treatment of other suitors (for herself and for Temple) that we see her *raillerie* at its most barbed, but given the fact that both lovers were under *huge* pressure to 'look elsewhere', the underlying good humour is much to be admired. Here is just one example:

> Your fellow Servant [Osborne's companion, Jane Wright] kisses your hands and say's if you mean to make love to her olde woman this is the best time you can take, for shee is dyeing; this cold weather kils her I think. it has undone mee I'me sure in Killing an Old Knight [Sir William Briers] that I have bin wayteing for this seven yeare, and now hee dy's and will leave me nothing I beleeve, but leaves a Rich Widdow for somebody. I think you had best come a woeing to her, I have a good interest in her and it shall bee all employed in your Service if you think fitt to make any addresses there. but to bee sober again, for god sake send mee word of how your Journy goes forward. . . . And of all things remember to provide a safe addresse for your letters when you are abroad. this is a strange confused one I beleeve, for I have bin call'd away twenty times since I sate down to write it to my father whoe is not very well. but you will pardon it, we are past Ceremony, and Excuse mee if I say noe more now but that I am tousjours la mesme, that is Ever
>
> Your affectionate freind & servant (Osborne 1928: 22)

By quoting this 'jest' through to the conclusion of the letter, I have, I hope, enabled readers to see the way in which the perpetual pressure on both Osborne and Temple to consider other suitors is converted into flirtatious intimacy. Even in the long Letter 3, in which she reviews the numerous suitors who were seeking her hand during Temple's absence, Osborne manages to keep the tone light; and – bearing in mind the effort required to keep up polite evasions for so many years – this is no mean feat. Only very occasionally, indeed, do we see the 'threat' of other suitors take on a darker edge, as in the sequence of letters (47–53) when she attempts to break off the engagement. At this juncture, her promise to remain a 'faithful friend' to William and assist a providential marriage elsewhere rings hollow ('Leave mee to this, and seek a better fortune' (Osborne 1928: 124)) and makes the reader realize that we are but a short step away from the emotionally perverse actions of Catherine in Emily Brontë's *Wuthering Heights* (1995a [1847]) (when she promises to help Heathcliff in his seduction of Isabella) or Kate Croy's efforts to bring about the marriage of Millie and Densher in Henry James's *The Wings of the Dove* (2004 [1902]).

One of the generic specificities of letter-writing that Osborne utilizes to maximum effect in her seduction of Temple is the text's inscription in a particular place and time. As Nick Cave observes in 'The Secret Life of the Love Song', one of the principal drives behind the writing of the love letter, like the love song, is to 'shorten the distance between the writer and the recipient' (Cave 2001: 15), and one of the most effective ways of doing this is for the writer to physically embody him- or herself in a particular moment of time that the reader (on receipt of the letter) will themselves be made a part of. There are frequent examples of this device scattered throughout Osborne's correspondence and, in particular, at the end of her more intimate letters. Once again, Letter 17 – written whilst nursing her father and drinking a quantity of ale – is one of the best examples, with the extended 'real time' of the composition contributing to its sense of immediacy:

> the turning of my paper has waked mee, all this while I was in a dream. but tis noe matter, I am content you should know they are of you, and that when my thoughts are left most at liberty they are the kindest. ile swear my Eys are soe heavy that I hardly see what or how I write, nor doe I think you will be able to read it when I have done. . . . [T]is like people that talk in theire sleep, nothing interupts them but talking to them again and that you are not like to do at this distance, besyd's that at this instant you are I believe more asleep then I, and doe not soe much as dream that I am writeing to you. my fellow watchers have bin asleep too until just now, they begin to stretch and yawne, they are goeing to try if eating and drinking can keep them awake and I am kindly invited to bee of theire company. (Osborne 1928: 36–7)

This extraordinarily intimate portrait of herself, half-awake and half-asleep, ends – as we have already seen – with one of Osborne's most candid pronouncements of 'kindenesse' for Temple; what creates the intimacy is thus not only what she says, but the location of herself in the telling of it. In the same way that writing to someone whilst in bed – and telling them you are – is clearly one of the most effective means of bringing them to you, so does Osborne's attempt to 'take William with' her as she falls in and out of consciousness likewise 'shorten the distance'. The compulsive appeal of this practice, meanwhile, is strikingly evident when reviewing Osborne's correspondence as a whole. Many of the letters refer directly to the *process* of writing (especially her tendency to lose her train of thought!), and the lover's desire to preserve for ever the precious moment is demonstrated in her tendency to write to Temple immediately after they have met and parted ("Tis but an howr since you went, and I am writeing to you already, is not this kinde?'(Osborne 1928: 129–30)). But probably the most intimate of all the self-portraits Osborne offers in this regard is the delight she expresses over a lock of hair he has sent her. By this point (Letter 58) the two are 'officially engaged', but the frank depiction of her barely sublimated desire is arresting – even today:

> twill be pleasinger to you I am sure, to tell you how fond I am of your Lock; well in Earnest now and setting aside all complement, I never saw

> finer haire nor of a beter Couler, but cutt noe more on't, I would not have
> it spoyled for the world, if you love mee be carefull on't. I am combing
> and Curling and kissing this Lock all day, and dreaming ont all night.
> (Osborne 1928: 146)

Apart from this lock of hair, the 'official' engagement of Temple and
Osborne is marked by the exchange of rings and portraits, all of which
enhance the physical materiality of the correspondence and underline this
undervalued aspect of letter-writing. In an age where electronic mail is
rapidly rendering postal delivery obsolete, lovers should possibly attend to
what they are set to lose when they are no longer able to 'reduce the distance' between themselves and the other by this particular form of
'gifting'.[7]

Yet as well as *performing* the intimacies of romantic love in one of the
most interesting of ways, Osborne's letters have a good deal to say on the
subject. In the first instance, there are pages and pages of thoughts on what
constitutes a 'good marriage' and what a 'bad one'. In Letter 43, for
instance, she makes the startlingly progressive suggestion that couples
should live together for a trial period before they marry ('for my part I
think it were very convenient that all such as intend to marrye should live
together in the same house some year's of probation and if in all that time
they never disagreed they should then be permitted to marry if they pleasd'
(Osborne 1928: 102)) and in Letter 44 offers an extended portrait of the
'ideal husband' (Osborne 1928: 105). Although very clearly scripted to
amuse Temple as much as to pronounce her true opinion, Osborne's list
of desirable qualities (that is, gentility, refinement of taste, temperance)
nevertheless provides us with a useful 'gallery' of the varieties of (in)eli-
gible bachelor on offer in the seventeenth century and makes a very particular connection between 'breeding' and 'education': what she cannot
tolerate, it seems, is boorishness ('he must not bee soe much a Country
Gentleman as to understand Nothing but hawks and dog's' (Osborne 1928:
105)). Her parting shot – that husbands and wives should also *love* one
another – is expanded upon on numerous other occasions (e.g. Letter 4),
but often with a caveat attached. She has, indeed, a particular horror of
respectable women (that is, titled aristocrats like herself) making public
fools of themselves in their pursuit of 'Love'. Lady Sunderland and Lady
Anne Blunt are both invoked frequently in this context, and the scandals
surrounding their liaisons are evidently a strong contributory factor in her
request to call off her own engagement. At a moral/intellectual level, then,
we may conclude that Osborne's views on the role of romantic love within
marriage conformed to the dominant ideology of her day: marriage

without love (however defined) was 'wrong', but liaisons undertaken purely for love – without regard for 'name', rank and fortune – were equally reprehensible. Once her own engagement has been formalized, indeed, Osborne speaks out repeatedly on the importance of a 'fair settlement' on both sides; despite the fact that she has recently declared that she will die a maiden if she cannot marry Temple, she is now determined that the terms and conditions will be in keeping if not with her family's *fortune* then at least with their *name* (Osborne 1928: 179). What is hard, and yet vital, for the twenty-first-century reader to grasp is the fact that the nexus of rank and fortune is a profoundly *moral* concern: wealth bought respectability in a way we simply do not understand today; indeed, in this respect it is clear that Osborne's romantic proclivities were constrained by the vital need for 'good sense' that typifies the Austen heroine (see Chapter 3).

At this point the reader may be forgiven for thinking that if this is the 'endgame' of Osborne's courtship, it is not much of a 'Romance Story' after all. What does all her 'kindeness' for, and affection towards, Temple amount to if it is bound by such material concerns? Is the 'gift of a name' truly the *only* sort of gift that is worth anything to her? The answer, happily, is of course not. As my discussion of her skilful deployment of the epistolary genre has already shown, Osborne's tireless pursuit of Temple was engendered not by the pursuit of rank, or fortune, but by *desire* pretty much in the sense that we understand the term today (see Belsey 1994: 7–10). The most fascinating passages in the correspondence on the subject of romantic love are thus not those in which she propounds orthodoxies, but ones in which she presents herself – and Temple – as the subjects of forces quite outside their conscious control. Nowhere is the struggle between the force of such feelings and the material constraints afflicting the lovers – what Osborne refers to repeatedly as their 'misfortunes' – so powerfully expressed as in the sequence of letters (47–53) in which she proposes that they break off the relationship, and it to these that I now turn. These are texts in which the discourse of romantic love (as propounded in the French romances) and that of aristocratic decorum themselves go to war.

The catalyst for Osborne's proposal that they end their engagement seems to have been their meeting in London in the February of 1652/3 after not seeing each other for at least eighteen months. The meeting also followed the period of their most intense – and intimate – letter-writing, and one can imagine that it was the subsequent realization of their physical desire for one another that made the situation newly unbearable. It is certainly immediately after this meeting that the word 'passion' enters Osborne's vocabulary (see quotation at head of this section) along with statements of self-mortification. G. C. Moore Smith explains the nature of this anguish as stemming partly from her religious conscience (Osborne 1928: xi), which may well have been activated by what she considered to be an inappropriate expression of physical intimacy. The terms in which she presents and analyses their passion are certainly remarkably frank – and, indeed, 'modern' – for a seventeenth-century Englishwoman. Especially striking in this regard is the way that she insists that passion *ought* to be able to be brought under the command of 'Reason', only to finally concede that it is *beyond* conscious control (see Letter 53). Hers is a text, indeed, in which the arguments of both eighteenth-century rationalists and twentieth-century psychoanalysts are unwittingly anticipated and put to the test.

This crisis-moment in the couple's relationship – which lasts almost exactly one month – begins with Osborne falling ill (see Letter 46) and consequently being plunged into a depression and spiritual crisis which she considers 'punishment' for placing her 'passion' for Temple above all other human regard:

> I think I need not tell you how dear you have bin to mee nor that in your kindenesse I placed all the sattisfaction of my life, 'twas the only happinesse I proposed to my selfe, and had sett my heart soe much upon it, that it was therefore made my punishment, to let mee see that how innocent soever I thought my affection, it was guilty, in being greater then is allowable for things of this world; 'Tis not a melancholy humor gives me these aprehensions and inclinations, nor the perswasions of Others, tis the result of a long Strife with my selfe, before my Reason could overcome my passion, or bring me to a perfect Resignation to whatsoever is alotted for mee. (Osborne 1928: 114–15)

The religiosity of Osborne's remorse is further confirmed by the fact that she likens their passions to other kinds of sin (for example, covetousness, stubbornness, pride) despite the fact that the thing they desired was, of itself, 'innocent'; it becomes a sin simply by their wanting it too much (Osborne 1928: 116). This is, of course, another astute psychological observation on the nature of romantic love when it is in danger of becoming pathological: a topic to which she returns – with even more desperation – in Letter 48:

> You must pardon mee I cannot bee reconciled to it; 't has been the ruine of us both; Tis true that nobody must imagin to themselv's, ever to be absolute Masters ont, but there is a great difference betwixt that and

yeelding to it, between striveing with it, and soothing it up till it grow's too strong for one; Can I remember how ignorantly and innocently I sufferd it to steall upon mee by degrees; how under a maske of friendship I cousen'd myself into that, which had it apeard to mee at first in its true shape, I had fear'd and shunn'd. (Osborne 1928: 118)

For the modern reader, Osborne's reference to romantic love/passion as 'it' is wonderfully suggestive, conjuring up as it does all manner of bestial 'others' and *doppelgänger*, not to mention a prefiguration of the Freudian 'id'. Even without expropriating the text from its historical moment, however, it would seem that Osborne's recourse to abstraction is her attempt to capture the irrational power, and strangeness, of the feeling she is dealing with. Towards the end of this letter, indeed, she invokes the further striking metaphor of her heart as the site of 'Civill War' 'where two oppos[e]ing Party's have disputed there right soe long till they have made it worth neither their conquests' (Osborne 1928: 119). The endless struggle between reason and passion has as powerfully 'ruin'd' her personal prospects as the recent war has divided the nation.

Although Osborne's analysis of romantic love at this moral/psychological level is probably the most fascinating feature of the text for the modern reader, it is important not to overstate the case. As we have already seen, her decision to call off the engagement was precipitated by concerns for her respectability as much as by existential and religious angst. In Letter 48 she cites concern for her reputation as the reason why, if they meet again, it be 'the last of [our] interviews' and reminds Temple that a respectable woman can have no excuse meeting someone if there is 'noe hope of ever Marryeng him' (Osborne 1928: 120). The letter also contains the first of what becomes a repeated appeal to Temple to 'master' his own emotions, and cites instances of others who have 'loved and lost' and then loved again. It is also worth nothing that this particular letter – Letter 48 – is over 2000 words long and therefore one of the longest in the correspondence as a whole. Indeed, there is good reason to consider it the defining letter of the courtship, marshalling – as it does – all Osborne's desires and fears together into a single resolve.

But resolve or ultimatum? There is certainly a temptation for the modern reader to interpret the text as Osborne's decision to 'up the ante' and compel Temple to make a formal proposal of marriage. This, at least, is what seems to happen with first Temple's father, and then Osborne's brothers, granting their approval. Before that happens, however, Temple appears to have been pushed to the verge of taking his own life ('I tremble at the desperate things you say in your letter' (Osborne 1928: 126)) and

Osborne to recant and re-affirm her passion for him. This happens in Letter 53 (after four much shorter letters in which Temple is urged to apply reason and see sense), where she finally concedes: 'I never had the least hope of wearing out my passion, nor to say truth much desyre, for to what purpose should I have strived against it . . .' (Osborne 1928: 127). Towards the end of the letter she affirms that – *vis-à-vis* the status of their relationship – 'wee are but where wee were' (Osborne 1928: 129), and within the same week Temple visits her at Chicksands, presumably in order to formalize the engagement. Although there was evidently some attempt to keep the news private for a while after this, by 2 April 1654 the engagement was public knowledge.

From this point onwards, and until their marriage on Christmas Day that year, the letters become shorter and less effusive, focusing increasingly on practical arrangements. Cynics would doubtless present this as clear evidence, if any were needed, that what fuels the love letter is not love, *per se*, but rather *seduction* and all the 'obstacles' entailed. It is certainly true that Osborne's letters work hard not only at entertaining Temple but also, as we saw in the earlier discussion, presenting her 'self' (her intellect, her accomplishments, her habits) in the best possible light; but this conscious display of 'the lover's art' is repeatedly undermined by her myriad unconscious desires and fears. In this regard, Letter 17 probably remains her single most memorable testament to the 'condition' of romantic love, betraying – as it does – love's compulsion to 'speak its name', and repeatedly.

III

The Gift Called into Question: Seventeenth-Century Women Writers on Love and Marriage

Although Dorothy Osborne's letters demonstrate the tensions, and occasionally the contradictions, between the official, 'marriage-bound' discourses of romance in the seventeenth century and its counter-discourses (originating in Courtly Love, French literature and unconscious sexual desire), they fall short of outright critique. The same cannot be said of a good many of her female contemporaries and immediate successors who, across a wide range of genres, expose the dark underside of the 'loveless marriage' and, indeed, the fate of women who enter into sexual liaisons outside of marriage. Taken together, these texts raise serious questions about the exact nature of the gift conferred upon women through marriage and suggest that their new names entail a debt rather than a bonus.

One of the texts to raise this spectre most spectacularly is Margaret Cavendish, Duchess of Newcastle's *The Convent of Pleasure* (2002 [1688]). Given the importance Cavendish herself evidently placed on her own 'family name' and good marriage (her autobiography is, after all, entitled *A True Relation of my Birth, Breeding and Life* (1989 [1656]), it is perhaps surprising to discover that in this 'closet drama', both the central action (the courtship of Lady Happy by a Princess who turns out to be a Prince) and burlesque 'play-within-a-play' (Act III, Scene II), the *price* attached to love's gift is violently exposed. The latter is, indeed, an effective catalogue of the various abuses and punishments women – *of every class* – may expect to endure subsequent to marriage. These include: the husband's adultery, whoring, drinking, gambling and debt; the wife's pregnancy, childbirth, infant mortality and the betrayal/death of children later in life. Within many of these scenarios there is also the heavy threat of physical violence, in the form of both beating and rape. In Scene X, for example, a 'Gentleman' is seen chatting up a 'fair young lady', and when she refuses his attentions, he concludes: 'You had best be content; for, otherwise he will have you against your will.' She consequently demurs and promises to let him have an answer tomorrow. This vivid dramatization of a notional gift of love turning, in an instant, to violent coercion can, moreover, be seen to prefigure Lady Happy's own fate. The moment her Princess is discovered to be a Prince, the mutuality of their relationship gives way to *droit de seigneur*: 'But since I am discovered, go from me to the Councellors of this State, and inform them of my being here, as also the reason, and that I ask their leave I may marry this Lady; otherwise, tell them I will have her by force of Arms' (Act V, Sc. I) (Cavendish 2002: 283–4).

The fact that when a woman married she lost all economic independence, including the marriage portion, or dowry, she brought with her, was also perceived as a gross injustice/inequality by many seventeenth-century women writers. Although Dorothy Osborne appears to have been prepared to strive for a fair settlement despite the fact that she herself 'owned' none of it, several of her contemporaries clearly felt differently. The issue is raised directly in another of the sketches in *The Convent of Pleasure*, where a Lady observes: 'But my Husband hath not only lost his own Estate, but also my Portion; and hath forc'd me with threats, to yield up my Jointure, so that I must beg for a living' (Cavendish 2002: 270), and is also a central preoccupation of another remarkable text from the period: Martha

Moulsworth's autobiographical poem, 'The Memorandum of Martha Moulsworth, Widdowe' (Moulsworth 2004 [1632]: 258–61).

With a boldness and sanguinity that has caused her to be compared with Chaucer's Wife of Bath, Moulsworth tells the story of her (unusually privileged) education and three marriages, making candid reference not only to the sexual fulfilment she found with her third husband ('a lovely man and kind, Such comeliness in age we seldom find' (Moulsworth 2004: ll. 57–8)) but also to her pride in having survived them all and emerged as a rich widow. Implicit in this text, then, is the thought-provoking conclusion that it is *only* a widow of a certain age (Moulsworth is 55 and thus safely beyond the reach of childbearing) who can enjoy the material gifts of love and marriage *in her own right*.

Even those seventeenth-century women writers who elected to write within the genre of romance were not unaware of the paradoxical constraints the gift of a name placed on the idealized gift of love. As has already been noted in Part I, the multi-volumed escapades of the heroes and heroines of the French romances may be seen, in part, as fantastical projections of the more material obstacles that frequently stood in the way of men and women from the propertied classes. Many of these romances (including their English equivalents, such as Robert Greene's seminal *Pandosto* (1588)) depended upon endlessly recycled stock ingredients such as: a jealous king who deals unfairly with his own family and others; an abandoned daughter, brought up by a poor shepherd; a prince disguised as a shepherd, who then courts the princess; the prince's travels and eventual restoration of identity/fortune; the death of the king, and the marriage of the lovers (see Newcomb 2002: 3–4). What makes these texts *romances* (and not critiques), however, is the fact that villainous *individuals* rather than systems are seen to be to blame. It could be argued, indeed, that there is a strong element of this sort of rationalization in Osborne's figuration of her own 'Romance Story' (where much is made of difficult fathers and wicked brothers), and other texts, both from this period and into the eighteenth century (for example, Mary Hearne's *The Lover's Week* (1718) and *The Female Deserters* (1719)), persist in the romance tradition of converting social/economic obstacles into adventure.

As I noted above, however, such displacements rarely account entirely for complex and contradictory positioning of the lover, either in material or in emotional terms. In this respect, Lady Mary Wroth's epistolary verse-romance, *Pamphilia to Amphilanthus* (2002 [1621]) is a nicely expressive text with which to end this chapter. Breaking with the tradition of its precursor texts like Sir Philip Sidney's *Astrophil and Stella* (1973 [1591]) by having the woman speak of *her* desire, the poem – like Osborne's letters – is clearly in search of gifts and satisfactions beyond those of a name:[8]

> Love is the shining star of blessing's light,
> The fervent fire of zeal, the root of peace,
> The lasting lamp, fed with the oil of right,
> Image of faith, and joy for womb's increase.
>
> Love is true virtue, and his ends delight;
> His flames are joys, his bands true lovers' might.
>   (Wroth 2002: 185)

Circumscribed by poetic convention as it is (see note 8), the female voicing of these lines lends its sexual objective an iconoclastic edge. As will be seen in the next chapter, the rhetorical admixture of the spiritual and the sexual that we find here becomes increasingly polarized in the course of the next century, and the residual ideology of courtly love will bear the echo of a bygone age. Although good feminist, political sense can be made out of the turn towards the 'companionate marriage' that aspects of Osborne's and Temple's relationship endorse, it failed to fully accommodate the 'passion' (sublimated and otherwise) that had been the life-blood of early romance.[9] The story of romance in the eighteenth century is, indeed, one in which the prudery of much courtship fiction severs sex from love and sends it underground, and we have to wait until the end of that century – and the beginning of the next – for Osborne's elusive 'it' to once again make its appearance.

3

Courtship Romance

The Gift of Companionship

I

For all those who, like myself, are fascinated by romantic love precisely on
account of its unpredictability, its irrationality and its ability to bring the
best of us to our knees, the English courtship fiction of the late eighteenth
and early nineteenth centuries is – at first sight – pretty miserable fare. The
novels, almost exclusively by women writers, represent what Jane Spencer
has identified as the dominant (and highly successful) 'didactic tradition'
during a period of intense social and political change (Spencer 1986: 108).
In their apparent conservatism and deference to patriarchal law they are
generally positioned *against* other sub-genres, such as the seduction novel
or the Gothic novel, which feminists have seen as inherently more subversive, even if the 'resistance' has to be gleaned symptomatically and despite
a notional 'happy ending'.[1] And whilst mainstream courtship fiction – in
particular, Austen's novels – has itself been 'read on behalf of feminism'
in recent times, there are many (myself included) who have found this a
somewhat deadly labour.[2] For all their sparkling wit, playfulness and
unquestionable irony, these texts can at first appear as airless and stultify-
ing a reading experience as the closed, claustrophobic worlds that they represent. Thus while it has become something of a commonplace to assume
that Austen and Burney (in particular) were offering critiques of the 'marriage markets' they depict with such acuity, there is a dissenting line of
critics who have refused to rescue these texts from their dominant conservatism. As Jane Spencer observes:

> Novels with reformed heroines were about learning to repudiate faults
> seen as specially feminine, and accepting male authority instead of chal-
> lenging it. This is a tradition of conformity and, significantly, it had a more
> continuous history during the eighteenth century than the tradition of
> protest, and led to greater achievements in the novel: Fanny Burney, Maria
> Edgeworth and Jane Austen all drew more or less extensively on this tra-
> dition. (Spencer 1986: 143)

Although Spencer herself goes on to qualify this generalization with the observation that 'the tradition of conformity is hardly ever simply that: some protest about female subordination could be mingled with it, to the extent that the author sympathized with her heroine's errors' (Spencer 1987: 143), her political assessment of the texts in question is, I think, a fair one. Even as the 'comedy of manners' enacted in Austen's novels is redeemed by the fact that it *is* comedy ('Romantic comedy becomes Austen's means of reforming her heroines without elevating the hero's authority. Elizabeth [in *Pride and Prejudice*] is reformed without being subdued . . .' (Spencer 1986: 172)), it fails to significantly challenge the *status quo*. For many theorists this is, of course, the limit-point of the comedic mode; even the most virulent irony and satire must be figured, ultimately, as expressions not of resistance, but of impotence (see Hutcheon 1994).

It would ultimately be wrong – in literary-historical terms –, however, to insist on an absolute separation of courtship fiction from the other eighteenth-century genres which deal with romance. Although ostensibly defined 'against' the seduction novel and the Gothic novel, for example, it is clear that most courtship fiction is in complex dialogue with such texts, and for this reason my reading of Austen's *Persuasion* in Part II of the chapter will make sense only when placed alongside the readings of the selection of Gothic and other texts performed in Part III. *All* the texts of this period are characterized by their struggle to explain, and give voice to, the as yet unnamed 'unconscious', and romantic love – as a consequence – is more or less a mystery for the authors concerned. What remains somewhat depressing about a good many of the courtship novels, however, is what is *substituted* for that mystery. Indeed, the 'gift' from husband to wife and vice versa in a good many of these texts is distinguished from those discussed in the other chapters precisely by the fact that it is a substitute *for love* rather than a supplement *to it*. As we shall see in the discussion that follows, the combined forces of familial duty, rationalist philosophy and the Protestant religion meant that, while young people were increasingly encouraged to make matches based on 'character' as well as wealth and status, these 'qualities' were often – though admittedly *not always* – figured as compensation for the lack of sexual and emotional compatibility (see Abbott 1993: 57–62).

The Consolation of Companionship

We need first to consider, however, the huge *improvement* in interpersonal relations signalled by the arrival of so-called 'companionate marriage' in the late seventeenth century. In *The Family, Sex and Marriage in England 1500–1800* (1979) Lawrence Stone is careful to emphasize how much progress is made in liberating relationships between the sexes in England in the period following the Civil War. Until this key transitional moment, marriage (for the propertied classes) was – according to Stone – truly no more than the 'gift of a name':

> Family relationships were characterized by interchangeability, so that sub-
> stitution of another wife or another child was easy, and by conformity to
> external rules of conduct. The family group was held together by shared
> economic status and political interests, and by the norms and values of
> authority and deference. . . . It was a structure held together not by affec-
> tive bonds but by mutual economic interest. (Stone 1979: 88)

Although many of these rules – economic and social – only had meaning for the classes who owned property, Stone has inferred, from the limited archival evidence available, that love – as we understand it today – was of equally limited importance to the peasantry. He concludes that 'so far as the surviving evidence goes, England between 1500 and 1660 was relatively cold, suspicious, and violence-prone' (Stone 1979: 80); 'at all social levels there was a general psychological atmosphere of distance, manipulation, and deference' (88). Starting from this standpoint, then, the increasing demand for affection and companionship in marriage (*as well as* eco-nomic/social status) must indeed be seen as revolutionary, even if the emotion that is sought, and traded, bears little resemblance to romantic love *per se*. The nation may still have been a long way away from the concept of interpersonal relationships based primarily upon sexual com-patibility, but notions of personality and moral worth gained increasing hold from the period of the Civil War onwards.

Writing as an historian rather than a literary/cultural theorist, Stone focuses primarily on the social/economic changes of the late seventeenth century that facilitated the growing importance of 'affect' for the proper-tied classes. These included: (1) the decline of kinship and clientage as orga-nizing principles of landed society; (2) the simultaneous rise in the powers and the claims of the state; (3) higher obligations to state and monarchy; (4) the growth of Protestant Christian morality (Stone 1979: 102). Whilst the first three changes impacted on relationships largely through extended kinship systems being replaced with what is now thought of as the 'nuclear family' (and affiliation to 'King and country' rather than kin and clan), the last worked directly at the level of ideology. Although still severely patri-archal in its analysis of relationships between the sexes, the new Puritan sects insisted that 'holy marriage' be predicated upon mutual affection and respect. Stone quotes Milton to illustrate this point:

> For him [Milton] the prime object of marriage was 'the apt and cheerful conversation of man with woman, to comfort and refresh him against the solitary life'. By minimizing the sexual and procreative functions of marriage he came to the conclusion that 'natural hatred is a greater evil in marriage than the accident of adultery'. On the other hand, Milton had very strong views about the subordinate function of women – 'who can be ignorant that woman was created for man, and not man for woman?' – and therefore demanded divorce only when the 'unfitness' lay with the wife, not with the husband. . . . Milton thus carried the Protestant concept of holy matrimony about as far as it could go, without abandoning the sexual superiority of the male. (Stone 1979: 102–3)

According to Stone, then, the discourse of companionship has its historical origins in the rise of the 'affective individualism' (Stone 1979: 103) that steadily gained ground in England in the latter part of the seventeenth century. It was for the most part, however, a discourse that was significantly at odds with the 'affect' associated with the romantic love of literature and legend, and thus raised questions about the type of affection 'appropriate' to married love. Romantic love was regarded by 'all theologians, moralists, authors of manuals of conduct, and parents and adults in general' as 'a form of impudent folly and even madness' (Stone 1979: 128), even though by the eighteenth century there was an 'increasingly open recognition and acceptance of sensuality' (Stone 1979: 149–50) in relations between husband and wife.

It is at this point in his discussion that Stone's otherwise invaluable assessment of the changing social and cultural climate of the period 1660–1800 reaches its disciplinary limit and sends us back to the literature that is the subject of the present chapter. Before constructing that alternative 'literary history', however, it is worth noting Stone's analysis of how *choice* did (or did not) revolutionize relationships between the sexes during this period. Moving on from his conclusion that, prior to the late seventeenth century, there was effectively *no* choice of marriage partner for either men or women, Stone observes the emergence of a new 'power of veto' from this moment onwards (Stone 1979: 181–2). Whilst plenty of marriages continued to be 'arranged' in the absolute sense – that is, the parents/kin alone were responsible for making the choice –, more liberal parents allowed their children a right to veto the prospective partner (even if this was a 'freedom' granted prospective husbands more often than prospective brides). We have, of course, already seen one late seventeenth-century woman – Dorothy Osborne – make repeated use of this indulgence, but, according to Stone, its application increased with time. Much rarer were the marriages where the bride and bridegroom chose each other and offered the *parents* the right to veto the match, though the establishment of the 'marriage markets' of the late eighteenth century and early nineteenth century were, in part, intended to make the young people 'do the looking' in a way that was inconceivable before.

This is, of course, the very historical and cultural moment that is presented to us in the courtship fiction of Burney, Austen *et al*. Were there *no choice* in the matter of marriage partners, these stories could never have been written, even if it is a much more conditional notion of 'choice' than the one most of us reckon with today. By the end of the eighteenth century, indeed, the opportunities for the propertied classes to identify marriage partners outwith their immediate social circle/geographical region had grown immensely. As well as the *'county* marriage markets' that may be historically identified by the building of Assembly Rooms the length and breadth of England, and the *'national* marriage market' centred on the 'seasons' at London (Spring) and Bath (Summer), card parties, annual fairs and horse-racing provided eligible young people with new opportunities to meet one another (Stone 1979: 213). In addition, the introduction of Lord Hardwicke's Marriage Act of 1753, which deemed a marriage 'official' only once it had been solemnized in church, removed parents' worries about secret, but binding, prior 'engagements' (Stone 1979: 213). Until this Act, indeed, marriage in the British Isles took many forms, with the 'spousals' (sometimes referred to as the 'handfast') representing the binding moment of union for many (Stone 1979: 34).[3] After 1753, the only way of securing a so-called 'clandestine marriage' was to travel to Scotland, which then, as now, operated according to a different legal system. This was, indeed, the moment in history when Gretna Green – the first town north of the border – became synonymous with elopement.

Such was the impact of this institutionalization of the marriage market in England in the late eighteenth and early nineteenth century that – according to Stone – foreign visitors began to look upon the nation with wonder. On the continent, marriages amongst the aristocracy and propertied classes were still entirely built upon family interests, and the notion of personal preferences entering into marriage choice was virtually unheard of. For travellers like the Duc de La Rochefoucauld, indeed, late eighteenth-century England offered an extraordinary insight into married life as a state of companionship and domestic bliss: 'Husband and wife are always together and share the same society. It is the rarest thing to meet the one without the other . . . they always give the appearance of perfect harmony, and the wife in particular has an air of contentment which always gives me pleasure' (in Stone 1979: 220).

With such evidence to hand, it is clear that an affective revolution of sorts did take place in England in the course of the seventeenth and eighteenth centuries and that – patriarchy notwithstanding – men and women of the middle and upper classes entered marriage with significantly higher emotional expectations. What remains unclear is the extent to which the resulting 'companionship' took account of sexual desire and/or the values associated with specifically 'romantic' love. Although, as we shall now see, the *literature* of the age inclined to new polarities on the subject, it is important to recognize that, for some, *companionship* signalled a new order of intimacy that was inclusive, rather than exclusive, of 'romance'. Austen's novels are, indeed, of considerable help here inasmuch as they can be see to offer examples of both 'radical' and 'compromised' companionship.

The Discourse of Companionship vs the Discourse of Romantic Love

Mary Wollstonecraft's biography, and the writings that shadowed it, encapsulate the war that was waged between these two contending discourses during the latter part of the eighteenth century. As Dorothy Osborne's letters (written over a century earlier) evince, it was a 'war' that had been going on for some time, with all those who experienced, within love, an element of 'passion' struggling to reconcile their feelings with doctrines (official and unofficial) that firmly rejected such intense emotion as the basis for marriage. Indeed, it will be recalled that during and after the crisis in their relationship, Dorothy agonized endlessly over the propriety of her and William's feelings for one another and repeatedly pitted the received wisdom of her peers against the love she had read about in the French romances. For Wollstonecraft, meanwhile, it was rather a case of Feeling giving the lie to Reason when she became involved with the French Revolutionary Gilbert Imlay, with whom she had an illegitimate daughter (see Wollstonecraft 1976: xiv–xv). Although Imlay later abandoned her, and Wollstonecraft went through a period of horrific personal distress (including several suicide attempts) before eventually marrying William Godwin, the experience convinced her of the centrality of sexual desire within love relationships. Thus the woman who, as a passionate advocate of Reason in the quest for personal and political justice, initially advised that 'a master and a mistress of a family ought not to continue to love each other with passion' (Wollstonecraft, *A Vindication of the Rights of Woman* (1792), quoted in Spencer 1986: 133) came to write – in her unfinished novel, *Maria, or The Wrongs of Woman* (1976 [1798]) – one of the most candid critiques of romantic love (its pleasures as well as its pains) ever penned. As Spencer concludes:

> Wollstonecraft went much further than her contemporaries in defiance of sexual mores. . . . She also went much further than earlier novelists in the tradition of protest, by criticizing not only the seducer and the social ostracism of his victim, but the very definition of seduction. . . .Without abandoning her feminist analysis of artificial sensibility, she developed a revolutionary view of sexuality which she expressed in her second novel. (Spencer 1986: 132–4)

I shall return to Wollstonecraft's extraordinary 'second novel' in Part III of this chapter, but we need first to look a little more closely at how the discourse of romantic love and its purported 'artificial sensibility' had been represented in the fiction of the earlier part of the century.

As was noted in the introduction to this chapter, eighteenth-century novels dealing with romance may be broadly categorized into three types: (1) the Gothic novel; (2) the seduction novel; and (3) the courtship novel. Although there is a good deal of overlap between these sub-genres at both a structural and an ideological level, it would also be fair to say that they are distinguished by different notions of love and a different gendered viewpoint. Whilst the seduction novel, in its original male-authored form, focused on the male lover's adventures and regarded the seduced heroine only as a function of her purity and virtue, both the female-authored versions of the seduction tale – for example, novels by Delarivière Manley, Eliza Haywood, Sarah Fielding and Mary Brunton (see Spender 1976) – and the Gothic novel dealt with the experience from the point of view of the heroine. Moreover, in terms of the *manner* of the love/desire under investigation, the Gothic novels may be seen to follow in the footsteps of both the medieval and seventeenth-century French romances, whilst the seduction novels were predicated upon an *ironic* treatment of the same. As critics such as David Fairer have noted, however, the extent to which eighteenth-century 'anti-romance' ideology rejects the earlier texts and their values is debatable (Fairer 2004: 197ff.). Excessive 'romanticism' (and, in particular, heroines' penchant for the reading of French romances) may be mocked, but (as Spencer concludes) 'sentimental writers copy the romance's submissive lover [male] in their own picture of [ideal] love relationships' (Spencer 1986: 184). It is thus only with the rise of the courtship novel *per se* that a new model of love and relationships finally emerges that is seriously at odds with that evident in the literature of earlier centuries.

Although the next chapter provides a more complete account of the Gothic as the genre that first grappled with the dark, unconscious underside of love and desire, it is necessary to say a few words here about its early eighteenth-century manifestation. Indeed, as is noted in Chapter 4, literary history has drawn a clear distinction between the 'terror Gothic', with its origins in the works of Ann Radcliffe and other female authors of the period, and the 'horror Gothic', which followed on from Matthew Lewis's infamous *The Monk* (1796). With regard to the 'terror' tradition, it is evident that the texts and authors are linked most closely with early romance not so much in their depiction of love but rather in their insatiable appetite for *adventure*. The *raison d'être* of these texts is very obviously not the marriage to the 'good prince' at the end (as Diane Hoeveler has noted, 'these marriages are less celebrations than they are quiet acceptances of their new keepers' (Hoeveler 1998: 38)), but the (spectacular) journeys on which the heroines are sent in their efforts to escape, and overcome, a persecuted past. Although these novels – and Radcliffe's in particular – thus resound with incidents and experiences of high emotional intensity, these are rarely visited upon the heroine's love-object *per se* but are sublimated, instead, in the (spectacular) forces of wild nature or the (hidden) terrors of a dungeon or subterranean passage. Indeed, the fate of the unwaveringly 'pure' heroines of Gothic texts is often indistinguishable from those of mainstream courtship fiction, even to the extent that their prospective husbands are often asexual, brother-like characters. This said, the locations and circumstances in which their romance takes place grants them an excitement wholly absent from the domestic interiors of London and Bath.

As already indicated, the eighteenth-century seduction novel – in both its male- and female-authored forms – is likewise unable to shake off the romantic love ideology of previous centuries as easily as it would like. One excellent – and textually complex – instance of this is Charlotte Lennox's *The Female Quixote* (1970 [1752]). Following in the tradition not only of Cervantes but also of Richardson and Fielding, Lennox presents us with a heroine who is both the dupe of romance (she is, first and foremost, an avid reader of French romances) and its defender. Clive Probyn describes the way in which the decision of its heroine, Arabella, 'to live not in the real world but in an already-written romantic narrative' (Probyn 2004: 253–5) may be seen not merely as escapism but as a canny strategy to preserve her independence and autonomy for as long as possible. Spencer for the most part echoes this sentiment, reminding us also that what sold the book to its readers was its subtitle (*'The Adventures of Arabella'*) and *not* the compromised and (for Arabella) chastening ending. Another especially interesting female-authored seduction novel is Mary Collyer's *Felicia to Charlot* (1744), which imitates Richardson in its epistolary form. Although, according to Spencer, Felicia's letters begin as a parody of the romance (especially in the portrayal of her less than heroic suitor, Lucius), in the end the heroine is forced to admit that: 'I seem to be writing one myself' (in Spencer 1986: 185). Like Glanville in *The Female Quixote*, Felicia simply cannot escape being positioned as a romantic heroine. It will be seen, then, that for all their ostensible critique of romantic – and, in particular, *chivalric* – behaviour, these seduction novels preserve an affectionate nostalgia for love as it was construed in former times.

Another way in which this residual ideology was preserved, and yet distinguished from the rationalist present, was through the mechanism of historical novels like Sir Walter Scott's. As Fiona Price has observed, putting romance in an explicitly party-political context: 'For Scott romance remains associated with Jacobitism, arbitrary authority, and the French influence, but belongs to a sublime past; legal and economic restraints form the unromantic present. Unlike Richardson's, Scott's account suggest that romance and the modern social contract belong to different historical phases' (Price 2004: 283). Playing the 'history' card was, then, one further way in which writers from the eighteenth century could hold on to a model of romantic love – and its attendant world-view – that had become deeply unfashionable in the contemporary intellectual world (see also Richter 1996: 102–5). The other option was to submit to the ideology of the times and attempt to modernize, and rationalize, beliefs and practices that were seen, by some, as no better than superstitious nonsense. Such a rationalization was undertaken by significant numbers of women writers working in both the seduction and courtship novel traditions and representing both conservative and emancipatory social groups. Mainstream Tories and proto-feminist educators were, indeed, united in their desire to rescue impressionable young women from 'romantic fantasy' and prepare them for the 'realities' of married life.

Mary Wollstonecraft's commitment to just such a cause was noted at the beginning of this section. Of Charlotte Smith's novel, *Emmeline* (1788), which includes elements of Gothic fantasy, she wrote: 'the false expectations which these scenes excite, tend to debauch the mind, and tend to throw an insipid kind of uniformity over the moderate and rational prospects of life, consequently adventures are sought for and created, when duties are neglected, and content despised' (Wollstonecraft in *The Analytical Review* (1788), cited in Spencer 1986: 208). Whilst this pious resistance to romance is resoundingly overturned in Wollstonecraft's later novels, the ideas and values she expresses at this earlier point in time had widespread currency amongst feminist educationalists. Indeed, the central focus on what constituted a young woman's 'proper' education and moral development within the genre of courtship fiction has caused some critics to argue they are better classified as *Bildungsromanen* (see Collins 2005: 102). Re-classifying women's fiction from this perspective certainly helps when one comes to those hybrids which follow the narrative structure of the seduction novel but trade in the moral/ideological values of courtship fiction. A good example of this, discussed by Spencer, is Sarah Fielding's *The Countess of Dillwyn* (1759), which deals with the story of a wife's seduction and infidelity, but within a highly conservative moral framework. Such 'values' were, of course, also circulated via the conduct books of the day, and on this point it is important to realize that the dialectic of entertainment and instruction formed part of a long tradition. Simons, for example, notes just how many of the chapbook versions of medieval and/or seventeenth-century French romances (for example, 'Guy of Warwick') effectively became *manuals* on 'how to conduct courtship' (Simons 2004: 181), quite apart from the literature written specifically for that purpose such as Dr John Gregory's *Father's Legacy to His Daughters* (1774) or Hannah More's *Cheap Repository Tracts* (1795–8) and *Coelebs in Search of a Wife* (1809). And while there is a significant ideological gap between the presentation of love and its 'conduct' in these two classes of literature, it is clear that the writers of courtship fiction were, in effect, the inheritors of both; their challenge, as it were, was to communicate the message of Dr Gregory within a storyline that held the reader's interest (albeit at the level of intrigue and comedy rather than passion) (see Spencer 1986: 110–11).

On the subject of romantic love *per se*, meanwhile, conduct books like Dr Gregory's were unequivocally repressive, and based their advice on the assumptions that: (1) respectable women did not suffer from sexual desire; and (2) love and affection were emotions that 'naturally' followed upon marriage. There is (in Gregory's text) also to be found the notion that an implicit narcissism causes women to love where they are loved: 'What is commonly called love among you is rather gratitude, and a particularity to the men who prefer you to the rest of your sex' (Gregory, *Father's Legacy to His Daughters* (1774), in Spencer 1986: 111). This, of course, links directly with the nature of the reform undergone by the heroines of most mainstream courtship novels: that is, the abandonment of coquetry

('The typical heroine in need of reform is a coquette . . . Vanity and unsteadiness were the coquette's distinguishing characteristics' (Spencer 1986: 142)). Reform, moreover, is nearly always brought about through the services of a 'lover-mentor': a substitute father (or brother) figure whom the heroine does not, at first, think of as a 'love-object' but eventually gives herself up to on account of the values he himself has educated her in. As Spencer further observes: 'Masculine guidance and protection are the answer to the heroine's problems, and she is given a substitute father to guard her from other men and from her own female nature' (Spencer 1986: 147). To this list may, of course, be added romantic love itself.

II

Jane Austen's Consolation Prize?

Returning to the philosophical models of romantic love discussed in Chapter 1, it is clear that one of the ways of understanding the phenomenon in Jane Austen's novels is as an almost fundamentalist expression of 'property-based love'. The following algebraic explication of that condition by Alan Soble reads, I would suggest, like a parody of the mad relay of character evaluation and preference that characterizes novels like *Pride and Prejudice* (1972 [1813]), *Emma* (1996 [1816]) and, indeed, *Persuasion* (1985 [1818]):

> Suppose that x's stated reason for loving y is that y has attractive quality P, but that (unknown to x) y does not in fact have P; nevertheless, suppose in addition that x is caused to love y by y's having some other property Q. There are in this scenario two causes for x's loving y: x's (false) belief that y has P (the reason-cause) and y's having Q, which operates behind the scenes of x's consciousness as a nonreason-cause. Hence x's love is both reason-dependent and property-based, but x's love is non-ideal because x makes two mistakes: x believes falsely that (1) y has P and that (2) y's having P totally explains x's love. (Soble 1990: 7)

Laying to one side the intricacies of the philosophical argument presented here, I would invite readers to focus merely on the rhetoric and consider: what does it *mean* for love to be based on, and defined by, a subject's ability to perceive, and evaluate, 'properties' in another? Further, what does it mean for that love to be contingent upon the subject's ability to judge both y and him/herself *accurately* and to avoid 'mistakes'? Can a relationship predicated upon semiology really aspire to the condition that human beings experience as love?

My own feeling – following on from the discussion begun in Chapter 1 – is that allowance has to be made for the *nature* of the property and how, or why, it has been given value. Although Soble does not himself reflect upon this variable, there is surely a difference between loving/desiring someone for an idiosyncrasy of appearance or character (see Barthes 1990: 18–21; Soble 1990: 89, 143), and loving them because of one or more qualities (for example, sensitivity, good sense of humour) that figure as a set of pre-conceived expectations or an ideology. It is, moreover, a difference that is crucial to our understanding of the somewhat 'muddled' (Butler 1975: 279–83) sexual/textual unconscious of Austen's *Persuasion* and explaining why this last novel, in part, goes beyond the arid equation of love with moral value/virtue that characterizes its predecessors. Anne Elliot and Frederick Wentworth may believe that they love one another because of a particular set of moral properties/values (Soble's *P*), but the unfolding of their 'second romance' reveals the operation of far more wayward and contradictory forces: forces that may be accounted for as either blessedly *irrational* sexual desire (Wentworth) or full-blown agapic love (Anne).

It will be recalled that Soble himself is a staunch defender of the view that 'personal love' is property-based and hence erosic: in philosophical terms, the agapic rationale is always in danger of collapsing lover and beloved and hence losing the specificity of what attracts one person to another and makes the latter the (apparently) 'unique' object-ideal. He does, however, allow that the discourse of specifically *romantic* love may contain agapic elements (for example, the 'illusion' of unconditionality, non-repeatability, irrationality and infinity) and also that a love which begins by being 'property-based' may *become* agapized. This last possibility remains my own first preference since it is clear that – at the level of *discourse* at least – human subjects *are* positioned to believe in love as unconditional and, ideally, non-repeatable. It would, however, be fair to say that the extent to which these agapic features are permitted to operate within property-based models of personal love varies historically. Whilst, from the mid-nineteenth century onwards, the fusion of the two models becomes increasingly common, for example, we must assume that Agape was anathema to the new types of affective relationship – including companionate marriage – that grew out of Puritanism. What the English Revolution heralded, in particular, was the equation of personal properties with moral – and specifically Christian – values; whilst tenderness and emotional/physical affection were given new importance (see Stone's argument above) they constituted an erosically *rational* (as opposed to an agapically *irrational*) 'gift'. As we saw in Part I of this chapter, both theologians and writers (including Milton) developed a very explicit check-list of the values that husbands (and especially) wives should bring to their relationships; the personal properties which best served God were also those which best served domestic patriarchy.

The personal properties most valued by Milton are those equally valued by Austen and her late eighteenth-century predecessors, but careful study of any one of her novels reveals that a vastly expanded taxonomy of desirable attributes has now been added to basic Christian qualities such as (for the female) modesty, honesty, obedience and grace. Indeed, the merry dance of courtship and match-making that all the texts deal in calibrate these properties with a niceness and precision that will be lost on the contemporary reader until s/he learns the 'code'. Moreover, as Marilyn Butler observes, what distinguishes these properties or values from *merely* Christian ones is their role in identifying – and maintaining – a rigid social hierarchy. The values that Austen's texts promote, and prize, the most are – in Bourdieu's terms – 'marks of distinction' that discriminate between one social class and another:[4]

> The familiar Austen moral abstractions avoid seeming abstract, so closely are they bound up with an orderly pattern of behaviour, a set of assumptions imposed by the material circumstances of leisured middle-class life. The nouns which convey her positives – 'powers' [*sic*], 'grace', 'elegance', 'understanding' – are general, but the effect is never cloudy. The syntax Jane Austen gives to those characters she favours is decided and clear, revealing that, for her, personal merit is bound up with perspicuity – the power to discern general truths. (Butler 1975: 1)

Considered *vis-à-vis* a cognate consideration of Austen's representation of romantic love, we must thus conclude that the personal properties she believes to be 'worthy of love' are those which most emphatically secure a subject's *gentility*; more, that this gentility will express itself in his/her ability to read 'marks of distinction' in others as well as to display his, or her, own.

Within this super-refined Austen dictionary, no term, indeed, is more loaded than that of 'gentleman'. The often poignant, frequently ironic, invocation of the term to expose the snobbery and/or misplaced values of certain characters is, of course, not unique to Austen, though its connotations for her heroines – operating within a ruthless, sometimes treacherous, marriage market – are especially intense. Although, for some of the less perspicacious characters – like Emma and Sir Walter Elliot in *Persuasion* – gentlemanliness is reduced to a matter of rank and breeding ('You misled me by the term *gentleman*. I thought you were speaking of some

man of property: Mr Wentworth was nobody, I remember; quite uncon-
nected' (Austen 1985: 52–3)), it is clear that – for prospective wives – something rather more is hoped for. Indeed, reading between the lines, I would
suggest that many of these women seem to be harbouring the desperate
hope that the refinement of manners and/or evidence of education that
are essential to the 'gentleman' are signifiers of a more material (indeed,
an explicitly *physical*) kindness and consideration. Observing to what extent
such kindness was frequently lacking in married life (see discussion of
Wollstonecraft's texts following), it is not surprising that there was a huge
investment in this particular personal property. Being married to a man
who was as gentle with his hands as in his speech was, one must assume,
a significant consolation for all those obliged to enter into partnerships
with little choice in the matter.

The problem with personal properties that are so obviously dependent
upon education and/or instruction in etiquette, however, is that anyone –
with access to that education – may learn them. The challenge that dom-
inates the lives of Austen's suitors (both male and female) is thus to distinguish between the true and false ownership of these properties on the
assumption that they are 'signifiers' which presuppose a 'signified'.[5] And
whilst today, with the hindsight of Saussure, we know that no such necessary link exists, Austen's characters (and especially her heroines) repeatedly gamble on a continuity between 'surface' and 'depth' – providing, of
course, the surface has been read correctly. In this regard, indeed, Austen
was an author for whom the notion of character was more akin to Renaissance humours than to post-Enlightenment psychology. As Juliet McMaster has shown in her study of the 'symptoms' of love in Austen's *oeuvre*,
the texts certainly exhibit a profound belief in the connection between the
conduct of the (outer) body and the temper of the (inner) mind (McMaster 1996: 130). In each and every one of Austen's novels, however, the *practice* of this semiology of 'manners and morals' looks forward to Derrida
rather more than it looks back to the Renaissance. Although all 'the best'
characters learn to read the runes correctly in the end (indeed, that is their
principal education), most of them make serious mistakes along the way;
mistakes that, for today's reader, signal rather less their lack of moral per-
spicacity than their entrapment in a world of simulacra. In *Persuasion*, the
dizzying impossibility of distinguishing moral depth from surface manners
is encapsulated in the figure of William Walter Elliot. His appearance is,
if anything, even *more* 'gentlemanly' than Wentworth's, and Lady Russell,
for one, is utterly seduced by a veritable excess of properties that render
him the most eligible bachelor in town: 'Every thing united in him; good

understanding, correct opinions, knowledge of the world, and a warm heart' (Austen 1985: 159). Quite apart from the fact that William Walter Elliot's superficial perfection is soon afterwards exposed (by Mrs Smith) as a complete and utter sham, Lady Russell's inventory of the most desirable – and 'marriageable' – gentlemanly properties also raises serious questions about the specificity, or uniqueness, of a suitor. The message here would seem to be that the more points a man can score on a checklist of this kind, the more desirable he may be supposed to be; even though properties reduced to manners must singularly fail to distinguish him as an 'individual' in the sense we understand the term today. Indeed, there is plenty of evidence – in both *Persuasion* and the other novels – to suggest that 'good' (that is, eligible) characters *are* virtually indistinguishable from one other: take, for instance, the assumed interchangeability between Edward and Robert in *Sense and Sensibility* (1990 [1811]); or, indeed, the difficulty the community has in deciding whether Henrietta or Louisa would be a more suitable match for Wentworth. Austen's texts must, of course, be read as *critiques* of such an instrumental approach to human nature whilst also bearing witness both to its practice and to its ideological sway.

As was noted in Chapter 1, any notion of personal love based upon the beloved's possession of particular properties will inevitably lead its advocate to the conclusion that y can be replaced by w, if w possesses some – or all – of the qualities possessed by y. And if properties are understood to equate with manners and morals, as they are in most courtship fiction, there is compelling evidence to suggest that love relationships, far from being unique, are easily repeatable. That Wentworth himself believes this is evident not only in the fact that, when he returns to the village of Kellynch, it is with the express purpose of finding a wife who will replace Anne in his heart's affections (Austen 1985: 86), but also in his later explanation for why he had not, during the eight-year separation, been in love with anyone else. In significant contrast to Anne, who – with all the exclusivity and non-repeatability of the agapic lover – has never ceased to love Wentworth *qua* Wentworth, he has merely failed to find someone with properties comparable to Anne's. As he confesses at the novel's denouement (via the reported speech of Austen's narrator):

> Of what he had then written [in his letter] nothing was to be retracted or qualified. He persisted in having loved none but her. She had never been supplanted. He never even believed himself to see her equal. . . . Her character was now fixed on his mind as perfection itself, maintaining the loveliest medium of fortitude and gentleness; but he was obliged to acknowledge that only at Uppercross had he learnt to do her justice, and only at Lyme had he begun to understand himself. (Austen 1985: 243–4)

And yet this, of course, is only half (that is, the rational half) of Wentworth talking, and only half (literally) of what he says on this occasion.
Excised by my own ellipses is a rare, but crucial, acknowledgement of the
role of the *unconscious* in matters of the heart. Although it would be a
mistake to consider Wentworth's love agapized to the same extent of
Anne's, Austen's choice of words suggests that for her hero, too, love exists,
and *persists*, beyond the realm of reason; witness the restored text:

> He never even believed himself to see her equal. *Thus much indeed he was
> obliged to acknowledge – that he had been constant unconsciously, nay uninten-
> tionally; that he had meant to forget her, and believed it to be done. He had imag-
> ined himself indifferent, when he had only been angry; and he had been unjust to
> her merits, because he had been a sufferer from them.* Her character was now
> fixed on his mind . . . (Austen 1985: 243–4, my italics)

Thus, despite the fact that Wentworth's unconscious adherence to Anne is
here given a quasi-rational explanation (it was precipitated by his hurt and
anger), the principle that human beings may love one another *in spite of*
perceived negative properties has been admitted.

What I am proposing here, then, is that *Persuasion* is the novel in which
Austen goes furthest in unsettling the notion that love is – and should be
– property-based, and explores the subversive forces of Agape. This is
subtly different from saying that this is the text which (along with *Pride and
Prejudice*) most frankly acknowledges the force of explicitly *sexual* desire,
even though the two are not, of course, unrelated. Yet Anne's love for
Wentworth is characterized by an outward motion and adherence to the
other '*qua* other' that escapes the more solipsistic workings of the sexual
drives and would appear to conform, most closely, to the paradigms of
Courtly Love. As the novel progresses it becomes clear that she is not insen-
sible to the charms and attractions (indeed, the 'properties') of other men
such as William Walter Elliot (Austen 1985: 125), but her early love for
Wentworth was so personally transformative ($x + y \rightarrow x' + y$) that it has
acquired a *singularity* that cannot easily be reproduced. The discovery of
such alchemy in a love-match is clearly inimical not only to property-based
theories of love which insist that x may love w as well as y (if w possesses
similar qualities to y) but also to drive-theories which argue that, given
time, a bereaved subject will seek out a new ideal-object (see discussions
in Chapter 1 and Chapter 4): x may well discover a new y, but what s/he
cannot necessarily repeat is the ensuing reaction – the [$'$].

Anne and Wentworth, happily, are spared the need to pursue the latter
experiment to its conclusion. Through the benign workings of chance and
circumstance (Wentworth's sister comes to live at Kellynch Hall), they are
thrown together once again and – in due course – the *same* spark [$'$] is

re-ignited. That this is essentially a resumption of their former relationship is evidenced by the fact that there is no second courtship as such; merely a sequence of supremely awkward meetings in which the two lovers barely speak to or look at one another. For several commentators, Austen's treatment of these encounters is the most distinctive feature of the text, so radically removed are they from the standard fare of courtship fiction. As Marilyn Butler observes:

> The intimacy with which Jane Austen approaches Anne's consciousness appears to be something extraordinary. So, too, is the effect of high-wrought nervous tension, compared to the mental worlds of the other characters, whose attention is dissipated among the trivia of their external relationships . . . There is nothing in subjective fiction in any other English novel to compare in subtlety of insight or depth of feeling with the sequence of nervous scenes between the hero and heroine in *Persuasion*. (Butler 1975: 278)

The most memorable of these 'nervous scenes' include: Anne's first fleeting re-encounter with Wentworth at the cottage when she is so flustered she barely sees him (Austen 1985: 84–6); the occasion on which he rescues her from the clutches of the infant Walter (Austen 1985: 102–4); the chance meeting in Bath in which she gets the 'advantage' by seeing him first (Austen 1985: 185); and, of course, the concert (Austen 1985: 194–9). The latter is by far the lengthiest direct conversation the couple share in the course of the novel, and one in which Anne – having correctly 'read' Wentworth's renewed feelings for her – has the greater control. This said, the event is still focalized through her significantly heightened and disordered consciousness:

> Anne saw nothing, thought nothing of the brilliancy of the room. Her happiness was from within. Her eyes were bright, and her cheeks glowed, – but she knew nothing about it. She was thinking only of the last half hour, and as they passed to their seats, her mind took a hasty range over it. . . . sentences begun which he could not finish – his half averted eyes, and more than half expressive glance, – all, all declared that he had a heart returning to her at least . . . (Austen 1985: 194–5)

Given the amount of emphasis that is placed in this, as in all Austen's novels, on the absolute importance of attentive observation, Anne's temporary blindness in this and the other encounters listed above is highly significant. As early as 1850, Charlotte Brontë had identified Austen's narrative mode to be 'all eyes' and 'no heart' ('Her business is not half so much with the human heart as with the human eyes, mouth, hands and feet' (McMaster 1996: 133)), whilst Marilyn Butler avers that this radical shift

from outer performance to the 'inner self' is something 'not even suggested in any earlier Austen novel' (Butler 1975: 278). Whatever the final
status of its sexual politics, then, *Persuasion* has a claim to true innovation
in this attempt to depict the condition of being in love through what we
might think of today as a 'stream-of-consciousness' technique. And whilst,
in the first section of the novel, Anne's desire for Wentworth is re-ignited
in the context of hopelessness and misery ('No; the years which had
destroyed her youth and bloom had only given him a more glowing, manly,
open look, in no respect lessening his personal advantages. She had seen
the same Frederick Wentworth' (Austen 1985: 86)), it is subsequently permitted to explode into a second, full-blown *ravissement*: 'Anne, who . . . in
spite of all the various noises of the room, the almost ceaseless slam of
the door, and ceaseless buzz of persons walking through, had distinguished
every word, was struck, gratified, confused, and beginning to breathe very
quick, and feel an hundred things in a moment' (Austen 1985: 192–3). Such
a heightened state of being, in which self, other (that is, the beloved object)
and the world are transformed into a fantastical alter-reality, accords
perfectly with Barthes's description of the climactic *coup de foudre* (Barthes
1990: 184–94), and, for all the perceived social conservatism of her novels,
Austen is certainly to be credited with giving this sublime experience one
of its earliest literary representations. Indeed, with this evidence to hand
it becomes easier to argue that Austen was ultimately an advocate *for*
romantic love being brought *within* companionate marriage (*Persuasion* is,
after all, the text in which the heroine is actively punished for following
her 'head' rather than her 'heart').

For all Austen's innovation in this depiction of the physiological experience of love's rapture, however, it remains difficult to read *Persuasion* – or
any other of her novels – as being *fully* committed to the idea(l) of romantic love. At an ideological level this is because, as Butler and her followers
have argued, she was a 'Tory' and a 'conservative' (Butler 1975: 2–3) who
believed that 'good marriages' were important not only for the individuals concerned but for the stability and prosperity of family, community and
nation; at a stylistic level, this is because her novels' distinctly Augustan
blend of realism and satire keeps all 'enthusiasms' firmly in their place
(Butler 1975: 1–2).

It is, indeed, in the depiction of the relationships that *surround* the fairy-
tale romance of Anne and Wentworth that we see that – even in this somewhat atypical last novel – Austen struggled to deviate from the didactic
tradition which advised young women that the *first* objective of 'intelligent
courtship' was not personal happiness and fulfilment, but consolation and

compromise. As well as the tragic 'mistake' Anne's own mother clearly made in marrying Sir Walter, we have countless representations of the sad mismatch of Charles and Mary, not to mention Mrs Smith's dark allusion to the tragedy of William Walter Elliot's first marriage:

> My heart bled for you, as I talked of happiness. And yet, he is sensible, he is agreeable, and with such a woman as you, it was not absolutely hope-less. He was very unkind to his first wife. They were wretched together. But she was too ignorant and giddy for respect, and he had never loved her. I was willing to hope that you must fare better. (Austen 1985: 216)

Although only a brief, unspecified allusion to marital cruelty (and, possi-bly, domestic violence), Mrs Smith's vignette sends a chill through not only *Persuasion* but, I would suggest, the whole Austen *oeuvre*. Aside from the depressing mismatches and 'mistakes', there lurks the very real threat of a truly bleak marriage in which loss of respectability (from the husband's drunkenness, gambling and debt) is combined with varying degrees of physical and mental cruelty. Mary Wollstonecraft, as we shall see in the next section, was one of the first women to write of such marriages frankly, but it may also, of course, be argued that the Gothic tradition had already made such horrors the stuff of fiction. When faced with *this* sort of prospect, it is not surprising that many of the female educators of the period looked with suspicion upon 'passion' in any shape or form and advo-cated de-sexualized marital affection instead (see quote from Woll-stonecraft cited above). In this context, sexual compatibility between husband and wife was necessarily chance, not choice; the desirable – but improbable – icing on the cake.

This last point inevitably leads us to the vexed issue of 'choice' in both *Persuasion* and Austen's novels generally.[6] Indeed, the issue for rather less liberal feminist readers remains the *nature* of the choice allowed to women in Anne's position and thus returns us, once again, to the emotional com-promise endemic to this particular version of property-based love. Bearing in mind the not inconsiderable constraints surrounding their choice of marriage partner (constraints of 'time' as well as of person, as Elizabeth Elliot's 'ticking clock' is repeatedly made to remind us), it is clear that women of this social class would have been under pressure to accept the *first* seriously eligible partner who came their way. And it was clearly this pressure that made an 'education in courtship' such an urgent priority: whilst it might take years to become a skilled semiotician in the Austen mode, suitors of both sexes – but young girls especially – needed a basic grasp of how to identify the 'properties' of prospective partners. Operat-ing in such a potentially dangerous environment, it is not surprising that desire, as we understand it today, was not a priority consideration or that the heroines of courtship novels repeatedly made what appeared to be 'safe', if unexciting, choices. Indeed, Joan Forbes – writing about the 'anti-romantic discourse' of courtship fiction as a form of *resistance* – has argued that this is precisely where the texts' feminism lies: 'The message conveyed is that, within a patriarchal society, romance and romantic love further threaten women's fragile autonomy and control. For women, already disadvantaged in a male dominated world, marriage is too important a life decision to be made on the basis of romance' (Forbes 1995: 301). This last point, it seems to me, is a fair assessment of the *dominant* ideology informing Austen's fiction and accounts for the fact that even (or, perhaps, especially) in *Persuasion*, where – as we have seen – sparks *do* fly, Admiral and Mrs Croft are the conjugal role-model that carries the day. Whether or not sexual desire or romantic love is, or has been, an important part of their relationship is unclear, and ultimately unimportant; the impossible to miss *gift* of their relationship, its rather less than ghostly supplementary value, is hearty *companionship*. Admiral and Mrs Croft may be man and wife, but what distinguishes them is that they go everywhere as *friends* ('They brought with them their country habit of being almost always together' (Austen 1985: 179)).

Whether we elect to regard the advocacy of these companionate relationships as feminist or otherwise must remain, of course, a matter of debate. For Joan Forbes, the anti-romantic/de-sexualized nature of such relationships is a price worth paying for the comfort and peace of mind it offers its heroines. On this point, she observes how many courtship novel heroines – including Austen's – end up marrying men who are *brother*-substitutes (Forbes 1995: 301). The fact that such men also begin life as 'mentors' tends to complicate the politics of this somewhat (see McMaster 1996: 150–2; Spencer 1986: 145), though the preference of *some* of the heroines for men who are symbolically – if not actually – 'asexual' is clearly a persuasive one in the context of the pressures such women were under. What complicates the issue, of course, are texts like *Persuasion* and *Pride and Prejudice*, where the fantasy of romantic/'passion'-love contends with the safer choices.

The problematic status of *Persuasion* vis-à-vis these two contending discourses (what George Paizis usefully distinguishes as 'marriage-love' and 'passion-love' (Paizis 1998: 117–19)) has been identified by Marilyn Butler, albeit in the context of a rather different discussion, as the novel's *failure* to 'integrate . . . two planes of reality' (Butler 1975: 279). By this she means the contrast between the innovative representation of the 'inner life' of the subject in the sequence of 'nervous scenes' discussed earlier, and the 'tradition of social comedy' – and, indeed, *satire* – that characterizes narration and plot. I would agree with Butler that *Persuasion* is, indeed, a text which strains apart stylistically in precisely this way, and with particular implications for the love story at its heart. Read through Anne's disordered, joyful and thoroughly agapic consciousness, this novel is, indeed, a true romance, and Wentworth less a man of 'properties' than the bright spark who not once, but *twice*, transforms her into a 'blooming' *new* woman. Read, however, through the playful yet cautionary consciousness of the *narrator*, it is a very different book indeed. Take, for instance, the latter's highly satiric comment on Anne's renewed belief that she is committed to Wentworth for life, come what may: 'Prettier musings on high-wrought love and eternal constancy, could never have passed along the streets of Bath' (Austen 1985: 200). With Anne's euphoria thus mocked, the reader is left wondering what fate *is* to befall the heroine and whether she could have exercised a failure of judgement for a second time. Despite the thrill and pleasure that accompany the *re-ignition* of Anne's spark ['], text, narrator and implied author all seem to lack the conviction that such delights can truly be brought within the steady companionship of marriage. In my reading of the text, then, Austen comes close to bringing a new romantic idealism to bear upon companionate marriage, but cannot quite trust the giddy irrationality of her infatuated subjects. The fact that Wentworth (like Darcy, in *Pride and Prejudice*) *turns out* to be a thoroughly good 'type' as well as an 'object-ideal' helps, of course; in the world of fiction, the romantic choice *becomes* the sensible choice and a truly ideal companionship is secured.

In conclusion, then, it would seem that Austen's anatomy of love and marriage figures 'companionship' as a fiercely contested site which encompasses 'compromise' and 'consolation' at one end of the spectrum and a radical, new heterosexual intimacy at the other. Companionship, in other words, is figured both as the consolation prize and as the gift.

III

Seduction and Sequel: The Other Side of Eighteenth-Century Romance

The extent to which the romantic love of courtship fiction has been de-sexualized – especially *vis-à-vis* the problematic oedipal 'protection' of fathers and brothers – is brought to shocking and spectacular attention in novels of one of the true 'bad girls' of eighteenth-century literature, Delarivière Manley. Consider, for example, the extract from one of the stories that comprise her blacklisted novel *The New Atalantis* (1709):[7]

> She took the book and placed herself by the Duke; his eyes feasted them-selves upon her face, thence wandered over her snowy bosom and saw the young swelling breasts just beginning to distinguish themselves and which were gently heaved by the impression Myrra's sufferings made upon her heart. By this dangerous reading he intended to show her that there were pleasures her sex were born for, and which she might consequently long to taste! . . . But the Duke's pursuing kisses overcame the thoughts of any-thing but the new and lazy poison stealing to her heart and spreading swiftly and imperceptibly through all her veins; she closed her eyes with languish-ing delight! delivered up the possession of her lips and breath to the amorous invader, returned his eager grasps and, in a word, gave her whole person into his arms in meltings of delight! (Manley 1991 [1709]: 35–6)

For those of us who have imbibed our literary history largely though the canonical texts of school and university syllabi, any encounter with the subcultures that have shadowed it comes as something of a salutary shock, and a text like Manley's – written a whole century before Austen sent the 'young people' of *Persuasion* off for a rather less than wild weekend in Lyme – is no exception. Moreover, the fact that Austen and her courtship-fiction-writing contemporaries are unlikely to have read it should not cause us to underestimate the extent to which such erotica was in dialogue with more mainstream seduction fiction throughout the period. When, for example, a text like Charlotte Lennox's *The Female Quixote* (1752) plays roguishly with Arabella's repeated fantasies of being 'Ravished' (Lennox 1970: 102), we may be sure that there was a cohort of readers who would cross-reference to *The New Atalantis* rather than to the rather less explicit French romances which had seduced the heroine. A knowledge of such texts is clearly also important if we are to fully understand the origins of twentieth-century Mills & Boon fiction. Whilst – as we shall see in Chapter 6 – most feminist criticism has regarded the genre as emerging directly out of nineteenth-century 'classic romance' (in particular, that of Austen and the Brontës), it is clear that its bodice-ripping, soft-porn elements owe a very obvious debt to these subcultural prototypes. In terms both of erotic scenario and, even more importantly, of the control of the protago-nists'/reader's gaze, Manley's story of the innocent – but infinitely cor-ruptible – young virgin, Charlot, looks ahead to any number of Mills & Boon fantasies in which a fatherly rake eventually has his wicked way with his initially resistant, but then yielding, object of desire:

Charlot no sooner arrived but, the weather being very hot, she ordered a bath to be prepared for her. Soon as she was refreshed with that, she threw herself down upon the bed with only one thin petticoat and a loose night-gown, the bosom of her gown and shift open, her night-clothes tied care-lessly together with cherry-colored ribbon. . . . She was quite astonished to see enter the amorous Duke. Her first feelings were all joy but in a minute she recollected herself, thinking he was not come there for nothing. She was going to rise but he prevented her by flying to her arms where, as we may call it, he nailed her down to the bed with kisses. His love and res-olution gave him double vigor; he would not stay a moment to capitulate with her. While yet her surprise made her doubtful of his designs, he took advantage of her confusion to accomplish 'em. Neither her prayers, tears, nor strugglings could prevent him, but in his arms he made himself a full amends for all those pains he had suffered for her. (Manley 1991: 39)

For although Charlot has just enough coyness and sense of propriety to make her fight off the Duke's ravishment, we learn that – soon after – she was 'not at all behindhand in ecstasies and guilty transports' of her own (Manley 1991: 40). In terms of the dominant reading position, this scene would thus not be seen as a rape, though readers should be aware that – through its framing 'documentary' (the stories that comprise the texts are narrated, and analysed, by three allegorical female figures) – the text is highly critical of the double standards that allowed a girl like Charlot to be exploited (and then abandoned) in this way. At the same time, the more enduring feminist legacy of the text must be seen in the way that it acknowledges the *existence* of female sexual desire: Charlot might have been seduced and manipulated into erotic consciousness in a questionable way, but there is no denying her pleasure. As Spencer concludes: 'Though Charlot's story depends on the idea of female innocence, Manley does not idealize that innocence. Nor does she feel the need . . . to deny that sexual desire is an element in her heroine's downfall' (Spencer 1986: 114). The crucial message of this text, then – and one that anticipates the later Woll-stonecraft – is that women cannot properly protect themselves from unwanted seduction unless they are brought up to acknowledge the strength of their own sexual desires. Such frankness may, at first, seem a million miles away from Austen's sanitized courtships, but disreputable males like William Walter Elliot clearly represent a similar predatory threat; Anne, it will be recalled, was interested enough to wish to know 'who he was' initially (Austen 1985: 125).

Bearing in mind the nature of the 'consolation' most frequently meted out to the heroines of courtship fiction, Manley's focus on a 'father-protector' figure in this text also deserves further attention. In stark opposition to the conceit that a women's best chance of a companionate marriage was to opt for a man who would offer her the notionally asexual care of a father or (as Forbes has proposed) a brother, Manley's text abounds with instances of fatherly men abusing their protectorate role (see Spencer 1986: 116). One of the most suggestive passages in the Charlot story, and one that looks forward to Angela Carter's story 'The Bloody Chamber' (Carter 1979), centres on the young girl's paternalistic induction into sexual knowledge. Like the heroine in Carter's story, Charlot is left alone in the Duke's castle/villa to 'discover her desire' in the form of erstwhile forbidden books and 'adult' clothes and jewels. This recognition of the corrupting potential of *books*, in particular ('He . . . had recommended to her reading the most dangerous books of love – Ovid, Petrarch, Tibullus' (Manley 1991: 37)), certainly wags a warning finger to all those eighteenth-century texts (such as Lennox's *The Female Quixote* (1752)) that presumed to *mock* the titillating powers of the romance genre so remorselessly.

At this point it is worth noting the extent to which this discussion of 'seduction' fiction as opposed to 'courtship' fiction has led us away from the discourse of romantic love to the discourse of sex. As I noted in the Preface to the volume, the two discourses are not as obviously interrelated as they might, at first, appear, especially at the level of narrative structure. The fact that the Ur-love story focuses on quest, fantasy and the ever-elusive object-ideal holds it in crucial distinction to the erotic text; it also helps to explain why so many philosophers have seen Agape (with its focus on aspiration and transformation rather than the fulfilment of desire) as the 'sign' of romantic love. Indeed, it is common knowledge that stories of romantic love have traditionally stopped short of the moment of consummation, marriage or, indeed, in Roland Barthes's taxonomy, the 'sequel' (Barthes 1990: 197–8). What writers in the seduction fiction – as opposed to the courtship fiction – mode could thus be seen to be doing is refusing to entertain any notion of romantic love which does *not* attend to the sequel: to insist that all the *sublimations* of sexual desire which fuel, and agapize, the process of falling in love – which generate the 'spark' – be at least *imagined* from a position of hindsight. What sexual desire 'means' in prospect is not at all the same as what it means in the act, or in retrospect.

Bearing this discursive and generic tension in mind, Mary Wollstonecraft's determination to deal frankly with both romantic love *and* sexual desire is truly remarkable. Although, as we have already seen, Wollstonecraft was a staunch anti-sentimentalist in her youth, the bittersweet experience of her own love affair with Gilbert Imlay resulted in her two fiction works – *Mary* (1788) and *Maria, or The Wrongs of Woman* (1798) – embracing all three 'acts' of Barthes's romantic 'adventure' (Barthes 1990: 197–8).[8] In both texts, the heroine is first attracted to the man who is to become her lover on account of his intelligence, knowledge and learning, and – even more importantly – on account of the reciprocal *intellectual* spark he ignites in herself. Of Henry, in *Mary*, the narrator thus writes:

> Henry was a man of learning; he had also studied mankind and knew the intricacies of the human heart, from having felt the infirmities of his own. His taste was just, as it had a standard – Nature, which he observed with a critical eye. Mary could not help thinking that in his company her mind expanded, as he always went below the surface. She increased her stock of ideas, and her taste was improved. (Wollstonecraft 1976: 27)

Darnford, meanwhile, the revolutionary hero of *The Wrongs of Woman*, introduces himself to Maria through his intellect rather than his person by sending her parcels of books. Darnford is a fellow-prisoner in the jail in which Maria has been incarcerated by her husband – the wicked and depraved Mr Venables. He and Maria first get to know each other through letters and, subsequently, 'literary' conversation. The latter, however, soon induces 'flashes of sentiment' (Wollstonecraft 1976: 94) and it is a small step here – as in *Mary* – for 'textual' to tip over into 'sexual' passion: 'He adverted to the narrative [of her life], and spoke with warmth of the oppression she had endured. – His eyes, glowing with a lambent flame, told her how much he wished to restore her liberty and love; but he kissed her hand as if it had been that of a saint' (Wollstonecraft 1976: 187). This is hardly great literary writing (and Wollstonecraft carefully avoided calling herself a 'novelist'), but it certainly goes further than Austen in understanding the febrile mix of intellect and sexual desire that so often lights the fuse of distinctly *romantic* love. Here, indeed, as in several of the paradigms we shall encounter in the chapters on twentieth-century romance, mutual creativity/productivity becomes the incomparable 'gift' of love.

Both in *The Wrongs of Woman* and in *Mary*, meanwhile, the hopeless and tragic circumstances in which *all* the protagonists find themselves (Maria and Darnford in the former are prisoners; Henry in the latter is suffering from TB and doomed to an early death) mean that the love of hero and heroine is effectively agapized at the same time that it is eroticized. As we shall see in Chapter 5 on 'Wartime Romance', the sexual consummation of relationships in circumstances where there is no necessary 'hereafter' lends the act a very different meaning to the one it assumes in marriage (that is, the 'door' to a life-time commitment). And it is precisely this 'out-of-time' triumph of passion – when it occurs as *mutual* sexual desire – that Wollstonecraft's two fiction works celebrate, notwithstanding the tragedy and betrayal that ensue. With an agency, determination and resolve unthinkable in the pages of *any* of the sub-genres of romantic fiction considered in this chapter, Maria 'gives herself' to Darnford in an act that is both personal and political:

> The lovers were, at first, embarrassed; but fell insensibly into confidential discourse. Darnford represented, 'that they might soon be parted', and wished her 'to put it out of the power of fate to separate them'.
> As her husband she now received him, and he solemnly pledged himself her protector – and eternal friend. (Wollstonecraft 1976: 188)

The contrast between this moment of 'yielding' and the one featured in Manley's text could, indeed, hardly be starker: where Charlot succumbs to seduction, Maria makes a *conscious* decision to enter into the relationship freely. The fact that it is a relationship that stands outside the law – that is both bigamous and adulterous – also makes it a very different order of 'choice' to the one exercised by Austen's heroines, as is made explicit in the stunning denouement of the text. Called up before a court of law to conduct Darnford's defence, Maria makes an impassioned plea for her 'right' to a sexual relationship with the man she loves rather than with him to whom she was 'married when scarcely able to distinguish the nature of the relationship':

> To this person, thus encountered, I voluntarily gave myself, never considering myself as any more bound to transgress the laws of moral purity, because the will of my husband might be pleaded in my excuse, than to transgress those laws to which [the policy of artificial society has] annexed [positive] punishments. – While no command of a husband can prevent a woman from suffering for certain crimes, she must be allowed to consult her conscience, and regulate her conduct, in some degree, by her own sense of right. The respect I owe to myself, demanded my strict adherence to my determination of never seeing Mr. Venables in the light of a husband, nor could it forbid me from encouraging another. (Wollstonecraft 1976: 197)

Such an extraordinary declaration of a woman's right to liberation from a loveless marriage – the statement concludes with a claim for divorce – would not be heard again for nearly two hundred years, its radical nature reminding us why, for many feminists, Wollstonecraft has become the defining figure of the Women's Liberation Movement.

Meanwhile, although a good deal of feminist interest in Wollstonecraft has rightly focused on her searing exposé of the reality of married life for vast numbers of women – both rich and poor –, the texts I have briefly considered here represent an equally bold endorsement of sexual/intellectual romantic love between the sexes. Tragic as the 'sequel' proved for both Wollstonecraft and her heroines, there is no flinching from her vision of such love as a supremely liberating and creative force that knows nothing of 'consolation' or 'compromise'. In a century where both sexual desire and sexual loathing were increasingly 'ob/scene' (see note 5 to Chapter 1), Wollstonecraft makes a fearless spectacle of both.

4

Gothic Romance

The Gift of Immortality

I

Both within and without the bounds of Gothic fiction, the nineteenth-century nexus of Love-and-Death has gifted us – its inheritors – an archive of extraordinary richness and complexity. The century that saw the scientific ordering and classification of all manner of things has also bequeathed us a monumental taxonomy of death, one drawer of which – the cross-listing of love with death – is piled high with literary exempla. So exquisite, indeed, became the codes and conventions surrounding death, the afterlife and mourning during this period that the twenty-first-century archivist will often find herself hard-pressed to decide what manner of love–death variant she is dealing with. The drawer, as it were, contains the casts of innumerable quirky creatures long extinct and barely recognizable to us today.

Some acknowledgement of the precision with which nineteenth-century society sought to collate and understand the processes of death is critical if we – as twenty-first-century readers and critics – are to move beyond analysing the tragic love stories of the era merely in terms of psycho-sexual drives. Whilst psychoanalysis clearly has a vital role to play in helping us understand these texts (indeed, post-Freud, it is virtually impossible to ignore the insights offered by such readings), attention to the specific beliefs, customs and rituals surrounding death reveals that it was far from being an abstract compulsion. Indeed, the fact that so many literary heroes and heroines are apparently willing to 'die for love' indicates that it was most certainly a sacrifice with a handsome gift attached. In this chapter I shall thus be arguing that, whilst this gift may be most obviously construed as 'immortality', this will have meant very different things to different people. The widely contested – and, indeed, wildly imagined – visions of the afterlife that characterize the century offer its subjects – and, in particular, its writers – a wide range of 'final resting places', from the divinely ethereal to the grossly material. Thus, whilst, for Freud, the death-wish might be explained as an unconscious desire for 'release' from the endless tensions created by the pleasure-seeking drives of life, for most nineteenth-century subjects death was not (consciously) perceived to be an end (or 'object') of anything (Freud 1984c [1920]: 275–338). For those willing to commit themselves to a belief in the (after)life of the soul, death was, indeed, the ultimate 'new beginning' whose own final resolution (that is, committal to heaven or hell) may be light-years away.

Before moving on to my analysis of Emily Brontë's *Wuthering Heights* – a text which manifestly demands both psychoanalytic and cultural-historical readings – I therefore offer a brief, introductory discussion of a range of paradigms that may usefully be invoked to better understand the grand investment in 'Love/Death' that stands at the very centre of nineteenth-century literature, art and culture.

The Landscapes of Love and Death

As was noted in Chapter 1, for Denis de Rougemont (1983), a concealed 'death-wish' is *the* force that drives, and explains, the literary/cultural history of romantic love from the thirteenth century to the present. He cites the obstructions that Tristan (and the hundreds of hapless lovers who have succeeded him) places in the way of sexual fulfilment as indicative of a profound paradox at the heart of romantic love. Whilst, on the narrative surface, the repeated distress and separation endured by the lovers is taken as evidence of their commitment to one another, it more darkly signals 'a desire for death and an advance in the direction of Death' (de Rougemont 1983: 45). In a further attempt to explain *why* this should be so, he invokes Freud to distinguish between 'actual death' and the 'ideal death' which is the object of the death-drive: it is 'a death that means transfiguration, and is in no way the result of some violent chance' (de Rougemont 1983: 45). The notion of death being rendered beautiful, and hence brought under control, by the processes of aestheticization and the sexual gaze is also the pivot of Elisabeth Bronfen's thesis in *Over Her Dead Body*:

> We invest in images of wholeness, purity and the immaculate owing to the fear of dissolution and decay. The function of beauty, Lacan suggests, is to point to the relation man has with his own death, but to point to this only as a dazzling sight. . . . Pleasure at the beauty of woman resides in the uneasy simultaneity of recognising and misrecognising it as a veil for death. (Bronfen 1993: 62–3)

For both de Rougemont and Bronfen, then, the *raison d'être* of romantic love is the 'management' of death. Although, for de Rougemont, this device is located in the spectacular obstacles/adventures of the 'love *story*' and, for Bronfen, in the *body* of the (beautiful, dead) 'beloved', both share the belief that – ultimately – love (which has the capacity to render all things lovely) is in the service of death. The emotion that in fairy-stories has the power to turn a frog into a prince, or a beast into a beauty, is also our best hope of averting the ugly decay and decomposition that is the end of life. All love stories that end in death are, according to this rationale, very obviously 'about' death and not love, with the beauty of the death and/or beauty of the (young) dead bodies denying the messy processes of ageing and death and focusing our attention, instead, on their instant/'wholesome' immortality. Thus whilst readers may naïvely read the resolution of such texts as the triumph of love over death, what they are really witnessing is the triumph of beauty – or the aesthetic act – over both. Keats's chilly 'Grecian Urn' inevitably comes to mind.

Whilst de Rougemont traces the symbiosis of love and death back to a wide range of texts (theological and philosophical as well as literary) from the Middle Ages, Bronfen identifies eighteenth- and nineteenth-century Gothic as its most obvious literary-cultural home. Edgar Allan Poe's observation that 'the death of a beautiful woman is, unquestionably, the most poetical topic in the world' (in Bronfen 1993: 59) was, indeed, the springboard for her study, which includes virtuoso readings of several nineteenth-century texts (British and American) which may broadly be said to operate under that sign. A few words are, however, also necessary on how eighteenth-century Gothic, with its origins in the work of writers like Horace Walpole (*The Castle of Otranto*, 1764), Ann Radcliffe (*The Mysteries of Udolpho*, 1794) and Matthew Lewis (*The Monk*, 1796), laid the ground for what followed. Whilst, from the perspective of the twenty-first century, it is tempting to read all this literature as Western culture's first concerted attempt to make sense of the darker reaches of the human mind – that wayward, irrational wilderness that we now think of as the unconscious –, recent commentators have emphasized the fact that the Gothic tradition comprises several sites of origin. Jerold Hogle, for example, points to the distinction between 'terror Gothic' and 'horror Gothic' (Hogle 2004: 225–8). Whilst the former (represented principally by the novels of Ann Radcliffe) tended to project its psychological and historical/cultural angst on external objects (which were ultimately 'explained' and conquered), the latter makes explicit the extent to which the perverse and 'unthinkable' reside *within* human consciousness. Needless to say, it was the 'horror' strand (with its apotheosis in Schiller, Lewis and Poe) that consequently proceeded to mix Eros and Thanatos most explicitly, though the obsession of *all* Gothic texts with the notion of *inheritance* means that their plots are inevitably compelled by the two drives.[1] Summing up the 'conventions' of the Gothic as instigated by Walpole's *Castle of Otranto*, Hogle pays particular attention to the way in which all the action, and all the horror, of these texts – including that undertaken in the name of romantic love – owes to some 'genealogical' crime or transgression in the past:

> The antiquated and haunted setting; some dark secret or secrets from the past hidden in the depths; the rising of these secrets in the form of some ghost or monstrosity; the pulling of the characters back to the past in a tug or war with their aspirations to transcend it; the problem of establishing the 'correct' inheritance so that present figures can seem to gain the support of something from the past while they leave it behind; *the determination of love objects more by these tensions than by preference* . . . (Hogle 2004: 219, my italics)

In other words, it is the (mis)alliance of sex and property in the lives of a previous generation that will determine the 'fate' of their successors, with the (justifiably terrifying) implication that 'the sins of the father' truly are visited upon his sons and daughters. Whether death is visited upon the protagonist in supernatural form or not (that is, as ghosts or revenants), the Gothic text thus sends out a clear message that it is never an 'end' but, rather, the means by which past grief *lives on* – be it in the genes (through some inappropriate 'mating') or through a more material form of cursed inheritance. The second-generation protagonists of *Wuthering Heights* are, as we shall see shortly, the victims of both.

Out of the convoluted, and often wildly improbable, plots of these early Gothic novels there therefore emerges one of humanity's darker psychological 'truths': the fact that the children of aberrant sexual unions will, themselves, struggle to find happiness in love. This is largely because, in their choice of love-object, they are always seeking to repeat – and finally 'lay to rest' – the mistakes of their forebears. In the history of Gothic fiction, including texts as various as Walpole's *The Castle of Otranto* (1764), Collins's *The Woman in White* (1860), Poe's 'Ligeia' (1845), du Maurier's *Rebecca* (1938) and *Wuthering Heights* (1847) itself, this dark legacy is seen in the figures of both 'doubles' and second wives/husbands whose own disturbing power/horror owes merely to the fact that they are inauthentic substitutes for the 'original'.[2] Hogle identifies this unease as a key factor in the ambiguous end to *The Castle of Otranto* in which Theodore's marriage to Isabella is overshadowed by the fact that she is a 'substitute' for the dead Mathilda (Hogle 2004: 220–1). Altogether, then, it is probably fair to say that although Gothic novels, past and present, invariably involve at least one love story, it is difficult to read them simply as romances. These are texts not so much about love as about love's fearful legacy.

As all those working in the field acknowledge, it is virtually impossible nowadays to read Gothic texts without reference to Freudian (or other) psychoanalytic models. In our attempt to make sense of the ways in which love and death are yoked together in their pages, the insights provided by psychoanalysis are, indeed, invaluable. We have already seen how convincingly de Rougemont was able to argue for Freud's 'ideal-death' being the covert object of the love story in Western culture, for instance; and an understanding of the precariousness of ego-development, and the inherent 'perversity' of the 'Family Romance', clearly helps explain *why* inheritance became such a compelling theme for the genre.[3] Also of crucial importance (as will be seen in the reading of *Wuthering Heights* that follows) is the way in which Freud's work on narcissism (Freud 1984a [1914]) sheds light upon the different ways in which subjects deal with 'lost [romantic] objects' (dead, or otherwise) and, tangential to this, his study of 'Mourning and Melancholia' (Freud 1984b [1915]: 247–68).

Inasmuch as the latter relates directly to my own thoughts on the link between the romance narrative and the narratives of death and dying that proliferated in the nineteenth century, it is necessary for me to briefly mention some of its key pronouncements here. The first of these is the obvious, but easily overlooked, observation that *mourning takes time*. In his summary of 'the work of mourning' Freud observes:

> Reality-testing has shown that the loved object no longer exists, and it proceeds to demand that all libido shall be withdrawn from attachment to that object. This demand arouses understandable opposition – it is a matter of observation that people never willingly abandon a libidinal position, not even, indeed, when a substitute is already beckoning to them. This opposition can be so intense that a turning away from reality takes place and a clinging to the object through the medium of hallucinatory wishful psychosis. Normally, respect for reality gains the day. Nevertheless, its orders cannot be obeyed all at once. They are carried out, bit by bit, at great expense of time and cathectic energy, and in the meantime the existence of the lost object is psychically prolonged. Each single one of the memories and expectations in which the libido is bound to the object is brought up and hypercathected, and detachment of the libido is accomplished in respect of it. Why this compromise by which the command of reality is carried out piecemeal should be so extraordinarily painful is not at all easy to explain in terms of economies . . . The fact is, however, that when the work of mourning is completed the ego becomes free and uninhibited again. (Freud 1984b: 252–3)

As well as echoing Heathcliff's memorable pronouncement that Catherine's was 'a strange way of killing, not by inches but by fractions of hairbreadths . . . through eighteen years' (Brontë 1995a [1847]: 291), Freud's text points more generally to the fact that the Victorians turned mourning into an industry: namely, 'death' was treated not as an end, but as a *process*, and for mourner and deceased alike.[4] Even as the bereaved has to learn to let go of his or her beloved bit by bit, so does the body take time to decompose, become spirit, and begin its long journey from earth to heaven (or hell). My own proposition here, moreover – as will be seen in the discussion of nineteenth-century eschatology that follows –, is that, *contra* Freud, this 'long goodbye' is as intensely pleasurable as it is painful; moreover, that it is in many ways a striking mirror-image of the (equally protracted) period of *ravissement* that signals the start of a romance.

The other aspect of Freud's essay that has proven crucially enlightening in my understanding of the love–death nexus in *Wuthering Heights* is the central distinction it draws between mourning and melancholia. As will be seen, my hypothesis here is that – despite the extremity/longevity of his passion – Heathcliff's behaviour is consistent with Freud's characterization of mourning, whilst Catherine's – both before and *after* her death – displays many of the symptoms of melancholia. *Vis-à-vis* the central motif of this chapter, however – that is, the notion that, for many Victorians, the 'gift of love' was commensurate with the 'gift of immortality' –, it should be noted that mourning and melancholia may both be seen as strategies to extend the 'life' of the lost object. Yet for the majority of nineteenth-century citizens, the promise (or threat) of immortality was regarded as an expression not of human, but of divine, will. In his book *Heaven, Hell and the Victorians* (1994), Michael Wheeler overviews the many different versions of the 'future life' that evolved in the course of the nineteenth century, paying particular attention to the role poets and novelists played in rendering visible (indeed, 'spectacular') the more abstract formations of the theologians.

Of all the 'future lives' available to humanity, heaven remained the most conceptually elusive by virtue of its claim to perfection: 'Just as it is easier to see hell on earth than heaven on earth, so is it easier to see earth in hell than in heaven' (Wheeler 1994: 183). The problem is also a feature of Western culture's most celebrated 'guide' to the afterlife, Dante's *Divine Comedy* (first published in the thirteenth century), in which the poet/pilgrim is shown around Paradise through a series of intellectual debates, in contrast to his rather more visceral experience of hell (Dante 2004 [c. 1308–14]). However, the fact that for Dante, and the majority of subsequent theologians, heaven was regarded as the absolute endpoint of the departed soul's journey permitted rather more successful imaginings of the intermediate states that preceded it. For some thinkers, indeed, heaven could, and should, be distinguished from 'paradise': an Edenic, but recognizable, landscape in which the soul prepared for its final delivery to the 'white light' of God.[5] Given that there was also much debate over whether heaven was a 'place' or merely a 'state' (Wheeler 1994: 131), the conceptual appeal of paradise, which was very definitely a *place* – and a largely recognizable one –, is clear. As Andrew Lincoln has observed, 'Most often [paradise] is heavenly in character, but it can also be earthly . . . or even combine elements of both' (in Wheeler 1984: 123): an alluring half-way house, then, that was 'imagined' most spectacularly in John Martin's painting of 1851–3, *The Plains of Heaven* (Tate Britain, London; reproduced in Wheeler 1994). This notion of paradise as an intermediate space/place that remains (for ever) 'this side' of heaven is, however, just one of many transitional states that the departed soul may enter. Indeed, going back to Dante and his nineteenth-century followers (see Ellis 1983), it becomes clear that transition is what characterizes *all* models of the afterlife: the soul's effectively *infinite* journey from this world to the next, no matter whether the final destination be 'good' or 'bad'. Apart from paradise, both purgatory and Hades (Wheeler 1990: 175–8) are expressly configured as intermediate states, whilst even a quick glance at Dante's *Inferno* will remind the reader that the journey to the centre of hell (like the journey through the spheres of heaven) is a long one. The crucial point that emerges here, then, is that – according to the Christian eschatological tradition in virtually all its variants – 'immortality' is something that is only very slowly *journeyed towards*; indeed, in the majority of these models the journey itself appears to constitute a notional *infinity*. This, as we shall shortly see, is a state of affairs that appears to have been willingly embraced by the star-crossed lovers of *Wuthering Heights* and also corresponds to certain readings of Brontë's own theology (see especially Marsden 2000).[6]

To conclude this introduction, however, I need also to say a few words about how these schemas of death and the afterlife may be linked to the narrative of romance. It will be recalled that one of the major break-throughs in the understanding of the 'deep structures' of romance was Janice Radway's (1984) discovery of the way in which most popular romances could be mapped on to Vladimir Propp's (1968) 'morphology' of the European folktale (see Chapter 1). Central to what Radway subsequently described as 'the narrative logic of romance' is the phase of obstacles, misunderstandings and enforced separation that follows the lovers' first encounter: a phase that might be resolved in a matter of weeks but – more usually – took months or years. If we trace this romantic interlude back to its literary origins in folktale / Arthurian legend, we discover, moreover, that it is likely to extend over *many* years – often counted in multiples of seven. In these texts the 'test' or challenge of the separation is thus made spectacularly explicit and often requires extreme acts of heroism and sacrifice on behalf of the protagonists. In classic and popular romance these challenges, whilst rather less extreme, are still present and – more often than not – continue to take the form of a journey / quest to – or through – another geographical location. According to this Ur-narrative, therefore, romantic love enacts the practices and rituals of mourning as part of its *first* 'progress' and, habitually, sends its heroes and heroines into locations that enjoy the same hallucinatory, phantasmagoric quality as the (Victorian) visions of Hades or paradise. Crucial to our appreciation of this romantic version of the 'intermediate state' is, indeed, an acknowledgement that its landscapes – though sometimes terrifying – are invariably sublime and full of wonder. Whether the dark forest in which Tristan and Iseult 'lose' themselves, or the wild heath that Jane Eyre is forced to cross before she hears Rochester's voice calling her home (Brontë 2000 [1847]: 444–5), or the more luxurious displacements of Mills & Boon fiction (see Pearce 2004), the spaces / places of this phase of the romance narrative are defined by the wonderfully heightened consciousnesses of the lovers, who, for all their grief, terror and anxiety, are simultaneously in a state of ecstasy. This last point is, I believe, crucial for our understanding of both *this* period of liminality and transition and the one experienced by the mourner and the deceased subsequent to death.

The similarities between the states of heightened consciousness experienced during the first spell-binding moment of falling in love and those associated with mourning have not, to my knowledge, been explicitly acknowledged elsewhere – though they are vividly *implicit* in Freud's analysis of 'the work' of mourning. In the same way that Barthes's moment of *ravissement* may be suggestively compared with the 'traumatic moment' (Barthes 1990: 188–94), so, too, may its ceaseless projections / introjections *vis-à-vis* the love-object be compared with the behaviour of the subject during the first weeks and months of mourning. Apart from *Wuthering Heights*, which offers a *tour de force* illustration of this state of altered consciousness, it is widely present – and explored – in the work of more mainstream nineteenth-century writers such as Tennyson (see Part III following). What I am proposing, then, is that there are striking parallels between the *landscapes* of *ravissement* and mourning inasmuch as the lover's intense focus on his/her 'lost' object fills everything around him or her with surreal brightness and significance. In this regard, indeed, Barthes's entry on 'The Ribbon', which explains the lover's hallucinatory relation to the external world in terms of *the fetish*, is especially germane:

> Werther multiplies the gestures of fetishism: he kisses the knot of ribbon Charlotte has given him for his birthday, the letter she sends him (even putting the sand to his lips), the pistols she has touched. From the loved being emanates a power nothing can stop and which will impregnate every-thing it comes in contact with, even if only by a glance. . . . Each object thus consecrated (placed within the influence of the god) becomes like the stone of Bologna, which by night gives back the light it has accumulated in the day. (Barthes 1990: 173)

This potential for fetishizing the world and everything in it is also another way of understanding what is more commonly referred to as the Roman-tics' 'sublimation' of the natural landscape.[7] Whilst it is perfectly plausible to explain Emily Brontë's poems according to the mechanisms of subli-mation, for example, this notion of the fetish perhaps takes us closer to an explanation of how these landscapes – and the ones in *Wuthering Heights* — are so intimately connected with the lovers who wander through them. Whether temporarily or permanently separated from their beloved(s), Brontë's heroes and heroines are expert in substituting them with a token of the landscape which will ensure their immortality.[8]

What, I hope, these opening discussions will have conveyed to the reader is the sense that nineteenth-century – and, in particular, Victorian – models of death and the afterlife would appear to be more focused (one might even say fixated) on the intermediate states between life and death, mor-tality and immortality, than on what was at the end of the journey. Whilst the popular imagination of the twentieth and twenty-first centuries has tended to equate this with a morbid, visceral fascination with the torments of purgatory and the journey through hell, Michael Wheeler's work has brought forward texts that suggest that other liminal states – most notably 'paradise' – might constitute an extremely desirable 'temporary home'. More important than the landscapes of these shadow-worlds, however, is the clear, structural wedge they would seem to have established between life and death. The fact that the departed soul, like the bereaved, could be expected to remain in this indeterminate state for years is a very different vision of death from that found in other religions and cultures, where the soul's release is instantaneous. It is thus my contention that, alongside the explanation for the love–death nexus proposed by de Rougemont and Bronfen – where the tragic love story is a means of aestheticizing, fixing and hence containing death – exists another model (typically Gothic, profoundly Victorian) which binds the two together in the processes of purgatory and mourning. Instead of death being defined by a moment of freezing – Bronfen's beautiful, youthful female corpse that will never decay – it is defined by a process of infinite deferral. Yes, the body decays (as Catherine Linton's body decays), but it also *survives*, in flesh as well as in spirit – and for upwards of twenty years (as dramatized by Heathcliff's declaration, following Catherine's exhumation, that her face was 'hers yet' (Brontë 1995a: 188)). The journey *towards* immortality thus becomes indistinguishable from the state itself. Moreover, in its perverse way – and I am using the Freudian term advisedly –, it is intensely pleasurable.[9] And so it should be. For the mourner's relation to the world, as to the body or his/her lost beloved, replicates the period when s/he was first discovered . . . and first lost. It is hardly surprising, then, that a pair of lovers like Catherine and Heathcliff – possessed of a consummately material belief in the afterlife as an indefinite intermediate state – should find its landscape so seductively familiar.

II

Wuthering Heights: *Love, Death and Everlasting Torment*

As one of the most fêted novels of English literature, *Wuthering Heights* has been the subject of a number of truly brilliant, virtuoso readings. Whilst deriving from many different schools of criticism – structuralist, Marxist, psychoanalytic, theological –, what most of these readings seem to share is a desire to *redeem* the text in expressly humanist terms. Despite Charlotte Brontë's famous pronouncement that 'Heathcliff stands *unredeemed*' (in E. Brontë 1995a: liii, my italics), no-one, it seems, wants to believe it; and this includes the most hard-nosed psychoanalytic critics such as Gilbert and Gubar and, more recently, Elisabeth Bronfen, who have dug deep into the perversity of the character's behaviour. For all these critics, it seems, there is a clear rationale for why things go so horribly wrong, be this identified as a corrupt, and confused, bourgeois marriage-market (Eagleton 1975), traumatic and incomplete psychosexual development (Gilbert and Gubar 2000 [1979]), or Brontë's Blakean attempt to interrogate and invert the Christian notions of 'good' and 'bad', 'heaven and hell' (Marsden 2000; Winnifrith 1973). What most of these readings conceal, however, is their own susceptibility to the discourse of romantic love: that is to say, the way in which the apparently overwhelming force of

Catherine and Heathcliff's love for one another becomes the text's baseline 'truth' and *raison d'être*. Take, for example, the following:

> What Heathcliff offers Cathy is a non-or pre-social relationship, as the only authentic living in a world of exploitation and inequality. . . . Catherine and Heathcliff seek to preserve the primordial moment of pre-social harmony, before the fall into history and oppression . . . (Eagleton 1975: 108–9)

> When Catherine associates Heathcliff with the eternal, she performs a metaphysical leap similar to that found in Schleiermacher's theology. At the heart of Schleiermacher's theology is the understanding of true religion as the personal experience of the infinite. This 'infinite' is sometimes called 'God', but is elsewhere defined as the universe, or, somewhat vaguely, as the eternal. . . . For Catherine, the totality is embodied in Heathcliff. (Marsden 2000: 58)

> Thus in her union with him [Heathcliff] she becomes, like Manfred [that is, Byron's *Manfred*] in his union with Astarte, a perfect androgyne. As devoid of sexual awareness as Adam and Eve were in the pre-lapsarian garden, she sleeps with her whip, her other half, every night in the primordial fashion of the countryside. Gifted with that unconscious, sexual energy which Blake saw as eternal delight, she has 'ways with her', according to Nelly, 'such as I never saw a child take up before'. (Gilbert and Gubar 2000: 265)

> Their relation is that of a symbiotic imaginary duality, where the beloved other is the same as the self, present as long as the survivor exists, absent or lost only by its absence. Their love establishes a notion of oneness that allows for difference only in the sense of annihilation. . . . A symbiotic love which cannot be sustained within the 'catastrophic' subjugation and prohibition that the social order required. (Bronfen 1993: 307)

Whilst working with, and within, very different theoretical paradigms, what all these celebrations of the Catherine–Heathcliff relationship share is a belief in its truth-value based on the fact that this is a union that apparently stands outside of, or anterior to, the constraints and corruption of what is generally encapsulated by the Lacanian 'Symbolic Order'. Whilst not disputing the appeal of such readings (and having performed similar myself in the past (Pearce 1994, 1996)), I am now inclined to present a rather less triumphant version of the relationship. By shifting our attention away from this (admittedly compelling) impression of Catherine and Heathcliff's early, 'oceanic' love for one another, and focusing, instead, on the moment of Heathcliff's return, it is possible to write a very different, and somewhat less redemptive, script. Thus whilst I still believe that each lover does, indeed, ensure the other's immortality, it is not according to any Platonic ideal.

The new story reads something like this: when Heathcliff re-appears at Catherine's front door (now Thrushcross Grange) after his long, unspecified absence, they are meeting as adults for the first time. Despite Catherine's superficially 'childish' delight in having her 'old friend' back, the reader – like Edgar Linton – should not be fooled into believing that they can still relate to one another as innocent children. Indeed, a close reading of the moment of their reunion makes it clear that – in Barthesian terms – this is another spectacular *coup de foudre*; strangeness is mixed with latent familiarity as the pair 'fall in love' with one another all over again:

> He took a seat opposite Catherine, who kept her gaze fixed on him as if she feared he would vanish were she to remove it. He did not raise his to her, often; a quick glance now and then sufficed; but it flashed back, each time more confidently, the undisguised delight he drank from hers.
>   They were too much absorbed in their mutual joy to suffer embarrassment; not so Mr Edgar, he grew pale with pure annoyance, a feeling that reached its climax when his lady rose – and stepping across the rug, seized Heathcliff's hands again, and laughed like one beside herself. (Brontë 1995a: 96–7)

What this scene heralds, then – and what most critical readings to date seem to have ignored –, is that this is now no longer a childhood (and hence 'innocent') relationship, but a mature and manifestly adulterous one.[10] The fact that here, and on other occasions, Catherine and Heathcliff manage to behave as though Edgar doesn't exist (literally as well as figuratively) is an illusion that cannot be sustained. Also overlooked in most readings of the text is the fact that the tragic outcome of Catherine and Heathcliff's romance can be traced to the moment when Edgar finally (if with the help of his 'men' (see Gilbert and Gubar 2000: 281)) throws Heathcliff out of his house and actively forbids Catherine and Heathcliff to see each other again:

> 'To get rid of me – answer my question,' persevered Mr Linton. 'You *must* answer it; and that violence does not alarm me. I have found out that you can be as stoical as anyone when you please. Will you give up Heathcliff hereafter, or will you give up me? It is impossible for you to be *my* friend, and *his* at the same time; and I absolutely *require* to know which you choose.' (Brontë 1995a: 117)

In this reading of the text I am therefore proposing that it is *this* moment – rather than the one in which Catherine famously declares 'it would degrade me to marry Heathcliff now' (Brontë 1995a: 81) – that ensures the tragic outcome of the story. Presented thus, the apotheosis of the relationship was not their childhood on the moors (the text provides plenty of instances of grief and cruelty to mitigate this myth), but the first few weeks and months of their adult 'affair'. Whilst one response to this proposition might be: 'OK: but why, then, did Catherine refuse Edgar's invitation to go with Heathcliff and hence "betray" her heart a second time?', I would argue that (illness and pregnancy and social consequence aside) within weeks the relationship had been recast according to the pleasures of its own perversity. For whilst Catherine and Heathcliff might have lived on – for a few months, or indeed years – in the 'fallen state' of their affair, theirs was no longer the all-exclusive symbiotic love of childhood. Indeed, the further twist to this 'adult' reading of the love story is that in their now explicitly sexual rediscovery of one another, Catherine and Heathcliff also discover their psychological differences *from* one another: differences which bring intense pleasure (psychoanalysis would argue that it is impossible to realize desire without them), but also acute distress. Thus when Edgar offers Catherine a second chance of leaving him for Heathcliff, the only adequate (re)union she can conceive is in death. This is because, as I shall now attempt to explain, Catherine and Heathcliff are *not* cut from the same 'eternal rocks' (Brontë 1995a: 82) and heath but are for ever psychically divided as the consequence of her narcissism.

Although previous commentators have observed that Catherine displays narcissistic characteristics, none – to my knowledge – has pursued this as part of a sustained analysis of her personality.[11] The moment in the text when she displays her egotistical apprehension of her relationship to the world, and everything in it, most frankly is in one of her (purportedly 'delirious') conversations with Nelly:

> 'If I were only sure it would kill him,' she interrupted, 'I'd kill myself directly! These three awful nights, I've never closed my lids – and oh, I've been tormented! I've been haunted, Nelly! But I begin to fancy you don't like me. How strange! I thought, though everybody hated and despised each other, they could not avoid loving me – and they've all turned to enemies in a few hours. *They* have, I'm positive; the people *here*.' (Brontë 1995a: 121–2)

Combining, as it does, delusions of megalomania ('If I were only sure it would kill him . . . I'd kill myself directly!') with a paranoid fear of harm and reprisal ('they've all turned to enemies . . . *They* have'), Catherine's outburst conforms perfectly to the pathological profile of the narcissist who – threatened with loss of power – projects her fear of perceived hostility onto others. Those whom she loved whilst they reflected back an ideal image of herself have – through their obstruction of her will / desire – suddenly ('in a few hours') become monsters. That which had been introjected in order to further boost her own ego (that is, the adoration of the Lintons) has become sullied and is now violently expelled. Love, in an instant, thus turns to hate, whilst revealing – all too tragically – the limitations of the narcissist's love. As Freud observes: 'The megalomania has no doubt come into being at the expense of the object-libido. The libido that has been withdrawn from the external world has been directed to the ego and thus gives rise to an attitude which may be called narcissism' (Freud 1984a: 66). What is implied here is that, in subjects whose 'primary narcissism' fails to redirect itself towards 'object-ideals' at the appropriate point in their ego-development, all possibility of loving and/or empathizing with other human beings – as separate beings in their own right – is lost. Although the adult narcissist may think s/he loves *y*, this is no more than a reflex of *x*'s desire for her own aggrandizement. Despite the fact that Freud problematically locates this tendency primarily (though not exclusively) in females, it is useful in helping to explain the *dynamic* between Brontë's two lovers:

> For it seems that another person's narcissism has a great attraction for those who have renounced part of their own narcissism and are in search of object-love. The charm of a child lies to a great extent in his narcissism, his self-containment and inaccessibility. . . . Indeed, even great criminals and humorists, as they are represented in literature, compel our interest by the narcissistic consistency with which they manage to keep away from anything that would diminish it. It is as if we envied them for maintaining a blissful state of mind – an unassailable libidinal position which we ourselves have since abandoned. (Freud 1984a: 82–3)

As elsewhere in his writings, Freud is careful to remind the reader that what may, here, be regarded as a psychosis is – when manifested less acutely – a widely experienced dynamic in interpersonal relations. Indeed, one may go as far as to propose that those inclined to narcissism (N) and those inclined to object-idealization (I) (where the object 'without alteration in its nature, is aggrandized and exalted in the subject's mind' (Freud 1984a: 88)) are likely to form a highly successful pairing. I's adoration will further exalt N's already-inflated ego-ideal and, at the same time – through the processes of projection and introjection – compensate for the loss of his/her *own* primary narcissism ($N + I \rightarrow NN + IN$). It will be noted that, in this equation, N is not required to contribute anything to the relationship other than the fact of his/her magnificent subject-plenitude.

Notwithstanding the fact that variations of this narcissist/idealist dynamic may be more widespread than is commonly allowed, many readers will doubtless already be resisting the possibility of reducing the apocryphal romance of Catherine and Heathcliff to its terms. Given the Western world's investment in the text as one of the great love stories of all time, this is hardly surprising, especially since the 'truth' and 'purity' of Catherine and Heathcliff's love has traditionally been invoked to excuse their crimes. As I noted at the beginning of this section, even those critics who have brought psychoanalysis to bear upon the text have tended to take their cue from Catherine's own, celebrated pronouncements (for example, 'Nelly, I am Heathcliff' (Brontë 1995a: 82)), leaving the image of the two star-crossed soul-mates intact. Whilst Eagleton, Gilbert and Gubar, and Bronfen (cited earlier) all allow that its strength, and extremity, owe in part to the *regressive* nature of the love (the terms 'semiotic', 'symbiotic' and 'primal' are variously invoked), they uphold the notion of its absolute 'equality' and 'mutuality'. Despite an acknowledgement of all the material things that separate them – class, gender, breeding (variously construed) –, the great romance of this text is that 'deep down' Catherine and Heathcliff are not only 'hewn from the same stone' (to invoke Catherine's metaphor (Brontë 1995a: 82)) but also *feel the same things* (about each other, and about the world). No-one has proposed, as far as I am aware, that their symbiosis is based on a rather *less equal*, rather *more complementary*, principle; or, indeed, that this difference becomes visible as a direct result of the sexual maturation of their relationship (that is, following Heathcliff's return).

Close examination of the scene when Catherine and Heathcliff are reunited reveals rather more, I would suggest, than their 'mutual joy' (Brontë 1995a: 97). Although undeniably enraptured by the sight of one another (see previous discussion), their ensuing conversation reviews both past and future as far as their interpersonal dynamic is concerned. For, from the first, Catherine is focused on how *she* is loved (or not): 'and yet, cruel Heathcliff! you don't deserve this welcome. To be absent and silent for three years, and never to think of me!' (Brontë 1995a: 97), while Heathcliff is intent on discovering if his love is, at last, returned:

> [W]hile waiting in the yard below I meditated this plan – just to have one glimpse of your face – a stare of surprise, perhaps, and pretended pleasure; afterwards settle my score with Hindley; and then prevent the law by doing execution on myself. Your welcome has put these ideas out of my mind; but beware of meeting me with another aspect next time! Nay, you'll not drive me off again – you were really sorry for me, were you? Well, there was cause. I've fought a bitter life since I last heard your voice, and you must forgive me, for I struggled only for you! (Brontë 1995a: 97)

What this speech (to which she never replies) confirms is the complete *lack of certainty* Heathcliff has in Catherine's love. Although the popular reading of this novel assumes that, whatever else, the passion the two lovers feel for one another is unwavering, the text's silence exposes Heathcliff's uncertainty. He knows not only that Catherine was prepared to marry another man largely because 'he [that is, Edgar] *loved her*' (see conversation with Nelly (Brontë 1995a: 78, my italics)), but also that she had always put her own needs before his in their own relationship. Although her warm reception enables him to briefly fantasize that she cares *for him* ('you were really sorry for me, were you?' (Brontë 1995a: 97)), subsequent events (and conversations) prove that this is not the case. Indeed, the narcissistic measure of Catherine's relationship to Heathcliff is confirmed in her *tête-à-tête* with Nelly later that night. Ecstatic as she is to have Heathcliff 'home', it is clearly not on account of his own well-being but because of the light he shines on her own ego: 'However, it's over, and I'll take no revenge on his [Edgar's] folly – I can afford to suffer anything, hereafter! . . . and, as a proof, I'll go make my peace with Edgar instantly – Good night – *I'm an angel!*' (Brontë 1995a: 100, my italics). With Heathcliff returned, and Edgar's devotion assured (not least by his jealousy), Catherine's ego is restored to its original plenitude and power. Her happiness and delight are thus not on account of Heathcliff himself but due to the supernatural transformation in her that he has enabled.

However, Catherine's joyful designation of herself as 'an angel' also points to another aspect of her person up to and including this moment in the story: her sexual immaturity. Indeed, following Freud, we might go so far as to suggest that the narcissistic dynamic she has enjoyed with others, thus far, has been focused on her 'ego-instinct' rather than her 'ego-libido' (Freud 1984a: 67–8). Even her attempts to understand Edgar's jealousy of Heathcliff are expressed through naïvely asexual parallels such as her own lack of envy at 'the brightness of Isabella's yellow hair' (Brontë 1995a: 98). Besides the fact that her narcissism has, up to this point, prevented her experiencing feelings of envy or jealousy for anyone, she is – as Nelly's retorts wryly suggest – entirely ignorant of the sexual fire with which she plays.

Catherine's sexual ignorance evidently does not persist for long following Heathcliff's return, however. Not only can their reunion, as I have already shown, be read as a moment of Barthesian *ravissement*, but the fact that Catherine is now 'a married woman' puts a touch-paper to Heathcliff's own sexual jealousy. This is manifested, some time after his return, by his perverse and (self-)destructive exploitation of Isabella's infatuation. Whilst both he *and* Catherine swear that they are emotionally indifferent to the liaison, it is hard not to read this as the moment Heathcliff succumbs to jealousy (seducing Isabella is an act of revenge against Catherine and her sexual relations with Edgar) and Catherine experiences it for the first time:

> 'Hush!' said Catherine, shutting the inner door. 'Don't vex me. Why have you disregarded my request? Did she come across you on purpose?'
>
> 'What is it to you?' he growled. 'I have a right to kiss her, if she chooses, and you have no right to object – I'm not *your* husband, *you* needn't be jealous of me!'
>
> 'I'm not jealous of you,' replied the mistress, 'I'm jealous for you. Clear your face, you shan't scowl at me! If you like Isabella, you shall marry her. But, do you like her? Tell the truth, Heathcliff! There, you won't answer. I'm certain you don't!' (Brontë 1995a: 112)

This is, I would suggest, the moment of 'the fall' for Catherine and Heathcliff. Readers who return to this scene (Vol. 1, Chapter XI) will discover that, after this first laying down of the gauntlet (on both sides), all hell is let loose. Heathcliff accuses Catherine of treating him 'infernally', with barely veiled allusion to her ability to flirt with him and have sex with Edgar at the same time ('And if you flatter yourself that I don't perceive it you are a fool – and, if you think I can be consoled by sweet words you are an idiot' (Brontë 1995a: 112)), whilst Catherine smarts under the suspicion (both Heathcliff's and her own) that she may, indeed, be jealous of – and unable to bear – his liaison with Isabella ('Oh, the evil is that I am *not* jealous, is it?' (Brontë 1995a:112)). Although both lovers, then, insist that it is impossible to be jealous of a woman they both despise, Isabella's ability to ignite a lifetime of sexual frustration casts her in the classic 'foil' role.[12]

Whether or not Catherine and Heathcliff's own relationship is ever consummated is, of course, another of the great secrets of this text. Whilst this silence must be taken as an assumption that it is *not*, the narrative does at least allow for the *possibility*. Not only does Nelly hint at numerous meetings – both at home and on the moors – whilst Edgar is away, but the denouement of the action reveals Catherine extremely alarmed at the prospect of Edgar over-hearing something Heathcliff has said. Twice, during this scene, does Catherine refer to the latter's 'outrageous talk' and on the first occasion observes: 'If he did overhear us, of course, he'll never forgive you' (Brontë 1995a: 115). Whilst such an unspecified allusion cannot, of course, be taken as *evidence* of anything (we, like Edgar, and – for once – like Nelly, 'hear nothing'), it nevertheless serves to make us wonder how physical (or not) the relationship had by this time become. In terms of the timescale there is even, of course, the possibility that Catherine II is Heathcliff's, and not Linton's, child. Both the genetic and narrative logic of the rest of the novel militate strongly against such a way-ward suspicion, however; and, in terms of my own reading, this is a Love-and-Death story whose afterlife makes much more sense if a *full* sexual consummation never happened.

This is, indeed, the moment in my own reading where the psychoana-lytic profile of the two lovers joins up with nineteenth-century eschatol-ogy once more. My proposal is that it is Catherine's unwavering narcissism – what Heathcliff, at her deathbed, refers to as 'your infernal selfishness' (Brontë 1995a: 161) – together with the unconsummated nature of their relationship, that effectively ensures their souls will walk the earth for ever. Although it remains unclear whether these wanderings take place in par-adise, or Hades, or purgatory, or limbo (and/or the Upper Circles of hell), the *psychological* narrative logic of the text suggests that the 'unfinished business' of their life has consigned them to an afterlife that is similarly without closure. Whilst various characters within the text (Nelly, Lockwood, Heathcliff himself) suggest that there is hope of 'peace' and 'rest' at last, nineteenth-century theology (as reviewed in the first part of this chapter) indicates that – for the likes of Catherine and Heathcliff espe-cially – this will be a long time coming. Their immortality is thus assured not by their fixed residence in heaven or hell, but through a destiny in which they are doomed to wander for ever but *never* arrive. Such a fate would, at least, be consistent with the rationale for hell outlined in Dante's *Inferno* – that is, that souls are punished according to the nature of their sins on earth (Dante 1984). In this last regard, indeed, it is interesting to observe that Dante's 'Second Circle of Hell' contains two souls who would seem to be the prototypes of Catherine and Heathcliff: the adulterous medieval lovers, Paolo and Francesca (see cover illustration and Preface). Once Paolo and Francesca (who has been married to Paolo's brother) fall in love they become 'inseparable' and, following their deaths (they are slain by Francesca's husband), this is figured as their immortal *punishment*: 'these two there were who move together/and seem to be so light upon the winds' (Dante 1984: V.l.74–5). The fact that Dante's pilgrim is, himself, dan-gerously enchanted by the image of these beautiful lovers also resonates with the ambiguous status of heaven and hell in Brontë's text. As has already been observed, many critics have concluded that the only way to make moral sense of *Wuthering Heights* is to see it as a 'Blakeian' inversion of the two 'Last Things' (Gilbert and Gubar 2000: 255; Marsden 2000: 72–3). What Dante's text reminds us is that there is plenty of scope, even within Christian doctrine, for hell to be heavenly; we may conclude that the souls of Catherine and Heathcliff *have* been consigned to hell, but (following Dante's model) only to its 'outer circles'. The fact that both

Catherine (in her dreams and deliriums) and Heathcliff (in his long years of mourning) repeatedly choose the torment of such a limbo over the peace of heaven makes the terms of their fate inevitable.

In conclusion, I offer a few words on how this willed, and wilful, destiny may also be seen as consonant with the characters' psychological profiles. The first thing to observe here is that, following the dramatic 'fall' brought about by the incursion of (mutual) sexual jealousy into their relationship, both Catherine and Heathcliff suffer severe ego-damage. With her narcissistic mirror shattered, Catherine succumbs to a severe melancholia that propels her towards a starvation-induced suicide. The psychoanalytic logic here is that one of the things that distinguish melancholia from mourning is the fact that 'the object-choice has been effected on a narcissistic basis' (Freud 1984b: 258), with profound consequences for the subject's own ego. With Heathcliff lost a second time, Catherine's ego is rocked to its core, and all her disappointment is turned self-destructively upon herself. In this respect, her earlier pronouncement about Heathcliff 'being more myself than I am' (Brontë 1995a: 81) becomes all too true. What is revealed at this crisis moment, however, is that rather than their interdependence being supremely 'romantic', it has always bordered on the pathological. The reason why Catherine cannot 'do' without Heathcliff is ultimately because he is the only mirror large enough, or deep enough, to give her back the vision of herself she needs in order to survive; and the reason Heathcliff cannot live without her ('I *cannot* live without my life! I *cannot* live without my soul!' (Brontë 1995a: 169)) is that he, too, requires the assurance of Catherine's undiminished ego in order to 'guarantee' his own. She is, and remains, his unmitigated 'object-ideal' ('she is so immeasurably superior to them – to everybody on earth; is she not, Nelly?' (Brontë 1995a: 51)) and, as such, compensates for his own lost ego-plenitude. The word 'symbiotic' does, therefore, sum up their relationship very accurately; the difference, in this reading, is simply that $x + y$ are bound together by (post-oedipal) *difference and complement* rather than (pre-oedipal) *similarity*.

Although neither Brontë nor her characters had the Freudian concepts and vocabulary to grapple with the perverse dynamics of their love in this way, the accusations that fly back and forth in the celebrated deathbed scene reveal that each was fully aware of the undisguised 'needs' of the other. Thus Catherine dies mourning not the loss of Heathcliff *per se* but the loss of her own ego ('"I wish I could hold you," she continued, bitterly, "till we were both dead! I shouldn't care what you suffered. I care nothing for your sufferings. Why shouldn't you suffer? I do!"' (Brontë 1995a:160)), whilst Heathcliff looks with terror upon the world that he (and his own mutilated ego) must inhabit without her in it:

'Are you possessed with a devil,' he pursued savagely, 'to talk in that manner to me, when you are dying? Do you reflect that all those words will be branded in my memory, and eating deeper eternally, after you have left me? You know you lie to say I have killed you, and, Catherine, you know that I could as soon forget you, as my existence!' (Brontë 1995a: 161)

And Heathcliff is also correct, of course, when he later asserts that Catherine has effectively 'killed herself' (Brontë 1995a:162). What he (the character, not the text) does not quite grasp is the extent to which this is as the direct result of her 'starving ego' rather than her marriage to Edgar; the reason why she 'betrayed her own heart' is not because she really loved Heathcliff better but that she needed him – and his mirror – more.

What, then, can these two souls – victims of an unresolved/fundamentally perverse desire and trapped in the unforgiving theology of the early nineteenth century – hope for after death? Are they truly consigned, in the manner of Paolo and Francesca, to a life of perpetual, insatiable wandering? Will Heathcliff be forced to concede that, even after death, there could be no final union with one who continued to love herself rather than him? Or will Heathcliff's reunion with Catherine in some intermediate state, in which she can become 'an angel' once again, be enough to restore them both to their former happiness? As I indicated at the beginning of this chapter, the closest we are likely to get to an answer is that Victorian eschatology appears to have been heavily invested in these intermediate, earth-bound states and the rather material immortality associated with them.

In this last respect, then, Brontë's lovers may not be as exceptional as they first appear, but represent just two of many souls who would endure any punishment in order to enjoy the tormenting joy of *human* existence a little longer. Whilst I therefore concede that Catherine and Heathcliff may well have secured a means of achieving '*their* heaven', I would also insist that its terms and conditions are indisputably those of hell. Inasmuch as the version of romantic love they have discovered is irredeemable, so – of necessity – are they.

III

'*Immortal Invisible*': Love, Death and Sublimation in Nineteenth-Century Literature

For all my efforts to resist a redemptive reading of *Wuthering Heights*, it is, of course, all too easy to find one in the 'corrective' affiliations of the second generation. After the relentless lust for cruelty and revenge which characterizes the second half of the novel – and it should be remembered that *all* the characters – and both narrators – are possessed by it –, even the most anti-humanist of readers is likely to feel his, or her, heart ease at the belated exchange of tenderness between Hareton and Catherine II. For those willing to take the long view of the novel, this new type of love-relationship – predicated very strictly on respect / affection for the other as an *autonomous individual* – holds out the hope that corrupt family lines may eventually be purged of their 'black blood' (genetic or otherwise). And freed from this Gothic attention to 'inheritance', romantic love – even in its relationship to death – is able to offer some more comforting visions.

A text which, on the surface at least, most certainly appears to offer the reader a proper Christian alternative to the wild irresolution of the relationship between Catherine and Heathcliff is Tennyson's *In Memoriam* (1974 [1850]). This Victorian best-seller, known in its day as the quintessential aid to mourning and famously patronized by Queen Victoria herself, tells the story of a successful resolution of love and loss. By the end of this long (131 cantos) poem, Arthur Hallam – the best friend and intellectual companion of Tennyson who died suddenly at the age of 21 – has been sublimated into a supernatural presence to whom the poet can relate with equanimity:

> Thy face is on the rolling air;
> I hear thee where the waters run;
> Thou standest in the rising sun,
> And in the setting thou art fair.
>
> What art thou then? I cannot guess;
> But tho' I seem in star and flower
> To feel thee some diffusive power,
> I do not therefore love thee less.
>
> My love involves the love before;
> My love is vaster passion now;
> Tho' mixed with God and Nature thou,
> I seem to love thee more and more.
>   Stanza CXXX (Tennyson 1974: 149)

For many readers, myself included, this joyful resolution – a veritable triumph of the 'work of mourning' according to Freud – nevertheless fails to convince. Doubtless there are very real theological issues here: in a poem which is as much about the Victorian crisis of faith and doubt as it is about personal love and loss, this account of Hallam's 'transubstantiation' is likely to find more ready acceptance amongst those practised in

Christian doctrine. Placed alongside the following early canto, however, my own 'cry' – like that of the lovers in *Wuthering Heights* – remains 'how?': how can we (as mourners) bear the sudden disappearance of a body into thin air? How can the 'white light' of something half-divine compensate for the loss of the specificity of a person?

> Dark house, by which once more I stand
> Here in the long unlovely street,
> Doors, where my heart was used to beat
> So quickly, waiting for a hand,
>
> A hand that can be clasped no more –
> Behold me, for I cannot sleep,
> And like a guilty thing I creep
> At earliest morning to the door.
>
> He is not here; but far away
> The noise of life begins again,
> And ghastly thro' the drizzling rain
> On the bald street breaks the blank day.
>   Stanza VII (Tennyson 1974: 79)

Even putting to one side the twentieth-century readings of the poem which focused on the intense homoeroticism of this image (see Craft 1988), it is surely hard to accept that the searing materiality of such a loss can ever be effectively sublimated and then memorialized. As we have already seen, however, according to Freud such a resolution is always possible, given time; and time is precisely, and painfully, what Tennyson's poem lays down as the fundamental requirement of mourning. Wait long enough (ideally, at least two years) and the libido will finally let go and direct its attention elsewhere; human love will, like the lost object, become comfortably 'immortal':

> Known and unknown; human, divine;
> Sweet human hand and lips and eye;
> Dear heavenly friend that canst not die,
> Mine, mine, for ever ever mine.
>   Stanza CXXIX (Tennyson 1974: 149)

As the title – 'Immortal Invisible' – to this chapter section suggests, I posit this transcendent model of 'immortal love' as the antithesis to the endless wandering in some intermediate afterlife 'chosen' by Catherine and Heathcliff in *Wuthering Heights*. I propose, also, that most nineteenth-century literature concerned with the Love–Death nexus swings between these two poles, but it is the latter that wins out. The – often spectacular – materialization of the afterlife that took place during this period would seem to be

part of a widespread (if unconscious) resistance to a 'quick exit'. Therefore, although *Wuthering Heights* is normally read as one of the great
maverick texts of the nineteenth century, I am suggesting that the indeterminate destiny it carves out for its lovers is consonant with the covert
preference of many writers who likewise desire an 'afterlife' without an
'end-to-life'.

Apart from the early Gothic fiction mentioned at the beginning of the
chapter, there is a strong poetic tradition – running from Keats and Byron
through to the Pre-Raphaelites – that was fascinated with those beings who
had become trapped between two worlds as the result of an unresolved,
or tragic, love affair. The Ur-text here – and, of course, for *Wuthering
Heights* itself – is Byron's tale of incestuous love, the closet-drama *Manfred*
(1996 [1817]). As numerous commentators have since observed, it is impossible not to see this as the primary source for Brontë's text, especially on
a rhetorical level. The language with which the half-crazed/suicidal
Manfred conjures up the spirit of his dead lover (and half-sister) Astarte
echoes Heathcliff's almost word for word: ('Speak to me! Though it be in
wrath; – but say –/I reck not what – but let me hear thee once –/This once
– once more!' (Byron 1996: 492)). Manfred's ghost, like Heathcliff's, shows
a spectre's 'ordinary caprice' (Brontë 1995a: 28) and grants her lover only
a handful of elusive words. However, for him as for Heathcliff, this proof
of her continued existence is enough to bring him peace ('There is a calm
upon me – Inexplicable stillness!' (Byron 1996: 493)) and a resolve to follow
her beyond the grave. Although we are not given any clear illustration of
the 'other-world' on which Manfred's eyes are set, moreover, the proclivities of his earthly (or 'earth-bound') soul figure a landscape of mountain
and cataract, wilderness and grandeur, in which all creatures are ever-
conscious of their 'freedom' (Byron 1996: 497). This, too, will find its echo
not only in *Wuthering Heights* but also in many of Emily Brontë's 'Gondal'
poems.[13]

This fantasy of miscreant lovers being finally reunited in a netherworld
that bears all the hallmarks of an earthly paradise survives, albeit in a
somewhat watered-down version, in the paintings and poetry of the Pre-
Raphaelite group. Whilst there is not space to survey even a small portion
of the relevant texts and authors here, Dante Gabriel Rossetti deserves
special mention because of his obsession with the story of Dante and
Beatrice. As illustrated by his hundreds of paintings and drawings on the
subject, the most famous of which is his *Beata Beatrix* (c. 1864–70) (reproduced in Pearce 1991), Rossetti rejoiced in the mythology of his poetic
namesake and created many lyrical images both of the lovers' reunion in

the afterlife and, indeed, of death itself. As I have argued elsewhere, the sublime – and sublimating – image of death found in this painting may be seen as typical of a somewhat troubling fascination with female illness and death by this particular group of artists (Pearce 1991: 51–2). It is certainly a perfect illustration of the 'frozen' moment of *ideal death* propounded by Bronfen and de Rougemont, and endorsed by Rossetti's own observation that the painting does not represent Beatrice's 'actual death' but rather the moment she is 'rapt visibly towards heaven'.[14] Returning to the image in the context of the present discussion, I find myself rather more fascinated by the background scenery and the glimpse this offers us into the afterlife of the Victorian imagination. The first thing that strikes the viewer in this regard is how Rossetti has used the blurred focus of background composition to 'half reveal and half conceal' his vision of this 'other world'. It is interesting to note that even in *Woman/Image/Text* I referred to this as an 'indeterminate space' in which 'float' the allegorical figure of Love, and the poet Dante (Pearce 1991: 53). Look still closer, however, and you will see that this indeterminate space also contains the ghostly outlines of buildings, temples, a bridge, and the trees and vegetation connotative of an Italian landscape. In other words, the world to which Beatrice is being 'visibly rapt' is purposefully confused with the one she is leaving behind: 'paradise', once again, is 'earthly'.

What has emerged here, then, is a theory that nineteenth-century literature and culture were heavily invested in keeping their dead alive for as long as possible; and this despite the Christian doctrine that counsels the bereaved to 'let go' of the departing soul in order to ease its passage towards God.[15] In the texts that I have focused on to date, the *means* of keeping the dead alive has depended largely on an imaginative belief in an extraneous afterlife. As the century progressed, however, there was an increasing tendency to internalize the process (and 'product') of death, and to move towards an acknowledgement that what is haunted is not the world but the human unconscious. Whilst it is, of course, quite possible to read the wild moors of Brontë's afterlife as a metaphor for the unconscious, the notion that ghosts are essentially a product of the imagination is made more explicit in the (many) Victorian texts dealing with death, love and *doubles*.

In terms of textual origins, this *doppelgänger* tradition returns us to *Faust* and the Devil's ability to take up temporary residence in the body/soul of a seductive 'other'. Within nineteenth-century literature, the replicant sometimes took the form of the protagonist's alter-ego (for example, Hogg's *The Private Memoirs of a Justified Sinner* (1824); Stevenson's *The*

Strange Case of Dr Jekyll and Mr Hyde (1886)) and sometimes that of a love-object. Edgar Allan Poe's short story 'Ligeia' (2003 [1845]) and Wilkie Collins's *The Woman in White* (1973 [1860]) are both fascinating instances of the latter, confusing – as they do – the power (and impotence) of sexual desire with the power of the dead. In both texts, a male lover is haunted and taunted by the 'double' of his (lost) love-object, though in Poe's story her 'likeness' to the original is not revealed until the sensational – and spectacular – end of the story. Sitting watch over the body of his second wife, the Lady Rowena (who had – for many days – been subject to uttering 'inexplicable sighs'), the narrator is, at last, confronted by her ghastly transformation into his first love, Ligeia:

> One bound, and I had reached her feet! Shrinking from my touch, she let fall from her head, unloosened, the cerements which had confined it, and there streamed forth, into the rushing atmosphere of the chamber, huge masses of long and dishevelled hair: *it was blacker than the raven wings of midnight!* . . . 'Here then, at least', I shrieked aloud, can I never – can I never be mistaken – these are the full and the black, and the wild eyes – of my lost love – of the Lady – of the LADY LIGEIA.' (Poe 2003: 387–8)

While the stuttering, hysterical nature of this revelation (which ends the story) is clearly intended to authenticate its horror, its convulsions also take us to the fear at the heart of the romantic 'double'. For Poe's narrator, as for poor Walter Hartright in *The Woman in White*, the anxiety that he himself has sinned (by allowing himself to be seduced by 'another woman') is compounded by uncertainties over which is the 'original' woman anyway. It is a fear which returns us not only to the psychic origins of love (the Freudian/Lacanian notion that all subsequent love-objects are but substitutes for the lost mother) but to one of its most abiding philosophical conundrums: that is, whether or not it is *repeatable* (see discussion in Chapter 1). The particular anxiety that emerges here, however, is that genealogy – as well as the irrepressible male libido – ensures that beloved objects can – and must — be replaced in the fullness of time. The interchangeability of Collins's Anne Catherick and Laura Fairlie, and of Poe's Lady Rowena and Lady Ligeia, thus amount to the same thing: a negation of what, for many, remains the first principle of love – its purported uniqueness.

This traumatized response to the fact that love might not, after all, possess an 'original' is also to be seen in Heathcliff's violent repulsion of Hareton and Catherine II at the end of *Wuthering Heights*. Both Eagleton (1975) and Gilbert and Gubar (2000) call into question the 'happiness' of the text's ending in this regard. The union of the new generation of lovers may please the reader, even as it pleases Nelly, but, for Heathcliff, its 'corrective' repetition of his own love is unbearable: 'Where C plus H equals fullness of being for both C and H, C^2 plus H^2 specifically equals a negation of both C and H . . . The illegitimate Heathcliff/Catherine have finally been re-placed in nature/hell, and replaced by Hareton and Catherine II – a proper couple . . .' (Gilbert and Gubar 2000: 301–2). It is hence interesting to observe that whilst Poe mixes the bodies of 'lover' and 'other' in such a way that the 'original' triumphs (Rowena's blue eyes are ousted by Ligeia's black ones), in *Wuthering Heights* it is rather a case that she (that is, Catherine) is subsumed or – as Gilbert and Gubar would have it – 'fragmented' by her *partial* replication in the next generation (Gilbert and Gubar 2000: 300). As Heathcliff so tragically observes: 'The entire world is a dreadful collection of memoranda that she did exist, and that I have lost her' (Brontë 1995a: 324). This, and not Poe's, is surely the truest 'horror': the notion not that things 'live on' in ghastly form, but rather that they change, mutate and are – eventually – lost for ever.

What has emerged from this overview of the dialogue that Brontë's text had – and continues to have – with its nineteenth-century contemporaries is thus a shared resistance to the finality of death. Whilst some texts – most famously, *In Memoriam* – have achieved (on a rhetorical level at least) a successful sublimation of both the deceased and the bereaved, others appear to find greater comfort in their 'unquiet slumbers' (Brontë 1995a: 337). This applies both to authors working within the Gothic tradition (such as Brontë, Poe, Collins) and to more mainstream classic-realist texts (Dickens, Eliot, Hardy). Indeed, one might go so far as to posit that there are few works of nineteenth-century fiction into which the 'hand of death' does not intrude with some degree of supernatural *frisson*. In many cases, also, it is a *frisson* indebted to the (spectacularly) un-smooth course of romantic love. Love – even when it becomes a 'curse' – is embraced for its 'gift' of eternal life, whilst eternal life – as envisaged by nineteenth-century eschatology – guarantees an everlasting home for Love. And whilst, as the century progressed, the sense that 'love lives on' focused increasingly on the haunting of the unconscious – Henry James's *The Wings of the Dove* (2004 [1902]) is a stunning case in point – the preference remained for the 'undead' to leave as many traces of themselves as possible; to refuse the finality of the so-called 'second burial'. Writing about the latter in *Over Her Dead Body*, Bronfen observes that it was a common belief that the 'deceased is no longer dangerous [only] when its body stops undergoing change, is stabilized into its last ossified state and when its image has receded and stops entering the survivor's dreams and memories' (Bronfen 1993: 296).

In the Victorian era's unprecedented obsession with the 'relics' of the dead, however, this 'stabilization'/'memorialization' of the beloved was often infinitely deferred, and things were locked away or buried repeatedly and exhumed. We need only be reminded of the savagery with which Heathcliff replaces Edgar's hair in Catherine's locket with his own to realize how much these things mattered (Brontë 1995a: 170). This was an era in which *things*, as well as people, were most emphatically not allowed to die.

5

Wartime Romance

The Gift of Self-Sacrifice

I

In this chapter we pursue romantic love into the early twentieth century but via a paradigm – wartime romance – that repeatedly claims to transcend historical and cultural boundaries. The reason for this will become clear in the course of the chapter: love that is born out of, and experienced within, the context of war actualizes the psychological trauma inherent in all romantic relationships to a truly spectacular degree. Wartime romance may, indeed, be thought of as presenting us with an X-ray of the body of love; of violently stripping the flesh from the skeleton[1] of desire and affiliation, and enabling us to see the many shocking un-saids (the chance, the fragility, the blindness, the transience, the limit-point) of love that all of us live with but repress most of the time. Wartime romance, then, not only takes us to the deepest of the deep structures of romance but – *vis-à-vis narrative* in particular – tampers with them. The love stories that are discussed in this chapter take on a different shape and form to those discussed in the other chapters; they occupy – in Bakhtinian terms – significantly different chronotopes[2] and pervert the narrative logic of romance through the cruellest twists of plot imaginable. War, then, whose bodily corpses serve to turn humankind's claims to civilization inside out, must necessarily wreak havoc also on the *mythos* of romantic love.

In the course of the chapter I turn the X-ray on wartime romance through, first, a close reading of Vera Brittain's war diary (1913–17) (Brittain 1981) followed, in Part III, by a comparative analysis of a selection of texts by modernist, and other, authors who were writing out of – if not always 'about' – the First World War. My objective here has been to illustrate the extent to which the (largely nineteenth-century) model of romantic love and sexual relationships which informs Brittain's text was in the process of being overturned by a new libertarian and post-Freudian consciousness whilst, at the same time, sharing in the same wartime dislocation of time and space. In other words, I attempt to disentangle the paradigm of wartime romance *per se* from the complex set of ideologies informing it. In Part III I also deal briefly with some texts from the Second World War – in particular Graham Greene's *The End of the Affair* (1951) – to further illustrate the way in which wartime so spectacularly uncovers the traumatic skeleton of romantic love.

Before moving on to these readings, however, I attempt a brief history of what happened to the representation of romantic love in literature during the latter part of the nineteenth century and *fin-de-siècle*, focusing in particular on the struggle between those writers who strove to understand it as a discourse or ideology (in particular, Christians, socialists, feminists) and those who engaged the work of the sexologists to pursue its status as an essentially irrational desire.

From George Eliot to Olive Schreiner: The Emergence of the 'Z' Factor

Across the many books that have sought to understand the extraordinary set of literary cultural and historical forces that gave birth to the nineteenth-century *fin-de-siècle*, one name, in particular, is invoked to represent the demise of the 'old order', and that is George Eliot. In her lifetime, Eliot quickly assumed Charles Dickens's mantle of Britain's leading novelist, and today's critics point to her death in 1880 as a symbolic watershed in the history of the genre in terms of both style (hers is, after all, the *classic* 'classic realism') and *zeitgeist* (see Showalter (1990: 59–75) and Bradbury (2001: 15–20)). This sense of Eliot's moral and political conservatism combined, as it invariably is, with acknowledgement of her carefully crafted studies of provincial life has made her the obvious target for all those looking for a symbol to set the turning world against. With respect to the cultural history of romantic love, however, I propose that her writings are much more a stepping-stone than an end-point, and especially with regard to what will emerge in the course of this chapter as the all-important 'z' factor: that is, a model of romantic love in which 'the gift' is conceived not in terms of what the lovers stand to gain (figured in previous chapters as $x + y \rightarrow x' + y'$), but rather what they – through collaboration – are able to *give* ($x + y \rightarrow x' + y' = z$).

Lloyd Fernando goes some way towards distinguishing Eliot's vision of women, love and marriage from the oft-invoked ideals of contemporaries such as Ruskin and Patmore. He observes that whilst she celebrates sexual difference and, in particular, women's capacity for greater emotional feeling than men, she nevertheless insists that this must be cultivated in tandem with the intellect (Fernando 1977: 28). Moreover, when this 'fully developed' woman subsequently joins forces with a receptive man, true moral and intellectual 'progress' will be made: 'The process begins with the individual, who has to achieve a blend of the two kinds of perception which will lead to the complete realization of his possibilities of growth and development' (Fernando 1977: 30).

If this vision of the ideal union between a man and a woman still sounds impossibly conservative to modern ears, it is worth considering the distance that it has come from the companionate marriages of Milton and his contemporaries. Within that paradigm, it will be remembered, what Eliot lauds as woman's special qualities (for example, gentleness and tenderness) are seen to be of value only in the *service and support* of the man. In Eliot's utopia, woman would deploy these qualities not merely to comfort her mate but also to produce 'z': their collaborative 'gift' to the world.

Within the universe of Eliot's own novels, however, 'z' is rarely achieved. Indeed, it could be argued that her greatest works – such as *Middlemarch* (1973 [1871]) – owe their classic status to the fact that she presents 'z' as an aspiration that forever beckons but ever eludes. For many critics, this supremely 'realist(ic)' vision of the present social order is evidenced by the fact that, in *Middlemarch*, the two characters who could most obviously achieve 'z' – Dorothea and Lydgate – are forever kept apart (see Fernando 1977: 47). This tragedy of the right woman failing to link up with the right man is to become, moreover, one of the most rehearsed destinations – or dead-ends – for romantic love at the end of the nineteenth century. It is only a small step, after all, from the tragic mismatches of Lydgate and Dorothea to the failed marriages of Hardy (*Jude the Obscure*, 1895), Meredith (*Modern Love*, 1862) and James (*The Wings of the Dove*, 1902). In the context of my present discussion, however, what is important is that this tragedy is conceived largely (though not wholly) in intellectual and social, as opposed to sexual, terms. The fact that Lydgate and Dorothea never get it together is less a loss to themselves and their desires (Dorothea, after all, would appear to discover genuine sexual compatibility in Ladislaw) than to the small town of Middlemarch and the larger world that both were so desirous to serve.

This notion of romantic love giving rise to 'z' – when 'z' is conceived as a social or intellectual mission that will serve, and prosper, humanity – is, as I hope will become clear in my reading of Brittain's war diaries that follows, a deeply significant residual ideology in a Europe where millions of men and women were about to make the 'ultimate sacrifice'. Before this particular 'gift of love' was refigured as the gift of *pro patria mori*, however, it was pursued further by middle-class feminists keen to make domestic life – and labour – somewhat more meaningful.

Chief amongst the writers and campaigners who sought to move the ideal heterosexual relation from $x + y \rightarrow x' + y'$ to $x + y \rightarrow x' + y' = z$ was Olive Schreiner. This woman, who, as we shall see, was to become Vera Brittain's lifelong role model and muse, stormed the world with her radical feminist/socialist vision through a series of generically diverse writings, including her best-selling novel *The Story of an African Farm* (1971 [1883]), her treatise *Woman and Labour* (1911), and numerous short stories/parables, essays and (latterly) her published *Letters* (1924). Viewed as a successor to George Eliot, Schreiner may be seen as the thinker who seized the '*z*' factor with both hands and gave it a name: *work*. Like many of the other feminists, suffragists and socialists of the late nineteenth century, she saw that until women (of all classes) were permitted to engage in meaningful labour (following an adequate education) they would never be fulfilled either as human beings or as citizens. Moreover, those middle-class women who not only failed to do meaningful work but also lived off their husbands were little better than 'parasites' (the title of one of her chapters in *Woman and Labour*) or, indeed, prostitutes (see Ledger 1997: 41–2). As she put such a premium on women's economic and social independence from men, it is perhaps surprising to discover that Schreiner nevertheless persisted in the notion of an ideal relationship between the sexes; but she did. In numerous letters with her friends in the contemporary feminist and socialist movements (including Karl Pearson, one of the period's outspoken advocates of 'free love'), she holds forth a vision – much the same as George Eliot's – in which properly matched men and women should be encouraged to unite, not only for their own comfort and satisfaction, but for the sake of '*z*'. Indeed – as revealed in the following letter to W. T. Stead – this also led her to conceive intellectual affinity as much more important than physical affinity in long-term relationships, and to the decidedly controversial extent that an 'adultery of the mind' was potentially far more disastrous a relationship than fornication:

> To me it appears that in a highly developed and intellectual people, the mental and spiritual union is more important, more truly the *marriage*, than the physical. I should feel it . . . a much more right and important reason for terminating a union, that the person to whom I was related had fuller, deeper and more useful mental union with another than that there should be a physical relation. Just the mental union 'for the begetting of

great works', to me constitutes marriage. . . . Continuance of the physical relation when the higher mental relation is not possible, and when the affection is given elsewhere, seems to me a more terrible because to me a more permanent prostitution than that of the streets. (Schreiner 1924: 217)

Despite the fact that, on other occasions, Schreiner seeks to mitigate the polarity of mind and body that she establishes here ('sexual love – that tired angel . . . shall yet, at last . . . leap upward with white wings spread, resplendent in the sunshine of a distant future' (in Ledger 1997: 43)), it is clear that the 'intellectual and spiritual' will always take precedence over the 'physical' in her view of human relationships precisely because their meaning and purpose is not self-gratification but 'z' (identified here *explicitly* as 'the begetting of great works'). This yoking of the function of 'the marriage of true minds' to intellectual and social endeavour clearly bespeaks the extent to which the nineteenth-century work ethic had combined with emerging Christian/socialist discourses to render all aspects of meaningful existence a 'mission'. When this world-view was linked, as it is here, to an equally radical feminism, it is easy to see why Schreiner's followers, Vera Brittain amongst them, were hooked: here, at last, was a vision of life – as personal and social aspiration and fulfilment – that made education essential *and* promised to redeem the institution of marriage. What the 'formula' (as conceived in the preceding quotation) also allowed for *theoretically*, of course, was the possibility of intellectually inspired same-sex relationships similarly capable of 'the begetting of great works', and – as we shall see in Chapter 6 – Brittain's life after the Great War was to be proof of it.

This supremely idealist vision of interpersonal love as 'a gift to the world' is, in effect, the limit-point of romance. Linking back, as it does, to Courtly Love (where the transfiguration of x has been conceived by commentators like de Rougemont as ultimately a 'gift to God'), this is another instance of the transformative power of love radically exceeding any notion of personal psycho-sexual satisfaction. Here, as in those discourses which link romantic love with immortality (see Chapter 4), the thrill of desire is predicated upon its capacity to reach *beyond the self*; its capacity, indeed, to take an individual 'out' of him- or herself. The dangers of such enthusiasm when exercised in the wider social/political arena will become obvious in the next section of this chapter, but it is also important to acknowledge the compelling strength of the vision at the cultural–historical moment when – I propose – the 'outward motion' of romantic love is first lost to the solipsism of the sexual self.

Sex, Sexuality and the End of Romance

As has already been observed, the discourse of romance and the discourses associated with sexuality and/or eroticism are not as closely aligned as casual observers might, at first, expect. Inasmuch as romantic love, as it is being investigated here, belongs to a long literary and cultural tradition which focuses on adventure, quest and the sublimation – rather than the consummation – of sexual desire, it stands to reason that those texts which turn their spotlight on the sexual act itself are invested in a rather different paradigm. This, I would suggest, is certainly the case with many of the writings which originate in literary modernism or whose characters are a direct response to the work of the sexologists and psychoanalysts (Krafft-Ebing, Havelock Ellis, Freud) who – from the 1880s – began to turn the world's understanding of both sexual identity and sexual desire upside down.[3]

Before addressing the consequences of this revolution for the discourses of romance and romantic love, however, it is important to say a few words more about those thinkers and writers in whose work 'the dream' does survive. First amongst these are the socialist reformers like Karl Pearson and G. R. Drysdale who argued passionately not only for the social, economic and legal equality of men and women but also for a similar freedom in sexual matters. What keeps Pearson's vision of 'free love' within the discourse of romance (in contrast to many of the exponents of the ideal which circulated in the 1960s and 1970s) is that it conceives monogamy and fidelity, rather than promiscuity, as the natural consequence of unfettered choice: 'The men and women who, being absolutely free, would choose more than one [lover], would certainly be the exceptions – exceptions, I believe, infinitely more rare than under our present legalized monogamy' (Pearson in Fernando 1977: 16). Pearson, then, like Olive Schreiner – his close friend and follower – held forth the vision that mutual love, freely given, would result not in sexual degeneracy but a life-long union that (for Schreiner especially) constituted not only a marvellous coalescence of the sexual and the spiritual but also the production of the all-important 'z' ('The union will be as long as each one feels they are expanding or aiding the other's life' (Schreiner 1924: 64)). Needless to say, this sanguine view of 'free love' and its consequences was not shared by the mass of the population, who clearly could not see the romance for the sex. This was true both of conservative despots like Walter Besant, who declared 'As for the freedom of love . . . It strikes directly at the family. If there is no fidelity in marriage, the family drops to pieces. . . . We will have none of your literature of free and adulterous love' (in Ledger 1997: 31), *and* many feminists who were terrified (justifiably) of having their campaign for 'equal rights' mixed up with a call for sexual libertarianism (Ledger 1997: 16).

The other cultural/textual arena in which the discourse of romantic love lived on was that which, since Lilian Faderman's ground-breaking study *Surpassing the Love of Men* (1985 [1981]), has enjoyed the title of 'romantic friendship'. Referring specifically to same-sex love-relations between women which may or – even more importantly – *may not* include a sexual dimension, the notion of romantic friendship is clearly as important to any attempt to write the history of romance as it is to an attempt to write the history of lesbianism. Thus whilst Faderman has frequently been criticized for her refusal to define lesbianism in sexually specific terms, I propose the counter-argument that – if anything – she could have gone further in teasing out what distinguishes the *romance* of these same-sex relationships quite aside from their significance in terms of sexual orientation. One special feature of the romance associated with romantic friendship that I deal with in this chapter, for example, is its commitment to the all-important 'z' factor. Although I have presented this, thus far, as an effect of a certain kind of heterosexual relationship, there is clearly a strong argument to be made that it is – from the mid-nineteenth century onwards – much more prevalent in relationships between women, and especially when it joins forces with the 'New Women's' campaign to grant middle-class women meaningful labour. As we will see in Chapter 6, Vera Brittain's relationship with Winifred Holtby is an example *par excellence* of the way in which the fires of romantic friendship can be fuelled by a shared mission to work, to produce, to create; and how this productivity, in turn, may be conceived as sublimated sexual desire.[4]

Yet if the discourse of romance may be seen to flourish, and carry forth into the twentieth century, under the banner of romantic friendship, the same cannot be said of the texts which deal with sexuality – homosexual *or* heterosexual – more explicitly. Even before the works of the sexologists earned widespread recognition, Britain and America had been forced to contend with the canon of European (primarily French) 'Naturalist' fiction which depicted sexual relations not only explicitly but, even more importantly, without the consolation of a moral 'purpose' or salvation. In the novels of Balzac, Flaubert and Zola, readers were often forced to confront sex without even a gesture of romance, and relationships which were manifestly stripped of any supplementary 'gift' other than tragedy and death. In Britain, this cold-eyed gaze at the human condition has been seen to feed directly into the tragic vision of writers like Hardy, for whom the sexual imperative rarely results in a happy romance and/or marriage. Most commentators cite his *Jude the Obscure* (1975 [1895]) in this context, on account both of its implicit critique of the legal system that bound men and women together in damaging, loveless marriages[5] and of its cutting-edge insights into some of the complexities – and perversities – of sexual desire. His portrayal of the relationship between Jude and Sue Brideshead is particularly ground-breaking in this regard, and is further evidence that romantic love may not necessarily articulate with sexual compatibility or desire (see Stubbs 1981: 64).

When we move from the nineteenth century to the writers and texts associated with literary modernism, moreover, there is a significant shift from an attempt to deal with the reality of sexual relations through *relationships* to one which focuses on the *sexual identity* of individual characters. Although the novels and short stories of D. H. Lawrence deal notionally with a variety of sexual relationships, both heterosexual and homosexual, for instance, it is largely in the context of *individual* sexual salvation. It is because of this, indeed, that it is possible for characters to be shown to be liberated, or saved, through the expression of their sexual desire even though the relationship which enables it is ultimately destructive (see Bradbury 2001: 122; Stubbs 1981: 227). Aside from the celebration of the sexual act (which may be read both as a frank engagement with the pervasive irrationality of the unconscious and as a nihilistic death-wish), Lawrence's work also displays a fascination with the nature of sexual difference. Although his (male) homosexual relationships are no more inclined to the paradigm of romance *qua* romance than his heterosexual ones, the often perverse twists and turns enjoined by the protagonists in their quest for 'sexual being' makes them rather more interesting. A good example of this is his short story 'The Blind Man' (1918), which has been identified by Trudi Tate (1998) as one of a number of texts in which the neuroses consequent upon the First World War initiate new understandings of masculinity and sexual desire. In this text, a soldier maimed and blinded in the war forces his wife's cousin to touch his mutilated face: an act which engenders both disgust and homoerotic desire (Tate 1998: 109). In the same way that, in this story, Bertie and Maurice 'use' rather than 'relate' to one another, so do many other early twentieth-century protagonists pursue their sexuality in largely solipsistic fashion (for example, Chopin, *The Awakening* (1899); H. D., *Her* (1927); Joyce, *Portrait of the Artist as a Young Man* (1916); and Woolf, *Orlando* (1928)).

One of the most notorious texts of the era in terms of its sexual politics was Radclyffe Hall's *The Well of Loneliness* (1994 [1928]). Although this novel may be classed as one of the twentieth century's first high-profile lesbian love stories, I would suggest – once again – that its focus is less on the romantic relationship between Stephen Gordon and Mary Llewellyn than on the former's *identity* as a sexual 'invert'.[6] What this text demonstrates, indeed, is the extent to which the sexologists' view of homosexuality as a *congenital* condition had the immediate effect of directing attention away from the homosexual *relationship* (including, interestingly, the sexual act) to the homosexual *subject*. In terms of *literary genre*, moreover, this shift of focus from the sexual relationship to the sexual subject was effectively a shift from *romance* to *Bildungsroman*, the long-term consequences of which I shall return to in the next chapter.

What I have proposed in this section, then, is that as the writers, philosophers and sexologists of the *fin-de-siècle* grappled ever more frankly with issues of sexuality *vis-à-vis* subjectivity, so did relationships – and, in particular, romantic relationships – temporarily slip from view. Inasmuch as relationships mattered at all to these thinkers it was in terms of how they defined (or not) one's sexual identity; what they might constitute, what 'gift' they might bring, in and of themselves was of little account, and perhaps especially because romantic relationships tend to mystify and sublimate sex rather than reveal it. Meanwhile, whilst one generic consequence of this shift of focus may be seen to be a shift from romance to *Bildungsroman*, another is clearly the demotion of the romance genre *per se* to the subcultural/popular underground. As a number of commentators have observed, where romance 'goes' at the end of nineteenth century is *not* into literary modernism but into the imperial 'quest' romances of Robert Louis Stevenson, Henry Rider Haggard, Joseph Conrad and, later, John Buchan (see Jones 2004: 406–23). Whilst there is not space here to explore this fascinating genre in detail, it is important to register the extent of its appeal and to propose a reason for it. For the majority of critics, these 'boy's own adventures' are best explained as literary escapism for middle-class men stultified by late Victorian society. As Bradbury observes: 'For once, this was an age when it was women writers who wrote bitter realism and men who wrote romance' (Bradbury 2001: 56). Yet the notion that these 'adventure romances' appealed *exclusively* to the boys is not strictly true. Showalter cites Elizabeth Bowen as an example of a woman writer who declares herself to have been hugely influenced by Haggard's *She* (1887) (Showalter 1990: 89). The crucial point, it would seem, is that the quest and 'grail' endemic to the romance narrative – the ['] and, indeed, the 'z' – are simply too compelling a fantasy for readers to do without for long. As well as the imperial or 'quest' romance, the 1920s and 1930s saw the birth and rapid development of the genres we know today as crime fiction and thrillers (see Bradbury 2001: 136), not to mention the Mills & Boon type of popular romance which I shall be exploring in the next chapter. Life without romance – in its post-Arthurian sense of adventure, spectacle, quest, heroism, triumph – is thus shown to be as hard as life without sex.

But before this readerly need began to be met by the myriad, popular post-romantic genres of the later twentieth century, there was the small matter of the Great War to contend with. This was, of course, the adventure to end all adventures and – as the ensuing reading of Vera Brittain's war diaries will I hope show – it enabled both romance and romantic love to persist in their unreconstructed forms for a little while longer.

II

Vera Brittain's War Diaries, 1913–17

I begin with two quotations:

> I wrote him a long letter this afternoon, enclosing the notices about Garrod and writing about him. I also talked about our present life – its agony & absence of ornamentation – its bareness of all but the few great things which are all we have to cling to now – honour & love & heroism & sacrifice. (26 May 1915; Brittain 1981: 202)

> As I stood there, the place was hallowed by the memory of his presence, so that even the bareness of the tree-trunks & the greyness of the distance which showed between them could not prevent my soul from making itself felt in a vague aspiring, and an intense inner consciousness of love & vital inner life striving for self-expression. I felt again keenly the desire to be able to stand alone & for the perfecting of the intellectual instrument through which it expresses and reveals itself . . . (24 March 1915; Brittain 1981: 165)

Between the two quotations with which I open this section swings the pendulum of Vera Brittain's attempt to make sense of the connection between love, war and (self-)sacrifice, which remained for her (as for her fiancé, Roland Leighton) the effective 'meaning' of life. Inspired by the traditions of a broadly conceived Christian socialism which took hold of certain sectors of the British, American and European middle classes in the latter part of the nineteenth century, Brittain was clearly born with a 'mission', and what we see in these remarkable diaries is her attempt to realize the 'vague aspiring' of her soul through the exigencies of war and romantic love.

Readers should be warned that Brittain's writings on this unique concatenation of desire and sacrifice (which, unlike the other romance narratives dealt with in this volume, are contained within the peculiar intimacy of the diary genre) are emotionally harrowing in the extreme. Written under conditions of heightened consciousness (first exhilaration, then grief), this roller-coaster of emotions is guaranteed to sweep away the most resolute of readerly defences. Speaking for myself, returning to these diaries after a space of twenty years was a reading event that shook me to the core: proof, if one were needed, that the paradigm of 'Love and War', even more than that of 'Love and Death', takes us to the very heart of all that is most unbearable about the human condition: namely that happiness is, *by definition*, un-endurable. Whilst falling in love with someone just as they are about to go off to the Front literalizes this threat in the most spectacular of ways, it is one that is common to *all* affective experience. As soon as we love someone, our greatest fear is necessarily that we will some day lose them; even though, in everyday life, we manage to hypothesize this as a (delusional) 'if' rather than an (inevitable) 'when'. For wartime lovers, however, 'if' is always-already-also 'when', and the provisionality of the relationship – however committed – a perpetual taunt.

In the days immediately prior and subsequent to Roland Leighton's first departure for the Front, Brittain probes deeply into what it means to love in the context of such radical uncertainty, but ultimately manages to persuade herself (and Leighton) that the risk is worth it; even if happiness *were* unfulfilled, it would bring about a condition of spiritual grace. In her diary entry for 19 March 1915 (Brittain 1981: 187), Brittain extols the benefits of such suffering and even adapts the cliché 'it is far better to have loved and have lost . . .' to the wartime context by substituting 'suffered' for 'loved'. Later, in her discussions and correspondence with Leighton, and via, in particular, their reading of their mutual 'bible', Olive Schreiner's *Story of an African Farm*, the link between love, suffering and some manner of spiritual redemption becomes even more explicit (see entry for 25 March 1915; Brittain 1981: 166) and is strikingly close to de Rougemont's (1983) explanation for why romantic love is, in effect, a disguised 'death-drive'. In the case of Brittain's diaries, however, we see the sacrifice of love (notwithstanding the promise of spiritual redemption) become rather less compelling as the spectre of death becomes increasingly probable and 'real'. In an entry for 17 April 1915, for example, she uses the image of the trap to describe her mounting feelings of frustration (some, explicitly sexual) about the way she and Roland may never have their happiness realized. This is apparently a state of mind more akin to the tortures of Dante's Hell (see Chapter 4) than a blueprint for spiritual salvation. Love with such a very slim chance of consummation becomes a torment indeed:

My eyes filled with most stinging tears, although I bit my lip to try & keep
them back. Sometimes I think it is less the thought of his danger than the
ardent desire for his presence which makes me so sorrowful, & when he
writes such things as this – & he has never admitted so much before – I
want him terribly badly, & the thought of what it may be if he returns but
is so likely never to be, is almost more than I can bear. At such moments
I feel as if I were shut in a trap from which there is no escape, & that I am
vainly beating my hands against the walls – a kind of fierce desperation,
which renders me incapable of doing anything but feeling acutely conscious of inward suffering. Well, I asked for the big things of life & now I
am up against them. (17 April 1915; Brittain 1981: 178)

It is my contention, then, that romantic love lived at this limit-point of
(im)possibility is qualitatively different from that experienced in everyday
life on account of the fact that one of the deepest, and most defining,
aspects of the condition – that is, its impermanence – is made so spectacularly visible. The illusions of futurity and permanence (the blind faith that
day will follow day) that enable us to function as human beings, and, in
particular, to enter into relationships, is ruthlessly stripped away. It is surely
for this reason that Brittain's diaries present the peacetime reader with such
a traumatic read, and also why – via a paradox I shall now attempt to
explain – the text itself attempts to understand love through ideological
rather than psychological means.

'Honour & Love & Heroism and Sacrifice': Vera Brittain and the 'Z' Factor

I was a good way through my reading of Brittain's diaries before it
occurred to me how far psychoanalysis was from my thoughts. Given the
apocryphally traumatic nature of the scenarios they describe, this, for a
moment, struck me as surprising. Other writers, like Pat Barker (see *Regen-
eration*, 1991), have, after all, used Freud *et al.* very effectively to explain so
much about the queer things that war does to the individuals concerned.
I have since come to the conclusion that the explanation for this readerly
blindspot rests with Brittain herself, who, notwithstanding intense emotional suffering, figures love as an essentially intellectual conundrum. Love
may be defined in relation to Death, yes, but in terms of ethics and
politics rather than psychic drives.

In understanding this aspect of Brittain's psyche, class and the historical
moment become vital elements in her biography. Born into a wealthy
upper-middle-class family from Buxton (her father owned a paper-mill),

Brittain presents her childhood and adolescence as privileged but stultify-ing. Her high-quality 'academic' education at St Monica's Girls' School, where she was a boarder, clearly made her severely impatient with the intellectual narrowness of provincial life, and the possibility that she might subsequently become an undergraduate at Oxford became a life-line. Although the text is littered with unconscious examples of her own class superiority (for example, references to 'the people' and later 'Tommies'), she also presents herself as a feminist, socialist and – at that time – atheist in the making.[7] Her overriding 'belief' from the age of about 17 onwards seems to have been in the intellect as the means of social and spiritual 'good', and allusions to Victorian writers and sages such as George Eliot and Tennyson give some clue to the origins of this thinking. In an early letter to Leighton (4 February 1913) she observes how she would like to become a character such as Felix Holt, for example (see Brittain 1981: 29). Soon after (and as the consequence of a gift from Leighton), her key point of moral and ideological reference becomes Schreiner's *Story of an African Farm*, of which she writes: 'It is a great book & has made my head almost ache with thinking. Religion – life – the position of women – one may contemplate them forever' (3 May 1914; Brittain 1981: 68).

Having divined the hold these residual ideologies of public service and self-sacrifice had on Brittain's psyche, there is rather less surprise at her sub-sequent rationalization of both love and war. In the second of the quota-tions which opens this section we see an early, and supreme, instance of how her love of, and desire for, Leighton literally *translates* into a creative act or 'production'. On the one hand, this may be read as a characteristic-ally egotistical moment of self-actualization, but – read in the context of numerous other entries – it is clear that this 'vague aspiring' is rooted in a wider social and artistic mission to 'make a difference' to the world. Indeed, one could argue that the existential peculiarity of loving someone in the context of their possible and, indeed, *probable* death plays havoc with the notions of both 'gift' and 'supplement' *unless* they can be converted into a meaningful third term, 'z'.

It is at this ideological point, however, that a 'symptomatic reading' (see note 1 to Chapter 3) quickly exposes strains and contradictions in Brittain's text. Although both she and Leighton *appear* to respond to the war patri-otically and imply that service to 'the greater good' is now coterminous with 'service to one's country', their discussions and correspondence betray considerable confusion. This is touchingly evident in the diary entries which pre-date Leighton's first posting to the Front, and in which both he and Brittain try to rationalize their support of the war and their readiness for sacrifice. In their first extended, intimate conversation (in the library at Buxton on the eve of Leighton's departure), Brittain sums up his reasons for enlisting thus: 'the vague moral sense of acting up to his faith in, his highest opinion of, himself – the worship & indefinite pursuit of heroism in the abstract . . .' (19 March 1915; Brittain 1981: 156). Although Brittain's concluding analysis ('the indefinite pursuit of heroism in the abstract') puts its finger, somewhat tragically, on what is effectively the *non*-reason why so many young men like Leighton died, at this point in her life she clearly does not see the ideology for what it is. Fired up as they both are by late nineteenth-century ideals of work, dedication and personal achievement, it is sadly inevitable that the 'object' of the endeavour should seem less important than the quest itself. That Leighton should put himself forward to be 'the best' officer (as well as the best scholar and the best poet) is as much a (self-)expectation as Brittain's ambition to become the best student of her year at Oxford and, in due course, a famous writer. It is, then, not so much heroism as '*ambition* in the abstract' that rules them at this stage in their lives and makes them willing to risk 'death' (also in the abstract) in the pursuit of glory.

Leaving aside, for the moment, the extent to which this general 'aspiration' and/or 'ambition' becomes increasingly confused with heroism in an explicitly militaristic sense, it is important that we first understand a little more clearly how all such idealism relates to Brittain's notion of romantic love, which is – I would suggest – a supreme example of the $x + y \rightarrow x' + y' = z$ function. Inspired as they both are by the characters of Lyndall and Waldo in Schreiner's *Story of an African Farm*, she and Leighton quickly utilize the capacity of love for both collaboration and (perhaps even more importantly) *co-validation*. Even during their early meeting at Uppingham, they talk frankly about their collective 'brilliance' and 'conceitedness' (Brittain 1981: 80) and look towards a future in which they can assist one another in their mutual quests. Whilst, once again, it is the transformative potential of love rather than the nature of the love-relationship *per se* that is the most exciting feature of the romance, for Brittain and Leighton the ['] is only *truly* meaningful when it can be realized – and made visible – in some *further* act, product or event: that is, 'z'.

Unfortunately, this further aspiration – the quest for 'z' – is all too soon overshadowed by the knowledge that, for Leighton, it can *only* be realized on the battlefields of France through feats of militaristic heroism. After his death, meanwhile (see entry for 25–6 January 1916), the knowledge that 'the ultimate sacrifice' had indeed been made becomes the coldest of comforts, if not a downright torment:

But during the night. . . . I thought of the Heroism, whether touched with recklessness or not, that caused Him to go out in the front of the line into the bright moonlight & led to the sacrifice of all that meant so much in the world, all that was so exceptional and brilliant & fine. And I looked out of the ward window to the tall church-spire & to the dark bands of clouds with rifts between them of bright moonlit sky, & cried in the bitterness of my heart 'Dearest – oh Dearest! Why *did* you?' (25–6 January 1916; Brittain 1981: 309)

So z has been achieved, but at a price that – for Brittain – is already beginning to seem too high.

The signal importance of the 'z' factor in Brittain's vision of life, and love, can only be fully understood, however, by surveying her relationships more generally. As we will see in Chapter 6, her subsequent (post-First World War) romantic friendships with women (and, in particular, Winifred Holtby) were also characterized by this sense of a shared 'mission' translated to a peacetime (or, more properly, 'post-war') context. Yet there is also little question that her early relationship with Leighton was the model for each of those that followed in this regard. In all her relationships, it seems, Brittain was in search of a mind that would not only match but also mirror back her own intellect, creativity and ambition. Not surprisingly, several of the female dons and tutors she met at Oxford displayed this potential (in particular Miss Lorimer and Miss Derbeyshire ('I almost worship expressed & powerful intellect, especially when I find it in women' (15 May 1915; Brittain 1981: 197)), and it is striking that even after her most thrilling secret rendezvous with Leighton (they meet on the train before he returns to the Front), she concedes that Miss Lorimer holds *some* fascination (see 16 January 1915; Brittain 1981: 149). The additional and/or 'permitted' sexual *frisson* in her relationship with Leighton causes heterosexuality to win out on this occasion, but it is arguable that there are more similarities than differences in Brittain's object-choices. In much the same way that biologists like to claim that we are attracted to individuals by specific, and complementary, genetic needs, so does Brittain repeatedly hone in on individuals who dangle the promise not only of ['] but also of 'z'.[8]

So far, in this section, I have focused on what defines the paradigm of romantic love for Brittain and how, in particular, its expressly aspirational nature – the desire to produce 'z' – is reconfigured in the context of war. I have shown how the pre-war abstract idealism of both Brittain and Leighton made them all too willing to sacrifice themselves to the supposed 'higher good' of war, and how their gift to one another ('The day will come

when we shall live our roseate poem through – as we have dreamt of it'
(21 March 1915; Brittain 1981: 163)) is treacherously sublimated into a
suicidal 'z': doing 'good *work*' (for one's country) is translated into doing
'good *war-work*' (for one's country), which, in turn, is translated into the
most sublime of all personal sacrifices: *pro patria mori*. I now turn my attention to what it meant to actually live out that paradigm in a world in which
all the usual co-ordinates of time and space holding romantic love together
– which, indeed, make sense of it for us through the conventions of *the
story* – are lost.

Time and Space in Times of War

Modern readers will doubtless be shocked to learn that, for all its status as
one of the great wartime romances, Vera Brittain and Roland Leighton
met each other on only *seven* occasions during the two and a half years
they knew one another, and for a total – according to my rough calcula-
tions – of just seventeen days. For the first three of those meetings (June
1913 to July 1914) they were, moreover, merely getting to know one
another, meaning that they shared less than a week of acknowledged intimacy in each other's physical presence. What kept them apart, moreover,
was more than the war. As I indicated at the beginning of this section, Brittain came from a highly respectable upper-middle-class family with all that
that entailed in terms of courtship etiquette. At times, indeed, the diary
of her 'coming out' years at Buxton gives the impression that little
had changed *vis-à-vis* the conventions of bourgeois courtship since Jane
Austen's day (what she wears to the Hospital Ball is, for example, reported
in the local newspaper! (Brittain 1981: 52)) and on her first 'day out' with
Leighton in London she is discreetly chaperoned by 'Aunt Belle' (Brittain
1981: 135ff.)). Indeed, the comparative *excess* of banal familiarity in twenty-
first-century relationships may, at first, cause readers to question the seriousness of the 'love' Brittain and Leighton lay claim to. There are different
routes to intimacy, however, and what this pair of lovers lacked in terms
of actual time spent together they more than compensated for in their
letters, which, for periods of time, were exchanged almost daily. Moreover,
as the fighting grew bloodier, and the risks to Leighton more imminent,
both he and Brittain committed their feelings to paper with a speed and
an abandon that would possibly *never* have happened in other circumstances. Recall, for instance, Brittain's response to Leighton's first long
letter from the Front (quoted earlier) in which she describes herself as 'shut
in a trap' *vis-à-vis* the desires he has awakened (in his letter, Leighton has

described himself 'kissing her photograph'), and what this will mean should he never come back (Brittain 1981: 178). The net result of all her turmoil, however, is that she writes back to him immediately and with a passion untypical of her self-avowed 'hard crust' (Brittain 1981: 124): 'the longing for his presence drives me very nearly desperate; I can scarcely keep it in check, much less face the thought that I may have to do without it for ever more. Thinking about that makes me feel utterly heart-sick & almost physically faint' (17 April 1915; Brittain 1981: 178).

Analysing this text with the eye of an outsider, one can measure the extent to which Leighton's absence is fuelling Brittain's desire. Not only does the written text seduce lovers into writing things they would never have said in person, but it refigures the romance as a fantasy (sexual and otherwise) with which no real-life courtship could ever compare. We have, of course, already seen one illustration of this in the love letters of Dorothy Osborne and William Temple, and many comparisons – not least the *length* of the more passionate outpourings! – may be drawn between the conduct of the two relationships. What propels the correspondence of Brittain and Leighton to an even greater pitch of frenzy, however, is the fact that the realization of their dream has become such an inescapable lottery. Either Leighton will come back and the relationship will be consummated, or he will die and all the sexual expectation the letters have whipped up will be violently aborted. No wonder, then, that Brittain describes herself as growing 'physically faint' at a situation that – outwith the context of war – would most certainly constitute a psycho-sexual *perversion* (see note 9 to Chapter 4). Brittain and Leighton are, indeed, trapped in a time where the limit-point is both absolute (death) and non-existent (there is no knowing if, or when, anyone will die); and in a space where they are both indefinitely separated (no-one knows for sure if, or when, Leighton will survive and / or get leave) and yet continually in touch (through their letters).

It is no surprise, then, that when the two *do* get to meet during the 'real time' of Leighton's leave, relations are – at first – somewhat strained. The people who meet and shake hands on St Pancras Station are *not* the personae who have corresponded in the letters, and the temporal horizon they occupy has suddenly shrunk from an unknown, and unknowable, moment in the future to a finite three days.[9] Brittain describes the excitement, trauma and unreality of the moment thus:

> The next moment I was meeting him face to face. Partly owing to his short-sightedness and partly to his inward abstraction he would have passed me by quite calmly if I had not asked him in an effort at amused scornfulness if he failed to recognise me. Then he stopped and we shook hands without

any sign of emotion except his usual paleness in tense moments. We stood looking at each other for quite a minute without moving. I scarcely realised where I was or what I was doing. It was difficult even to realise it was he.
(20 August 1915; Brittain 1981: 235)

The struggle to reconcile the Roland of the letters with the physical presence of the mature, war-stained man sitting next to her becomes even more intense when they are left alone together on the train; and, not for the first time, she hints at a element of fear and repulsion (see entry for 20 August 1915 (Brittain 1981: 231) and also 16 January 1915 (Brittain 1981: 148)) being mixed with the thrill and desire. What is especially fascinating about this emotional confusion is that the strangeness – and, indeed, 'stranger-ness' – that Brittain feels in the presence of Leighton is the result of more than the shock of his physical (and manifestly sexual) being; it is also – and perhaps more profoundly – a disorientation of time and space. Try as she might, Brittain cannot fully grasp the fact that the man sitting beside her in a swiftly moving train was in France – that is, in the trenches – only three days previously; the two chronotopes are so at variance (moving, enclosed, 'here' versus stationary, exposed, 'elsewhere') that she is overwhelmed by a sense of unreality that extends to her own person.

The disorientation Brittain describes on this occasion was, of course, far from unique. Indeed, one of the many paradoxes surrounding wartime romance is that situations that are experienced by subjects as so far outside 'every-day reality' as to seem exceptional are, in fact, some of the most commonly shared. Although not explored in the same depth as Brittain's account, many of the letters reproduced in the volume *Forces Sweethearts* (Lumley 1993) comment on a similar sense of confusion and unreality. What all the women left 'at home' seem to have struggled with most is the *disruption of their waiting*. Agonizing as the wait may be, it acquires its own normalcy and routine: one in which 'the next letter', or piece of news, substitutes for both the presence of the beloved and the fiction of 'the future'. The fantasy of waiting is thus absorbed into the fantasy of every-day life (as a series of repetitive, and forward-moving, events), providing the subject with the illusion of continuity in a context of monstrous uncertainty. It is not surprising, then, that the sudden/temporary reappearance of the beloved 'on Leave' should produce not comfort, but trauma: the fantasy of waiting is suddenly exposed for what it is, and the (temporary) presence of the beloved only serves to make spectacularly visible his impending absence and possible/probable death.

Needless to say, the long-feared death of the beloved in action brings with it an even more traumatic dislocation of time and space for the bereaved. For each of the passionate cries associated with the truly agonizing loss of the beloved as a physical presence, there is another which grapples with the dizzying discontinuities of 'here' and 'there', 'then' and 'now', 'this month' and 'last month', 'this year' and 'last year'. For Brittain, as for so many thousands of bereaved wartime lovers, what is experienced as most cruel – and, at first, most incredible – about the death is the way in which it makes a mockery of the 'time before'. Her closing observation in the entry for New Year's Eve 1915 reads: 'And I, who in impatience felt a fortnight ago that I could not wait another minute to see Him, must wait till all Eternity. All has been given me, and all taken away again – in one year' (31 December 1915; Brittain 1981: 297). Seen from the perspective of this new present in which all has been 'changed utterly', what she felt – and looked forward to – a fortnight previously is stripped of all credibility. Far from being able to turn to her memories of happier times for comfort, Brittain sees only her own, foolish naïvety at trusting in a future that turns out not to exist. This pain of 'not having known' is especially acute in a case like Brittain's where there is a four-day lapse between the moment of death (Leighton died of his wounds on 23 December 1915) and when she hears of it (27 December). In a rationalization typical of the newly bereaved, she attempts to comfort herself with the thought that he could not possibly have *known* he was dying or else she, and his family, would have been aware of the moment. The fact that a person *can* be preoccupied with her everyday life – secure in her own chronotope – whilst her beloved, in his, is dying is, understandably, unthinkable. In this text, indeed, it is hard to pinpoint what Brittain finds hardest in the months immediately following Leighton's death: is it the loss of his presence, the loss of their future, or – perhaps even more desperately – her loss of that treacherous past which *she imagined* they both shared?

> At present it gets worse every day. In the utter blackness of my soul I seem to be touching the very depths of that dull lampless anguish which we call despair. . . . Little, sweet, phrases from His letters keep coming always to my mind – & I just cry and cry. (28–9 January 1916; Brittain 1981: 313)

What Brittain is mourning here – and what, more than anything, drives her to despair – may thus be figured as the loss of romance itself: the 'roseate poem' that their correspondence created and in which they dwelt until a stray bullet blew it, and Roland Leighton, asunder.

I began this reading of Brittain's diaries by sharing my surprise at the fact that a text about being in love in such expressly traumatic circumstances should resist psychoanalytic interpretations, especially when the links between the terrors of war and the terrors of the human psyche are all too plain to see. I then proposed that this is largely on account of Brittain's own determination to align love with sacrifice and to account for both under the panoply of moral philosophy; romantic love is seen as a force that can inspire the individuals concerned to create, and collaborate, and leave their mark upon the world through a gift of mutual (self-)sacrifice. For Brittain as for thousands of her contemporaries, however, the temporal dislocations of wartime romance made stories with happy endings increasingly hard to believe in. Although she and Leighton managed to create, and sustain, the fantasy of love as *meaningful* sacrifice in their letters, the latter's death exposes the ideology for what it is. Despite some desperate attempts to reconcile herself to Leighton's loss through a celebration of his heroism (see in particular 25–6 January 1916; Brittain 1981: 309 and 26–7 January 1916; Brittain 1981: 311), the diary entries following his death reveal Brittain to be increasingly sceptical that he – or, indeed, 'they' – ever achieved, through their love, the elusive 'z'. By the time the war ended in 1918, she *knew* they had not; and by the time she came to write *Testament of Youth* (1929–33; see 1979a [1933]), she had already determined to dedicate the rest of her life to ensuring that such wanton sacrifice should never happen again.[10]

III

The End of the Affair *and Post-Wartime Romance*

Graham Greene's *The End of the Affair* was not written until 1951 but tells the story of a wartime romance – indeed, an affair – which spanned the years 1939–44. This, then, is not only a wartime romance told significantly after the event, but one that transports us from the cultural-historical moment of the First World War to the Second. This said, the paradigms of romantic love it enacts, and interrogates, are recognizably similar to those we have already encountered in Vera Brittain's war diaries. Once again, love is lived at the limit-point of an uncertain future; once again, time is seen to stand still; once again, present, past and future all exist to be rewritten as a consequence of which way the die does, or does not, fall. What Greene's novel does, however – and does superbly –, is illustrate how all these conditions of wartime romance, how all these distressing temporal dislocations, are also the *a priori* conditions of a clandestine relationship. 'The affair', save for some miracle, bears the same death penalty as the wartime romance: the probability that, at some as yet unspecified point in the future, it will be brought to an abrupt and violent end.

The deep, dark psychological twist Greene gives to this state of suspended animation, meanwhile, is to convert the threat of the impending
ending into an occasion for sexual jealousy. From the moment Bendrix falls
in love with Sarah, he knows he stands to lose her, and this fear is trans-
ferred onto all those things – both animate and inanimate – that keep her
from him in the present *and* conspire to take her away in the future. In particular, he develops an immediate, paranoid suspicion of 'other men':

> And yet there was this peace . . .
>
> That is how I think of those first months of war – was it a phoney peace
> as well as a phoney war? It seems now to have stretched arms of comfort
> and reassurance over all those months of dubiety and waiting, but the
> peace must, I suppose, even at that time have been punctuated by misun-
> derstanding and suspicion. Just as I went home that first evening with no
> exhilaration but only a sense of sadness and resignation, so again and again
> I returned home on other days with the certainty that I was only one of
> many men – the favourite lover of the moment . . . (Greene 2001: 47–8)

That the thing which ultimately 'steals' Sarah from Bendrix is not her
husband, or the non-existent 'other man', or even God (the God who
compels Sarah to forfeit Bendrix in a 'metaphysical wager' to save his life
(Bradbury 2001: 293)), but *Death* (from tuberculosis) is, of course, a final
twist that directs the reader (if not the hero himself) to the true nature of
his hates and fears. Himself a survivor of the Spanish Civil War, Bendrix
represses his more primitive fears about the faithless transience of life –
and love – in elaborate fantasies of jealousy and revenge. But read as a
wartime romance (rather than simply as an *adulterous* romance), what we
see in this text is an instance of the combatant's post-traumatic inability to
believe in the certain future of anybody, or anything. As Malcolm Bradbury has observed when writing of this historical moment:

> Pre-war [that is, pre-Second World War] fiction – for all its interest in the
> new, 'the abstract', 'the inhuman' – generally had the spirit of liberal
> humanism as its companion. It accepted progress in history, human devel-
> opment, the advance of the spirit as the motors of culture, and sought to
> see it 'whole'. . . . But war seemed to abstract and empty life itself, creat-
> ing a landscape of violence and uncertainty . . . (Bradbury 2001: 142)

By 1945, indeed, war had challenged the Western world's faith in humanity and history-as-progress not once, but *twice*. Whereas Brittain, writing
from *inside* the experience of *the first* war, preserved a fantasy of the future,
Bendrix (and, indeed, Greene, as 'implied author') had been stripped of
that (necessary) illusion. Indeed, the reason his relationship with Sarah is
an 'affair' and not a 'romance' has arguably less to do with the fact that

she is married and/or they engage in sexual relations almost as soon as they meet, and more to do with the fact that it is *for Bendrix* so unequivocally a relationship *without a future*. As we have already seen repeatedly in the course of this volume, romantic love is (ideally) a *prospective* emotion: its joy depends upon the fantasy that its desires will be fulfilled in some near, or distant, future. Sexual encounters which exist only in the present belong, rather, to the theatre of the erotic; indeed, it is often their detachment from any narrative/emotional context that is part of their thrill. Bendrix, a man without any faith in futures, is thus unable to (re)figure his relationship with Sarah as a romance and fails to be positively transformed by the experience (*x* never becomes *x'*). Consequently, her gift of love (which is genuine) is lost on him, and by the time he *is* convinced of it (through the retrospective reading of her diary) her illness is terminal. *Vis-à-vis* any definition of romantic love, the message is simple: love *requires* blind faith in the future, not evidence from the past.

For many of the novelists writing in the wake of the First World War also, the *recollection* of wartime romance was a much sadder, more complicated, matter than its experience at the time. A particularly fine illustration of this is Winifred Holtby's short story 'So Handy for the Fun Fair' (1995 [1934]), in which the first-person protagonist makes a return visit to the French town where she enjoyed a brief – unconsummated – love affair. Like Greene's novel, and like so many other post-war romances, the message of this text is that the 'meaning' of the relationships lived in those extraordinary conditions are often not known until years afterwards. In the same way that the combatants of both world wars were notoriously kept in the dark about what was 'really happening' or, indeed, how they were contributing to it, so, too, did wartime lovers have but a vague sense of how their behaviour was part of a major social-sexual revolution. As even the more popular books on the subject point out (see Lumley 1993), things happened in wartime that had been previously unspoken and/or unseen: for example, romances across race and class (including those with 'the enemy'); sex before marriage; adultery (both the men at the Front, and the women left at home); women taking the sexual initiative; the burgeoning of homosexual relationships. The element common to all these scenarios is, of course, a notion of 'sexual freedom', even if – as we have already seen in the case of Greene's novel – it is accompanied by unprecedented levels of angst and emotional confusion. In Holtby's touching story, meanwhile, it is romance across nationality that specifies the love (the protagonist is serving with the Women's Army Auxiliary Corps in France and falls in love with the son of a local farmer), together with the (retrospective) realization that the desire she felt for him was of a completely different order to anything she had experienced before. Indeed, the burden of the story – its small tragedy – is the protagonist's confession that, despite the fact he only kissed her once, she has lived the rest of her life (including her marriage) feeling that she has somehow *betrayed* François (Holtby 1995: 63). For this lover, then – as for many thousands of other women –, wartime was synonymous with the awakening of a proactive sexual desire that raised huge questions about both agency and entitlement: was it possible / desirable that women should assert themselves in sexual relationships?

A similar tale is told in Radclyffe Hall's short story 'Miss Ogilvy Finds Herself' (1995 [1934]), even though the desire here is homosexual rather than heterosexual and the 'romance' even more unspecified. Like Stephen Gordon in Hall's *The Well of Loneliness* (1928), Miss Ogilvy is a sexual invert in the Havelock Ellis mould (see note 6) for whom service at the Front has permitted the pursuit of an explicitly masculine identity. With her hair cut short and her hands thrust perpetually in her jacket pockets, Miss Ogilvy is seen to 'find' her true lesbian identity even without the experience of an actual lesbian relationship. Indeed, what is most significant about this representation of sexual desire is how it revolves around an *absence*: the relationship Miss Ogilvy has never had. For although attractions are hinted at, none are followed through and Hall is obliged to grant Miss Ogilvy her consummation via a surreal dream sequence in which she takes on the persona of a (male) Ancient Briton(!) who is adored by a 'little girl companion'. This scenario is certainly a long way – in every sense – from the First World War and the Front, but speaks volumes about the freedoms and fantasies which the war unleashed and the peace ended.

At the risk of generalization, it would, indeed, seem fair to say that, for the post-First World War generation of writers, 'innocent' romance was a thing of the past. Most of the novels and short stories written during the inter-war years and, indeed, during the Second World War seem to focus on relationships with a 'twist' to them. In contrast to the heroic, fixed-point passions of Vera Brittain's war diaries, we see writers attempting to match the perversity of the wartime situation (especially *vis-à-vis* the dislocations of time and space discussed earlier) with perversities of emotion and sexual desire. Even in women's magazine fiction, there is considerable fascination with the way in which the heart ceases to behave as it should; as, for example, in Ruth's outburst of disappointment and grief at her fiancé's unexpected return from a posting overseas in Molly Panter-Downes's 'Goodbye, My Love' (2003 [1941]), or in Dorothy Parker's similarly ironic 'The Lovely Leave' (2003 [1943]), which details the distance and alienation that has grown between a wife and her GI husband during his few, brief hours of leave.

For the writers who themselves served at the Front in the First World War, meanwhile, it is the *cruelty* of the battlefield that resonates most in their representation of human relations. One of the texts referred to most frequently in this context is Rudyard Kipling's 'Mary Postgate' (1995 [1926]), which explores a young woman's undisguised sexual pleasure at witnessing the death of a German airman. As Tate observes: 'The airman's death seems to have awakened Mary's dormant sexuality, an idea which the story finds fascinatingly disgusting' (Tate 1998: 38). Other 'survivors', like Ford Madox Ford, appear to have struggled hard to imagine redemptive relationships between the sexes. In his celebrated trilogy *Parade's End* (1924–8), Ford chronicles the rise of a relationship between his central protagonist, Christopher Tietjens, and the suffragette Valentine Wannop, at the same time as charting the demise of his marriage to the seemingly poisonous Sylvia. Interwoven as this personal story is with some of the most visceral and harrowing descriptions of conditions at the Front, it would be hard to afford this new relationship the status of 'romance', even though the final novel – *Last Post* – ends with a vision of redemption (see Bradbury 2001: 160).

It should be clear by now that, were we to focus exclusively on the 'high' literature of the post-war period(s), romance as a genre, and romantic love as an ideal, would be seen to have died their own deaths on the battlefields of France. For all 'serious' writers – modernist and non-modernist alike – life and love could never again be used to make sense of one another through the legacy of romance-as-adventure. Two world wars put an end to the notion that feats of heroism and bravery would be rewarded by a beautiful 'princess'; or, equally (from the woman's point of view), that waiting patiently would necessarily guarantee a 'soldier's return'. Instead, both life and love had become obscure, vastly unpredictable entities and – from the 1950s onwards – (hetero)sexual relations increasingly occupied the symbolic site of grief, anger and confusion as humanity's existential crisis got mixed up with the proverbial 'kitchen sink' (see Bradbury 2001: 315–17). In this 'fallen world', romance – both as *mythos* and as genre – was forced to move underground and join the ranks of other 'light' and popular entertainment. Whilst this may be seen to echo the declining status of the French romances in the seventeenth and eighteenth centuries (see discussions in Chapters 2 and 3), the great difference is that, at some point in the early twentieth century, faith in the transformative potential and/or essential 'good' of romantic love had itself also been lost.

As the subtext to this chapter will, I hope, have shown, this turning away from love as the means of both personal, and social, salvation is expressly linked to the birth of sexology and psychoanalysis: to a newly sophisticated understanding of the supreme irrationality and perversity of sexual desire. Romantic love as a means to something *other* than sex – the fuse which can light ['] or inspire 'z' – is a conceit that will come to appear increasingly naïve and/or utopian; which is not to say that it is killed off completely. In the next chapter, I track the course of romantic love both *underground* (in its most popular and deviant forms) and *overground* (in middle- to high-brow literature) from the post-war years through to the sexual revolution of the 1960s, and propose that, whilst the (all-female) 'romantic friend-ships' of the 1930s quite possibly constitute the end of 'z', the allure of ['] survives, albeit in a newly individuated and solipsistic form.

6

Modern Romance

The Gift of Selfhood

I

The story that most literary and cultural historians of the early twentieth century now choose to tell is that the First World War threw the citizens of the Western world into such social, moral and existential panic that all human relations – romantic love included – were sent reeling. As T. S. Eliot's *The Waste Land* ventriloquized: 'On Margate Sands / I can connect / Nothing with nothing' (Eliot 1961 [1922]: 62). Yet if the 'human' cost of the First World War was great, then that of the Second was – arguably – even greater. As Bradbury observes:

> When across Europe a post-war literature did begin to emerge, its writers often found their task difficult and paradoxical, their traditional humanism put on trial, their language and forms inadequate to deal with the horrors that had been witnessed and the sense of nihilism and absurdity they felt . . . [it was as if] human nature had betrayed itself, human character had collapsed, the human scene had gone. (Bradbury 2001: 263)

Here was a world event from whose devastation and *shame* – especially in relation to the Nazi Holocaust – humanity could never hope to recover; here was the *absolute* heart of moral darkness in which all innocence was finally lost.

Told this way – as it repeatedly is – the social and cultural history of the twentieth century is inevitably reduced to a cliché. For many of the writers and artists who have struggled to position themselves within the new world order, however, even the cliché is symptomatic rather than problematic. *Of course* the 'grand narratives' of our times are clichés: the (post)modern condition is such that we can now only ever know the world darkly, as a simulacrum, and never face to face.[1] In so 'fallen' a world, it is little surprise to discover that the twentieth century also sees romantic love assuming the status of a cliché; not everywhere, of course, and not immediately, but it is evident that by the end of the century – the millennium door through which we have now passed – love had been thoroughly 'outed' as the ideology it undeniably is. We can (and must) still experience love; we can still, if we wish, *believe* in it as a discourse that facilitates pleasure rather than pain. But to pretend that it exists as a quasi-divine force outside ourselves – that is, outside the combined forces of our egos and our culture – is wilful fantasy. Or is it? In the rest of this chapter – and, indeed, through into the next on postmodern romance – I shall attempt to chart some of the ways in which romantic love and its literary aficionados have attempted to defy the knowingness and cynicism of the modern age in this regard. The success of formula romance – Mills & Boon, Harlequin and their more 'middle-brow' variants – would, indeed, suggest that for literally *millions* of women, romantic love still promises salvation. In the face of existential crisis, a newly sexualized form of romantic love appeared to offer a way out; but it was – as we shall see – more often the way to the self, and not to the other; the way to (orgasmic) oblivion, rather than meaningful relationality.

But such prognosis is to leap rather too quickly ahead in what, after all, is a long and momentous century in terms of changing affective relations. Although the greater part of this chapter will focus on a mid-twentieth century census point (my close reading is of Jane Rule's lesbian romance from 1964, *Desert of the Heart*), this part attempts to sketch in some of the ways in which – during the inter-war years and after – the 'self' gradually displaced 'self-sacrifice' as the paradigmatic 'gift of love' and how, during the 1950s and early 1960s, sex and sexuality were seen increasingly as the gateway both to the individual's 'self-actualization' and his or her emptiness and existential despair.

From Romantic Friendship to Formula Romance

In terms of my own story of the cultural history of romance, I acknowledge that I am in danger of portraying the Western world before the two world wars as something of a 'golden age' for romantic love. It could, however, be argued that it was during the *inter-war* years in particular that – for certain individuals, and groups of individuals – romantic love as a gift of self-sacrifice found its most profound expression.

This could certainly be said to be the case with regard to the group of women writers and political activists associated with the periodical *Time and Tide*. As I have already indicated in Chapter 5, the 'romantic friendships' enjoyed by such women as Vera Brittain, Winifred Holtby, Lady Rhondda, Storm Jameson and Stella Benson managed to combine personal and professional interests to extraordinarily creative and productive effect.

Although, as Clay (2006: 39–40) observes, there is often the temptation for the post-Freudian reader to read the 'work' exchanged and produced within these relationships as the sublimation of repressed sexual desire, it is undeniable that important things (in the form both of writing and of political action) were achieved. In the context of the inter-war period, the friendship between Brittain and Holtby is exemplary in this regard, with both women becoming fiercely passionate about and committed to the pacifist cause. Both *Testament of Experience* (Brittain 1979b [1957]) and *Testament of Friendship* (Brittain 1980 [1940]) paint compelling portraits of the two women united in a life of fervid activity with *a cause*, whether that be giving public lectures, participating in the inauguration of the United Nations, writing articles for *Time and Tide* or (latterly) becoming involved in the Peace Pledge Union.[2] The way in which all this activity contributed to the sweetness of their shared life together is, of course, complex, but there can be no doubt that 'work' and companionship validated one another in a special way: 'Neither of us had ever known any pleasure quite equal to the joy of coming home at the end of the day after a series of separate, varied experiences, and each recounting these experiences to the other over late biscuits and tea' (Brittain 1980 [1940]: 117). This, then, is romantic love (albeit in the guise of 'friendship') unequivocally defined by the 'z' factor (as formulated in Chapter 5). In what way, or to what extent, the love between Brittain and Holtby is sexual matters far less than its *purpose*; the ['] that each lights in the other is, after all, not ultimately 'about' the self, *or* the other, but the z which that collaboration can produce.[3]

Yet whilst studies like Clay's and Faderman's (*Surpassing the Love of Men*, 1985 [1981]) make a strong case for why romantic friendship is its own unique paradigm, it is important to recognize that the inter-war years produced some remarkable heterosexual 'z'-oriented couples. One of the most glamorous of these is, of course, the long-term, non-conventional relationship between Simone de Beauvoir and Jean-Paul Sartre, for whom 'z' ranged from existential philosophy and social psychology to the 'war against Fascism' in the Second World War. The experimental lifestyle of the pair (both had other lovers) was undertaken, in part, in accordance with their liberationist politics, yet one could argue that, once again, what *defined* their romance was the productivity and political commitment they inspired in each other. A clear-eyed understanding of this is conveyed in de Beauvoir's novel *She Came to Stay* (1984 [1943]), in which infidelity in the form of triangular and/or 'open' sexual relationships fails to undermine the enduring significance of 'the marriage of true minds' enjoyed by the central protagonists. It is, I would argue, only by acknowledging the profound idealism of these relationships lived under the sign of 'z' that we can fully appreciate just how solipsistic the romantic love of the latter half of the twentieth century becomes. As indicated above, I believe there is also a good argument for seeing this solipsism in the discourses of sexual liberation (feminism, gay liberation) as well as in those perpetrated by the forces of social conservatism and popular romance, but it is to the latter that I shall first turn.

The story of how Mills & Boon became the brand synonymous with romance in its most 'degenerate' form (Pearce 2004: 521) is itself a fascinating one. From different perspectives, and with different political agendas, a good many critics have now had a go at telling it: from Tania Modleski (1982), Janice Radway (1984) and Mariam Darce Frenier (1988) in the feminist context of the 1980s, through to the more recent recuperative studies of jay [sic] Dixon (1999) and George Paizis (1998). It is another, earlier, book that offers the most useful insight into the *origins* of popular romance as a genre, however: Rachel Anderson's *The Purple Heart Throbs: The Sub-Literature of Love* (1974). By beginning her account of the mass-popularization of romance back in the nineteenth century with a discussion of female writers like Charlotte Yonge, Rhoda Broughton, Ouida and Mary Brandon, Anderson makes clear that Mills & Boon *inherited* a genre and a market rather than manufactured one. Her vivid summaries of a number of these texts also make explicit their links with the eroticism of eighteenth-century 'seduction' novels (see, for example, my discussion of Delarivière Manley in Chapter 3), even if this inclined increasingly towards euphemism and innuendo. An author who turned the latter into something of an art form was Marie Corelli, who, according to Anderson, 'wrote about everything . . . with the same crusading and evangelizing zeal' (Anderson 1974: 150). Here is a short extract from one of her many best-sellers, *The Life Everlasting* (1911), in which venal lust is (barely) disguised as 'mystical effusion' (Anderson 1974: 165):

> All at once I saw a vast Pillar of Fire which seemed to block my way –
> pausing a moment, I saw it break asunder and form the Cross and Star! –
> I gazed upward, wondering – its rays descending seemed to pierce my eyes,
> my brain, my very soul! I sprang forward, dazed and dazzled, murmuring
> 'Let this be the end!' (Cited in Anderson 1974: 167)

Although this is intensely comic to the contemporary, post-Freudian eye, Anderson is probably correct in her speculation that Corelli 'did not understand' her own blatantly 'erotic symbols' (Anderson 1974: 167). Pseudo-sexual rhetoric of this kind had been part of evangelical religious discourse for so long that it would have been quite possible for a writer like Corelli to replicate its passion without understanding its source. In terms of the literary history of popular romance, however, it demonstrates what I believe to be the single most determining feature of the genre: namely its equation of love with *the moment* of sexual consummation and the limit-point that that moment (albeit temporarily) supplies. Moreover, the fact that more recent popular romances feature story-lines in which the hero and heroine consummate their relationship *many times* does nothing to undermine this proposition; indeed, in these texts there is rather less chance of escaping the message that love, so defined, is essentially a drug, and those addicted are ever in need of their next sexual fix.

Such an assessment admittedly overlooks the hard work undertaken to recuperate popular romance and its readers by theorists from Modleski and Radway to Dixon and Paizis. In particular, it fails to acknowledge that the surface story-lines of these texts – which are, after all, romantic *comedies* – repeatedly show the heroine triumphing over the hero in bold and spectacular ways. Approaching the relationship between hero and heroine via the 'deep structures' of fairy-stories, Modleski famously identified this conquest as the heroine's 'taming of the beast', whilst Dixon is quite clear that both authors and readers see the conquest (even today) as the triumph of *love* (the heroine's objective) over sex (the hero's objective). She writes:

> The underlying philosophy of the novels of Mills & Boon is that love is omnipotent – it is the point of life. It is the solution to all problems, and it is peculiarly feminine. Men have to be taught to love; women are born with the innate ability to love. This love, power and femaleness are inextricably linked in Mills & Boon novels. Every novel is pervaded by female power because the base plot is the triumph of female love over male lust. (Dixon 1999: 177)

The fact that this 'triumph of female love' also secures, for the heroine, a respectable social and economic identity (she becomes, or is reinstated as, a happily married woman) matters, for Dixon, far less (Dixon 1999: 176). Although elsewhere in her text Dixon puts considerable emphasis on the social and economic independence of the heroines before they enter into the romance (from the 1930s onwards they are mostly 'working women'), she nevertheless insists on seeing the 'gift of love' consequent upon it in affective rather than material terms; what is traded between hero and heroine are two types of relationality in which 'true love' (figured as maternal care) triumphs over crude sexual desire.

George Paizis also seeks to show the heroines as the winners in romantic fiction, but makes a rather more complex and sophisticated argument

for the trade between sexual desire ('passion-love') and desirable social relationships (the objective of 'marriage-love'). Following de Rougemont
(1983) and Rousset (1981), he sees popular romance texts as attempting to
mediate the sexual desire and social aspirations of both the hero and the
heroine in such a way that the heroine secures the social esteem she
deserves and desires. He concludes that, for this to be achieved, the admittedly powerful forces of 'passion-love' have somehow to be brought under
control (Paizis 1998: 117). For Paizis, then, the heroine might be as vul-
nerable to the temptations of passion-love as the hero, but is obliged to
resist them in order to manufacture a relationship which recognizes her
social esteem. This is achieved by the triumph of her 'qualities' – the traits
of tenderness, nurturance and self-sacrifice commonly associated with love
in its feminine form – over the hero's social, economic and sexual 'power'
(Paizis 1998: 162).

Whilst I agree that, at this superficial narrative level, the heroine of the
majority of popular romantic fiction texts appears not only to have 'got
her man' but also 'got him where she wants him', there remain, for me,
several arguments against this being an unequivocal triumph (even if it
goes a long way to explaining why women readers have remained so faithful to the genre). First amongst these is the feminist perspective, which
raises serious questions about the political desirability of both the 'special
qualities' (pre-eminently, the capacity for love and self-sacrifice) that the
heroines are seen to already possess and the *nature* of the esteem conferred
upon them at the story's resolution. In other words, it is agreed they
'triumph' – but as *what*? As Germaine Greer observed way back in 1971:
'In sexual relationships, the confusion of altruism with love perverts the
majority. Self-sacrifice is the *leitmotif* of most mental games played by
women. . . . Women are self-sacrificing in direct proportion to their inca-
pacity to offer anything else but this sacrifice – they sacrifice what they
never had, a self' (Greer 1993 [1971]: 151).

More profoundly, there is the contingent question of whether the
triumph of one *self* over another is recognizable as 'love' anyway. As we
saw in Chapter 1, the classic formulations of both erosic and agapic love
keep the love-object in view, either as a set of (ever-)desirable qualities or
as a fixed point of desire and devotion. In the stories of popular romance,
by contrast, the final, social transformation of the heroine (through marriage) would appear to be the limit-point of love. Although critics like
Dixon may talk about the endings of more recent Mills & Boon texts
representing married life as an 'equal partnership', this does not concur
with the (far stronger) story-line of personal triumph. Indeed, implicit in

Dixon's own analysis is the notion that these heroines are not so much 'looking for love' as 'looking to *use* it'; and it is their capture of the hero, rather than 'love' of his 'properties', that is crucial in their self-actualization. Presented as a variant of my baseline equation $(x + y \rightarrow x' + y'\ [= z])$, this – admittedly rather ungenerous – reading of the Ur-Mills & Boon romance would thus amount to $x + y > x'\ (-y)$, where x is the superficially self-fulfilled heroine and y the ultimately dispensable hero. Whilst for some readers and critics this will be perceived as a positive – and possibly 'feminist' – outcome for the heroine, for others – myself included – it will be seen as a failure of love in its more ideal form(s). In such circumstances, *the self* – both social and sexual – is truly the limit-point of love; which is why the sexual act, and its temporary oblivion, is its most consummate metaphor. Love which ends with the self, and not with the other, is also, inevitably, the end of the story, the end of the relationship: a little – and maybe not so little – death.

From Popular Romance to Romantic Angst

In writing about romance it is – as the whole of this book attests – extremely difficult to resist the lure of the 'deep structures'. Even when attempting to present romantic love and its attendant genre(s) as a culturally and historically specific phenomenon, we are drawn, inexorably, to its skeleton, believing that there, perhaps, we may discover an all-encompassing answer to its omnipotence. Of the recent wave of theorists and critics who have tackled the subject, it is only those who have avoided the fascinations of these narrative and psychological depths that have gone some way to registering how – in social and cultural terms – popular romance *has changed*. Anderson (1974), Darce Frenier (1988) and Dixon (1999) all insist that it is a genre which takes its cue from the historical moment in which the texts are being written, and point – in particular – to the impact that the sexual revolution and the women's movement have had on the representation of the heroine, her needs and desires. Dixon, moreover – who focuses on the development of Mills & Boon from 1909 to the 1990s – identifies distinguishing features for *all* the decades (see Dixon 1999: 7). In the 1980s and 1990s, for example, the firm diversified into a wide range of sub-genres (for example, 'Contemporary', 'Love Affair', 'Temptation', 'Masquerade (historical)', 'Medical') distinguished by different sorts of story-lines and various degrees of sexual explicitness. Whilst I shall return to the implications of these last, post-1970s changes in the next chapter, the most important development for this is clearly the conservative backlash that Dixon has identified in the thirties, forties and fifties. Whilst the 1940s seems to have had its fair share of titles dealing with adulterous relationships, the virtues of domesticity still reigned supreme. Moreover, although the Second World War itself was rarely dealt with in a substantive way, woman's ability to create a haven of peace in the midst of horror and uncertainty (and its aftermath) became the heroine's most distinctive quality; *her* 'gift of love'. It could be argued, then, that these particular decades were ones of unprecedented empowerment for those women who sought to seduce, and conquer, their men through 'home-making'; the years, indeed, which saw the steady rise of what Betty Friedan (1963) labelled 'the feminine mystique'.

In addition to detailing instances of Mills & Boon texts from these periods which nevertheless deviate from the 'mystique' (especially in their representation of women out at work as well as in the home), Dixon observes the radical stance of the popular romance industry *vis-à-vis* divorce. Having provided evidence that it is not only post-1970 that Mills & Boon have featured heroes and heroines who are already married or who have been married previously, Dixon argues that '[d]espite, or perhaps because of, a total adherence and commitment to the ideology that love should be present in all marriages, Mills & Boon novels are strongly pro-divorce. They have always argued, along with some feminists and often against prevailing ideology, for no-fault divorce' (Dixon 1999: 163). She observes that divorce was a hot topic in the novels of the 1920s and 1930s in particular, and again in the 1960s, when the 1969 Divorce Act finally brought about the change that those abhorring the 'loveless marriage' had always craved (that is, that marriages could be terminated simply on the grounds of 'incompatibility'). The social and moral implications of this long-delayed legislation are also central to my reading of Rule's *Desert of the Heart* which follows.

Yet despite this evidence of historical sensitivity to *some* of the changes that have impacted on sexual relations over the past hundred years, the mass-market end of popular romance – namely Mills & Boon, Harlequin and Silhouette – has remained resolutely silent on issues of homosexuality and race. Although Dixon remarks upon this more than once, she struggles to offer an effective explanation for it other than (*vis-à-vis* the former) that 'it would not fit with the book's ideology that men have to be socialized through a love relationship into the female sphere' (Dixon 1999: 163). The further conclusion that can be drawn is that popular romance will entertain historical/cultural change only if this still ends in a *marriage* that is literal as well as symbolic. Gay relationships are, even now – in the twenty-first century –, struggling to achieve this sort of endorsement. An important coda to this homophobia within mainstream formula romance, however, is that – from the 1950s onwards – gay men and lesbians began to produce their own 'pulp fiction' (see discussion of Ann Bannon in Part III of this chapter). What Bannon's texts reveal, in particular, is the extent to which the deep narrative structures of formula romance are necessarily expressions of *heterosexual* relationships. Whilst several feminist critics have made strong arguments for homosexual liaisons shaking the 'literary' novel to its very core (for example, Butler 1993; Farwell 1990; Sedgwick 1985, 1994, 1997), the structural subversiveness of gay/lesbian pulp fiction is more questionable. On the issue of race, meanwhile, it should be noted that although all the heroes and heroines ultimately 'prove themselves' to be white, Mills & Boon/Harlequin have enjoyed a long tradition of exotic 'dark-skinned' male lovers who might at first *appear* to be black or mixed-race but who ultimately turn out to be no 'blacker' than Mediterranean (for example, the hero of the infamous best-seller *The Sheik* (1919), who is ultimately revealed to be not an Arab but half-Scottish and half-Spanish (Anderson 1974: 187)). This returns us, once again, to the measure of prescriptiveness in formula romance and, indeed, helps us begin to distinguish Mills & Boon from the thousands of 'middle-brow' romances that were also produced during the first half of the twentieth century.

Besides *Rebecca* and *Gone with the Wind* (both discussed in Part III), the first part of the twentieth century abounds with romances which fall into the 'middle-brow', 'middle-ranking' category. Nicola Beauman's *A Very Great Profession* (1983) pays tribute to a good many of them in her chapters on 'Romance' and 'Love' and notes how writers like Rosamond Lehmann and Elizabeth Bowen in particular 'just about' made it into the 'high-brow' category (Beauman 1983: 173). Even in the twenties and thirties, it seems, romance as a genre had effectively 'degraded' itself and authors writing on the theme of love were lucky to be taken seriously.

Angst, Irony, Despair – and Occasional Redemption

As has already been observed in Chapter 5, the 'great Victorian novel' was instrumental in bringing new psychological depth and complexity to the condition of romantic love at the same time as relativizing it: love is central to the human condition, but it is not the whole of it. In the twentieth century, meanwhile, this de-centring of romantic love has, I would suggest, been taken several steps further – which is not to say that it is entirely without significance. Indeed, it could probably be argued that as the narrative centrality of love has diminished, so has its symbolic / tropic value increased. 'Serious' writers from the forties and fifties onwards might have been less inclined to write 'about' love, but they certainly make use of it (especially *vis-à-vis* sex) at a metaphorical level. For those writers most despairingly inclined, romantic love – in its most lost, broken, depraved, violent and perverse forms – becomes the quintessential figure of the fallen human condition.

As was noted at the beginning of this section, the dominant reading of literary history in the period following the Second World War is of authors, and readers, unable to recapture their 'faith' in humanity. And the crucial emphasis here, of course, is that what the Western world was unable to bear most of all was the experience of an atrocity *repeated*. For those who had fought in, or lived through, what they believed to be 'the war to end all wars' (that is, the conflict of 1914–18), and then campaigned – as Vera Brittain did – in order that its horrors should never happen again, the truly industrial warfare of 1939–45 (46 million people lost their lives) provoked understandable despair. Indeed, from the perspective of the twenty-first century, it can perhaps be argued that the most profound moral and political consequence of this second war so close upon the heels of the first was resignation to the fact that such horrors cannot – even with the best will in the world – be *prevented*. According to Bradbury, the Western world – and perhaps especially those nations who were occupied by the Nazis – responded to this failure of agency with writing that favoured the cryptic, the cynical and the absurd:

> The Holocaust imprinted its lesson everywhere. Forty years on Martin Amis still proclaimed he lived in a time of 'Einstein's Monsters', his work shaped by the Holocaust and the nuclear age: 'It is the highest subject, and it is the lowest subject. It is disgraceful, and exalted. Everywhere you look there is great irony: tragic irony, pathetic irony, even the irony of black comedy or farce; and there is the irony that is simply violent, unprecedentedly violent . . .' (Bradbury 2001: 257)

Jane Rule's *Desert of the Heart*, to which we shall shortly turn, puts the question of whether humankind can, or cannot, rise above the condition of 'absurdity' and 'farce' at its moral core. The fact that it is also, very explicitly, a romance – and, indeed, a *lesbian* romance – illustrates perfectly the existential crisis personal relationships began to pose for people in the postwar period. Published in 1964, but clearly looking back to the 1950s, what Rule's novel seeks to dramatize is far more than the social risks one took in entering into a homosexual relationship; the greater romantic angst, as we shall see, concerns itself with whether – in an age of such profound alienation – it is possible to love at all.

Other writers to famously, or infamously, put love on trial in this way include Samuel Beckett, Harold Pinter, Evelyn Waugh and Graham Greene. The latter's *The End of the Affair* (1951), which we considered in the previous chapter, may, indeed, be seen as the quintessential 'crisis' text in this regard, revolving as it does around a 'metaphysical wager' (Bradbury 2001: 293) which tests one's belief in love as surely as it tests one's belief in God. Where love does survive in these texts it is by a thread, and often in the face of all manner of human cruelty. Without wishing to take this particular 'grand narrative' to too bleak an extreme, it would seem fair to say that – from the 1950s onwards – Western literature has been more concerned with what pain and suffering human beings can inflict upon one another 'in the name of love' than in love itself. A particularly British expression of this was, of course, the so-called 'kitchen-sink drama' made famous by playwrights such as John Osborne. In these hard-hitting texts, 'the sex war' and 'the class war' were brought together for the first time (Bradbury 2001: 315), and audiences were obliged to grapple with scenes of rampant heterosexuality and violence to which there were few 'happy endings'. Unlike the typical outcome of a Mills & Boon, these 'beasts' (that is, the macho heroes) are rarely tamed (see Modleski 1982). America, too, saw sexual politics mix with existential angst in a heady new mix, with authors like Norman Mailer and Henry Miller exploring the limits of human depravity and despair through a supposedly high-brow engagement with pornography.[4]

Aligning such wholesale political and personal despair in the 'high literature' of the forties and fifties with the simultaneous explosion of romantic pulp fiction is, admittedly, a tall order. The easiest way to make sense of the binarism is clearly, as has already been indicated, to acknowledge that they are, indeed, 'opposite' responses to a moment of social and political crisis. Faced with the question of whether humankind does, or does not, possess agency and/or free will, either one can concede defeat and content oneself with representing the world as it bleakly is, or one can retain faith in some notion of a salvation (albeit limited) in the personal sphere. The latter, supposedly, was the creed favoured by Mills & Boon and its readers; the erstwhile civilized world might be fallen and humanity proven to be impotent, but within the covers of a romantic novel heroes and heroines still retain the will, and the power, to act upon one another and to achieve lasting permanent fulfilment.

Or do they? As I have already suggested in my discussion of the nexus of love and the 'little death' in the popular romance genre, the co-incidence of the moment of self-fulfilment and self-annihilation in these texts is a disturbing one. However various in other ways, the structural feature which most universally applies to popular romance is its insistence on a proper *ending*. Regardless of whether or not we are given glimpses of a 'happy ever after', the climax of all the stories expresses the heroine's triumph as a finite limit-point. She is most 'fulfilled', therefore, at the moment that both her 'story' and her 'relationship' (as it is understood in the space of that story) end. Presented this way, the 'actualization' of the self at the expense of one's relationship (to one's lover and/or the wider world) would seem to me to emerge from the same fountain of existential despair as those texts which confront the demise more honestly. Indeed, it is not difficult to stand the binary on its head and proclaim the more ostensibly 'hopeless' texts the happier ones. For if the *raison d'être* of the Mills & Boon romance is its 'sense of an ending', then that of the contemporary existential tragedy (variously defined) is surely its purgatorial *un*-endingness. What unites the relationships of Beckett, Osborne and Pinter is the knowledge that their problems will go unresolved, both for worse – and, I am tempted to suggest, *for better*. But it takes a work of literature as outstanding as Jane Rule's *Desert of the Heart*, to which I now turn, to make this a truly convincing argument.

II

'For an Indefinite Period of Time': Lesbian Romance in 1950s America

I begin with an extract from the final page of Rule's novel:

> They stood together in the warm, morning sun, looking down at the bridge and the river. A couple of old men, sitting below them, turned to stare and then turned away again. Evelyn looked up at the clear, immense and empty sky. Then she turned to Ann and saw in her eyes the darker color of the day.
> 'It's a terrible risk, Ann.'
> 'And the world's full of mirrors. You can get caught in your own reflection.'
> 'And destroyed?'
> 'Or saved.'
> 'And I'm afraid of the one, and you're afraid of the other. We're a cryptic cartoon, my darling. It should be one of your best.'

'I'll only draw it if I can live it.'

'In a house by the river with me and your five photographs of children?'

'Anywhere.'

'For the while then,' Evelyn said. 'For an indefinite period of time.'

And they turned and walked back up the steps toward their own image, reflected in the great, glass doors. (Rule 1992 [1964]: 221–2)

Jane Rule's novel is very determinedly a love story *without an ending*. Although, as we shall see, it conforms to the classic/popular 'narrative logic of romance' (Radway 1984) in many ways, in this refusal of a happy ending predicated upon a *certain future* it breaks the number one requirement of formula romance; furthermore, it refuses any notion of lasting self-fulfilment. Ann's cryptic observation that 'you can get caught in your own reflection' (which makes sense only in the context of the novel's extensive use of this and other tropes) is endorsed by the 'corrective' image which brings the story to its temporary conclusion: Evelyn and Ann mirrored in 'the great, glass doors' not as individuals, nor as reflections of one another (despite the fact that they appear to all the world as 'mother and daughter'), but as a 'newly wed' *couple* seen only by themselves.

To understand the mastery of this final stroke in conceptual terms, readers unfamiliar with the novel need also to know that 'the great, glass doors' are the doors of the court-house in Reno, Nevada, where Evelyn – a university professor in her forties – has just been granted a divorce from her husband, George, on the grounds of (his) mental cruelty (Rule 1992: 219–20). She has being staying in Reno for six weeks previous to this in order to achieve the status of residency required to file for the divorce, and, in order to obtain it, has had to affirm that she intends to stay living there 'for an indefinite period'. The ambiguity which hangs over the notion of this 'indefinite period' *vis-à-vis* the divorce becomes the thing that enables Evelyn and Ann to 'commit' to one another (Ann is the 25-year-old stepdaughter of Frances Packer, the owner of the boarding-house where Evelyn has stayed). Both women are scared, for different reasons, by the implications of such a commitment, but the sense of provisionality engendered by the phrase paradoxically enables it; they thus leave the court-house (where Ann has acted as Evelyn's 'witness') effectively 'married' by the legal loophole of a Reno divorce. In narratological terms it is, indeed, an inspired stroke.

But the provisionality that characterizes, and enables, this relationship is about far more than resisting the happy endings of popular romance and insisting upon the future freedom and responsibility of the lovers 'to make it work'; it also – and rather more darkly – speaks to the text's concern with the nature of 'modern love' itself. In so 'fallen' a world (Evelyn's husband, George, is a veteran of the Second World War), with the greed and cruelty of humanity so recently exposed, what does love mean? What 'gift' can it possibly offer? The text's ending is underwritten by this deeper level of conditionality in the 'queer' marriage of another couple, Silver and Joe, which takes place a few days before Evelyn's divorce. Silver is an ex-lover of Ann's who has worked with her, for many years, in one of Reno's large gambling casinos ('*Frank's Club*'), and whose masquerade of vulgar, big-hearted and determinedly promiscuous female sexuality may be seen to symbolize – in the first part of the text – the de-mystification of romantic love. For Ann, indeed, Silver's version of love is wholly commensurate with the life of the desert; in the absence of all natural resources, humanity has somehow figured out an 'unnatural' solution: 'The earth's given out. Man can't get a living from it. They have to get it from each other. We can't have what we need, but we can take what we want' (Rule 1992: 103). Rather than seeing the gambling casinos of Reno as a symptom of humanity's failure and degradation, Ann insists on seeing them as a sign of its ingenuity; and – until she meets Evelyn – the philosophy of (self-)survival ('We can't have what we need, but we can take what we want') sums up her view of interpersonal relationships also.

In the wedding service which marries her to Joe, however, Silver – and all the members of the congregation – are swept up in the very discourse of romantic love (as exclusive, and gratuitous, and 'forever') that her person, and lifestyle, have so resolutely denied. And Rule, with a campness that anticipates the novels of Angela Carter, presents this as a very queer turn of events indeed:

> Then Joe, as easily as if it had been planned, walked up the aisle to her and offered her his arm. They walked down the aisle together, and the women in the congregation began to weep their easy tears of vicarious relief and triumph. One more among them was about to be saved. Even Ann's throat tightened as that ridiculous pair arrived before the minister to take the vows they neither believed nor clearly understood for reasons their unborn child only partially explained, for reasons neither they, nor those who witnessed this marriage, would ever quite believe or understand. (Rule 1992: 195)

Thus, despite the fact that immediately prior to her walk down the aisle, Silver had angrily expostulated to Ann, 'the bride and the groom have the privilege of at least fifteen minutes in which to contemplate what a sick, sick, fucking Christ-awful thing getting married is' (Rule 1992: 194), both she and Ann are forced to submit to the power of love as an involuntary act of faith, however blind. Indeed, the winning paradox here is that love imposes its power upon subjects *despite* the fact they don't 'believe'.

At this point in *her* story, Evelyn, however, remains defiantly sceptical (at least, at the level of her superego). Soon after Silver's wedding, it emerges that the citizens of Reno – and, in particular, Ann's ex-lover Bill – have found out about the relationship between herself and Ann, and Evelyn is thrown into a crisis over what she should do. With a psychological subtlety characteristic of the whole text, Rule makes it clear that Evelyn's conscious response to this crisis (as the moment she must 'take responsibility' for Ann's future, if not her own) is *not* what is really freaking her out. Although she subsequently persuades herself – and attempts to persuade Ann – that they must end their relationship for reasons of social and moral propriety ('It isn't right. It isn't natural. I can't go on with it.' (Rule 1992: 214)), her deeper and darker dilemma, like Ann's, concerns the nature of love itself. The more fervently she denies its authenticity as an emotion, the more she reveals herself to be in its possession, as illustrated in this 'hidden polemic' (Pearce 1994:52) against Frances:

> Frances had already excused her. She wanted love for Ann and did not much care how she got it. Had she no capacity for moral indignation or at least moral doubt? Did it never occur to her, because of the sentimental trash that filled her head, that love might be a devastating obscenity? Frances cherished convention. How could she then so willingly trade her dream of Ann's white wedding for what might turn into a vicious absurdity in the public courts of law? (Rule 1992: 200)

The phrases 'devastating obscenity' and 'vicious absurdity' ricochet through Evelyn's angry, cornered consciousness through the next few pages of the text, only to be shot down by her *unconscious* at the moment Ann (apparently meekly) accepts her decision to end their relationship. At this point she is finally forced to concede that 'viciously absurd' as the *institutions* of love, marriage, divorce and the dysfunctional nuclear family are, romantic love continues to present itself to individual subjects as the most natural, most innocent, thing in the world: 'Why didn't you argue, even a little? There isn't any argument for a lie. And it is a lie, my darling. Nothing else I've ever known has been as right and as natural as loving you. And there isn't anything I wouldn't risk . . . Except you' (Rule 1992: 214). In terms of the argument I have been conducting here, it is clear that 'the lie' to which Evelyn refers is much more than a personal lie; it is also the lie of a post-war, post-Holocaust world which has yielded to cynical *disbelief* in human nature (love included) in order to protect itself from further shame and suffering. Despite the period (that is, 1950s) tendencies of both

Evelyn and Ann to subscribe to such sentiment and philosophy, this, then, is a text in which the inexorable human spirit just about reasserts itself . . . just in time.

This frail, faltering belief in the authenticity of love is afforded spectacular resonance in the text's desert imagery. Although, on her visit to Pyramid Lake, Evelyn attempts to protect herself from Ann's seduction by declaring 'I live in the desert of the heart . . . I can't love the whole damned world' (Rule 1992: 108), nature (both human and terrestrial) steps in to show her there is no such thing. Even in the very heart of the desert, there is water, there is sex, and there is life (Rule 1992: 111). Whilst Rule runs the risk – surely a calculated one – of bringing her metaphor of 'romantic love vs. romantic angst' to the point of cliché, it is also no surprise that she makes Pyramid Lake, on the occasion of their second visit, the site of Evelyn and Ann's most spectacular love-making (spectacular unto themselves, unto the reader, and unto the two helicopter pilots who are later willing to give testimony to their 'unnatural passions'):

> The candor of Ann's absolute nakedness . . . aroused in Evelyn an arrogance of body, a lust that burned through her nerves like the fire of the sun they both stood in. This was the freedom she wanted, an animal freedom exposed to the emptiness of sky and land and water. (Rule 1992: 169)

The intellectual climax of an elaborate deployment of desert imagery on the theme of romantic love and the human condition, this extract also invites the reader to consider the dependence of this fine text on the codes and conventions of popular romance. In terms of its representation of sexual desire, it could be argued that what we have here is as crude, and as typical, as Rule's vocabulary: Evelyn and Ann are 'reduced' to their animal desires, no more and no less; both seek dominance, both seek self-gratification, both enjoy the Mills & Boon moment of orgasmic oblivion (Rule 1992: 169). Aside from the fact that we know them to be two women, there is nothing in particular that distinguishes this as specifically lesbian love-making. The vocabulary may be more sophisticated, and the imagistic context better prepared for, but in other ways this extract would not seem that out of place in the pages of a Mills & Boon.

Elsewhere, however, Rule's depictions of sexual and emotional intimacy differ markedly from those found in pulp romance and *do* acquire a lesbian specificity. The first, and most distinctive, of these is focused on the quasi-maternal nature of the relationship between Evelyn and Ann. Evelyn is just about old enough to be Ann's mother, and they look spookily alike (Rule 1992: 9); moreover, as the story unfolds, it is revealed that Ann's psychology is defined, in part, by desire for her lost mother, and Evelyn's by desire for the child she has never had. The fact that this is a dynamic that has been played out in countless lesbian love stories since, and has been made a founding principle of many psychoanalytic accounts of lesbian sexuality, should not be allowed to detract from the fact that at the time Rule was writing it was both new and shocking.[5] By the 1940s and 1950s, the paradigm most commonly invoked to understand female homosexuality was that of 'butch' and 'femme' (see Faderman 1991), and what is immediately obvious about the relationship between Evelyn and Ann is that it is not gendered in this way. Whilst Ann's femininity may be less orthodox than Evelyn's (she works as a 'change apron' in a casino and wears cowboy boots), this can also be interpreted as generational difference; neither is there any real evidence of her playing a masculine role *vis-à-vis* Silver's 'phallic mother' (Rule 1992: 40–1). Moreover, at the start of the story she has only recently ended what appears to have been a relatively successful heterosexual relationship with the casino manager, Bill. Bi-sexual and non-monogamous she may be, but a stereotypical 'invert' or 'butch dyke' Ann most certainly is not. The need that fuels her desire is ostensibly one of similarity rather than difference, and – more than once – Silver teases her for what she perceives to be infatuation with her latest mother substitute (Rule 1992: 79). Evelyn, meanwhile, the apparent essence of genteel femininity in many ways (the text pays a good deal of attention to her dress, her manners), is, as noted earlier in the chapter, a more powerful swimmer than Ann, and – at her own admission – a woman who has effectively emasculated her husband through her intellectual superiority and competence (see discussion between Evelyn and Ann; Rule 1992: 162–3). And Evelyn, too, has already had some experience of lesbian relationships *vis-à-vis* her wartime friend, Carol (Rule 1992: 114–16). Neither woman, then, can be seen to occupy a position of fixed gender-difference *vis-à-vis* the other, but both *do* have histories which indicate an inclination to the mother–daughter dynamic (Evelyn's one erotic episode with Carol positioned her in the mother's role). The real interest of Rule's text in this regard, however, is that it is a dynamic that is set up only to be taken apart again. Unlike the subsequent lesbian-feminist texts which raise the mother–daughter paradigm to almost holy status, *Desert of the Heart* resists the conclusion that *this* is the authentic face of romantic love.

By understanding Rule's complex positioning of the mother–daughter paradigm, we can also go several steps further in understanding the wider relationship between sex and love in the text. As has already been noted, both Evelyn and Ann come to their relationship with the experience of this particular dynamic, and the 'first step' towards intimacy for each of them is acknowledgement of this. For Evelyn, it is forced upon her consciousness when she reluctantly resists Ann's advances at Pyramid Lake ('Evelyn looked at Ann, the child she had always wanted, the friend she had once had, the lover she had never considered. Of course she wanted Ann' (Rule 1992: 109)), but it has already been prefigured, at an unconscious level, during her bout of 'altitude-sickness' at Virginia City. Here, as elsewhere in the text, Rule signals her characters' more repressed thought processes through a stream-of-consciousness type of free indirect discourse:

> 'Well,' Evelyn said, straightening up, 'how I welcome the convention of time and space.'
> 'Have you been dizzy before?'
> 'Umhum. It must be altitude.' Evelyn turned to Ann and smiled an apology. 'I don't awfully like . . . heights.' Or the adolescent depths of eyes, child, grown child. That will do. (Rule 1992: 65)

Once her desire for Ann has been raised to the level of *full* consciousness, however, Evelyn is able to start analysing her resistance and – perhaps surprisingly – begins to relax it. This narrative trajectory is, of course, in significant contrast to the Mills & Boon prototype, where emotional reactions (and their consequences) go completely unexplained in psychological terms. Just a week after the first visit to Pyramid Lake, Evelyn has already taken an impressive grip on the struggle between her ego and her id and is now able to acknowledge her desire for Ann ('Evelyn had established a new, tentative and precarious balance between what she called nature and will' (Rule 1992: 119)).

Even more significantly, however, this 'decision' has been made possible, in part, by Evelyn's recognition that her desire for Ann *exceeds* the bounds of the mother–daughter paradigm. She and Ann are separate, fully autonomous individuals and their desire for one another is predicated upon difference as much as similarity: 'Sitting across the dinner table from Ann, Evelyn studied her with the intensity and distance she might have given a painting. What she saw was no longer an imperfect reflection of herself but an alien otherness she was drawn to and could not understand' (Rule 1992: 117). That this 'otherness' is psychological rather than physical also goes to the heart of the text's stance on the dynamic between sex and love. Physical desire may ignite one's interest in an/other, yes, but the quest for *intimacy* goes way beyond the strangeness and/or familiarity of their body. From this moment in the story onwards, Evelyn's desire for Ann is most especially a desire to know her in her psychological/moral otherness and – in significant contrast to popular romance – this is indicated by moments in the text where intimacy climaxes not in sex but in psychological revelation. Probably the most explicit illustration of this is the end of Chapter 6, when Ann first shows Evelyn her cartoons. For Evelyn, this first glimpse into Ann's intellectual and political singularity is as surprising, and delighting, as her first encounter with her body; and Ann, likewise, takes pleasure from her innermost self being seen and understood (Rule 1992: 155). For Ann, similarly, any hope of a lasting relationship with Evelyn has to begin with a conscious acknowledgement of the desires and fears she retains *vis-à-vis* her lost mother. With the help of Silver's cod psychology, she is finally forced to admit a degree of perversity in her pursuit of mother substitutes to date (that is, she pursues them in order to prove that she can do without them, rather than as an acknowledgement of her need). As her relationship with Evelyn progresses, however, Ann realizes that she cannot sustain this lie any more and is given to conclude: 'If, in making love with Evelyn, her body yearned for obscure intimacies, they must no longer be substitutes for, a defense against, intimacies of person with person' (Rule 1992: 148). As in Evelyn's case, this moment of *conscious* revelation has nevertheless been preceded by a turbulent *unconscious* one (represented, once again, through stream-of-consciousness free indirect discourse):

> But, as she closed the front door behind her, she knew she had hop-scotched to the final square. 'The game's up,' she said in her sheriff's voice, but it really was. 'I didn't hear you, Mother, until the fourth time you called. And now I'm on the first step. And now I'm on the second step . . . Evelyn?'
>
> Evelyn opened the door and took Ann in her arms. (Rule 1992: 145)

Like Evelyn, Ann also recognizes that any further step towards intimacy will take her from the body's lust to the deeper waters of the mind: 'She was going to court Evelyn, not simply her body, but her mind and her heart' (Rule 1992: 148). Presented thus, it would be easy – at first glance – to read this as a simplistic dualism of 'body = lust', 'mind + heart = love', were it not for Rule's care in depicting the convoluted mind-games that have preceded it. For, ultimately, this is a text in which the two women discover love not in the gratification of the self (either sexually, or in terms of psychological reification) but in an on-going exploration of the other's unique difference and peculiarity: a classic illustration, in fact, of my baseline equation $(x + y \rightarrow x' + y')$, providing we understand the emphasis to be on the transformation of the self *in relation to* the other rather than (as in Mills & Boon) the transformation of the self *at the expense of* the other.

Posed in terms of the specific 'gift' lesbian lovers may be seen to give each other, I would thus venture that what Rule's text has envisaged, and endorsed, is a refined version of self-actualization. Although, in feminist bookstores across the world, *Desert of the Heart* may well take its place alongside other classic 'coming out' romances (in which the protagonists 'discover themselves' as a consequence of discovering their true / 'authentic' sexuality), the *conditionality* of Ann and Evelyn's selves and the *provisionality* of their future relationship ensure that this is a love story firmly rooted in the cultural-historical moment of the 1950s. Evelyn and Ann may have found a metaphorical Pyramid Lake in one another, but they remain surrounded by a desert that is fundamentally inhospitable and mocking of humankind's achievements. Ann's particular gift to the relationship, indeed, is her insistence that this context should always be kept in view; hence her passionate, repeated, desire that Evelyn should come and live with her in the desert rather than them both flee to California. Her success as a cartoonist has depended upon her determination to make the unnaturalness and absurdity of human endeavour (as symbolized by the casino) part of her daily life, and this is what she also wants for herself as a perverse kind of existential protection. After years of working in *Frank's Club*, Ann has truly internalized the panopticon of its mirrored ceiling and insists, just as the ending of the novel insists, that human beings keep their lives, and their loves, steadily in view: 'What a device of conscience that mirror was, for behind it, at any time, might be the unknown face of a security officer, watchful, judging; yet she could not see it. You could not get past your own minimized reflection' (Rule 1992: 28). This, after all, is the 1950s, and the romantic love of a newly fallen world.

III

As I observed at the end of Chapter 5, the birth of psychoanalysis changed for ever the Western world's understanding of the sexual self, whilst the reconfigurations of wealth and class after the Second World War effected a reconceptualization of the *social* self as radical as that wrought by the Industrial Revolution. And although a good deal has since been written on why these changes were rather less liberating for women than for men, from the perspective of the so-called 'sexual revolution', women's 'return to the home' was of complex significance.[6] In the last section of this chapter, I have therefore elected to focus on those texts – both popular and middle-brow – in which women's quest for an authentic *sexual* identity may be seen to challenge, displace or otherwise absorb their concern for social status. My hypothesis is that these texts may be seen to shift romance away from the achievement of a fulfilling and / or inspiring *relationship* to the production of a sexual self whose need of the other is primarily instrumental. Read in, and against, this context, readers will also be able to see more clearly what an exceptional text Rule's *Desert of the Heart* is. Even a modest review of 1950s and 1960s literature would seem to confirm Betty Friedan's argument that, during this period, women were 'successfully reduced to sex creatures, sex seekers' (Friedan 1963: 228):

> Are they using sex or sexual fantasy to fill needs that are not sexual? Is that why their sex, even when real, seems like fantasy? Is that why, even when they experience orgasm they feel 'unfulfilled'? Are they driven to this never-satisfied sexual seeking because, in their marriages, they have not found the sexual fulfillment which the feminine mystique promises? Or is that feeling of personal identity, of fulfillment, they seek in sex something that sex alone cannot give? (Friedan 1963: 226)

The texts I bring to this discussion range from the popular (Mills & Boon and their lesbian pulp equivalent) to the high-brow (the writers and philosophers who attempted to make sense of the dark night of the twentieth-century soul), whilst paying particular attention to the so-called 'middle-brow'.

Romance and the Sexual Self

In Part I of this chapter I propounded a theory for why the moment of sexual orgasm, and its attendant oblivion, has such huge symbolic significance in women's formula fiction. Although the more ostensible objective of these romances may be seen to be the restoration (or creation) of the heroine's *social* identity through marriage, this is invariably figured through the simultaneous limit-point of a sexual consummation which signals that the 'work' of the relationship is over. This, in every sense, is the end of her story.

From the era of the sexologists onwards, however, there began to emerge a body of fiction in which the quest for the sexual self was unburdened by the social concerns of class or caste. This was clearly due, in part at least, to the fact that many of the writers concerned were themselves comfortably provided for with respect to both wealth and ego, including those writing on gay and lesbian subjects. Several such authors were invoked at the end of Chapter 5, and the point was made that for many (for example, Radclyffe Hall) the quest for identity became inextricable from the realization of one's sexual identity; and although sometimes this was bound up with romantic love, often it was not.

This, I would suggest, is one of the ways in which the lesbian pulp fiction of the 1950s and early 1960s differs from its heterosexual counterpart most distinctly. *Beebo Brinker* (1962) by Ann Bannon is one of a best-selling series of novels featuring the eponymous heroine and is very much the story of her 'coming out' rather than a romance *per se*.[7] Although, in the course of the story, Beebo confirms her sexual orientation through, first, her desire for Mona and, subsequently, her relationships with Paula and Venus, it is clear that her identity as an 'invert' began way back in her childhood:

> 'I was kicked out of school,' she went on hesitantly, 'because I looked so much like a boy they thought I must be acting like one. Chasing girls. Molesting them. Everything I ever did to a girl, or wanted to do, or dreamed of doing, happened in my imagination. . . . My father tried to teach me not to hate myself because I looked like hell in gingham frills. . . . But when you see people turn away and laugh behind their hands . . . It makes you wonder what you really are. (Bannon 1962: 50–1)

As Beebo's adventures in Greenwich Village notch up, it is also obvious that her lesbianism is to be defined in terms of *generic* rather than subject-specific love or sexual desire:

> The floor was jammed with a mass of couples. . . . A mass of girls, dancing, arms locked around each other, bodies pressed close and warm. . . . Beebo watched them for half a minute, all told: but a minute that was transfixed like a living picture in her mind for the rest of her life. (Bannon 1962: 41)

Thus, although the word 'love' is used to describe Beebo's feelings for both Paula and the film-star Venus, it does not denote either exclusivity or permanence (see discussion of these values in Chapter 1). Indeed, the pace of her sexual adventures – once they get going – is impressive: she makes love to Paula within one hour of meeting her, transfers her attentions to Venus after just a few days, spends one month in California with the film-star (and another getting over her) before successfully reuniting with Paula again. And whilst this itinerary does, of course, comply with a popular stereotype of gay lifestyle and culture (Beebo's friend and mentor, Jack Mann, regularly 'fall[s] in love twice a year' (Bannon 1962: 22–3)), it also speaks more deeply of the correlation between love and subjectivity in this particular genre. There is a distinct impression in Bannon's text that the lesbian identity depends upon repeated – and spectacular – performance for its validation, and that this is perhaps even more true for 'femmes' like Mona than for more visible inverts like Beebo.[8] Despite the sexual and emotional gratification she receives from Paula, it is therefore no surprise to see Beebo resist the further step of moving in with her: 'I don't know. It would give her the right to expect me to be faithful. I can't imagine a lovelier girl. But I hardly know her. And there are so many damned girls in the world . . .' (Bannon 1962: 111). My point here, then, is that this is more than the expression of promiscuous sexual desire; it is also about Beebo's need to visibly perform her fledgeling sexual identity in an arena outwith Paula's cosy domesticity. Moreover, although the end of this particular novel sees Beebo reunited with 'the lovely Paula', who 'incredibly learned to love her [Beebo] in three days and loved her still after three months' (Bannon 1962: 227), we *know* that it will not be the end of her amorous adventures. Beebo's selfhood *is* her sexuality, and this can only be sustained through reiterative performance.

The 'sexual picaresque' also enjoyed a renaissance in the gay male fiction of this period. In his *History of Gay Literature* (1999) Greg Woods observes that 'the 1950s amounted to a virtual festival of queer self-assertion' (Woods 1999: 289) and points to the emergence of writers like Ralph Ellison, Chester Hines and Donald Webster Cory to illustrate his point. Although none of the works produced by these men would be thought of specifically as romances, they initiate a newly explicit focus on homosexual desire and, indeed, love. However, despite the fact that the heroes of these texts experience no shortage of relationships, few are lasting and a good many end tragically. It is also clear that the most interesting gay male writing of the fifties period is that which correlates repressed/frustrated sexual relationships with the American 'Cold War' psyche in a noir-ish vision. Baldwin's *Giovanni's Room* (1957) and *Another Country* (1962) are both classic gay texts in this respect, and additionally important for their representation of black characters at this sensitive moment in America's history.

Having already established that heterosexual formula romances rarely allow the heroine's sexual identity to subsume her social identity to quite the extent that Beebo Brinker does, I now turn to a significant subcategory within middle-brow fiction: namely the woman's novel of marital infidelity. As Nicola Beauman (1983) has shown, the 'domestic revival' of the inter-war period meant nothing if not boredom for a large number of housewives. Including, for the first time, women from the lower as well as upper classes, these 'kept women' led lives which combined the stressful, largely invisible, management of the domestic household with a dearth of stimulating activity or social contact. She quotes E. M. Delafield's *Diary of a Provincial Lady* (1930) to make her point:

> Every morning you awake to the kind of list which begins: – Sink-plug. Ruffle-tape. X-hooks. Glue . . . And ends: Ring plumber. Get sweep. Curse laundry. Your horizon contracts, your mind's eye is focused on a small circle

of exasperating detail. Sterility sets in; the hatches of your mind are bat-
tened down. Your thoughts, once darling companions, turn into club bores,
from which only sleep can bring release. (Beauman 1983: 9)

Given such a context, it is hardly surprising that, in the fantasy world of
literature at least, women took lovers and sought a new identity for themselves, even if it necessitated social scandal and shame.

An indication of the extent to which romance had become the vehicle
for the actualization of a sexually transgressive self-identity may be seen
by comparing what are probably the two most famous middle-brow
women's novels of the Second World War and its aftermath, Margaret
Mitchell's *Gone with the Wind* (1974 [1936]) and Daphne du Maurier's
Rebecca (1992 [1938]). In contrast to the nineteenth-century Brontë sisters'
novels (*Wuthering Heights* and *Jane Eyre*) which are their templates, these
two thirties novels (and their associated films) focus on the heroine's
pursuit of an explicitly sexual identity in the context of marriages that
threaten to render them anonymous and invisible. The fact that du
Maurier's nameless heroine is obliged to pursue this sexual self via vicarious identification with Rebecca, the dead wife of her husband, Maxim, is,
of course, a fabulously inventive twist to the proceedings. Through the
eyes of this mousy *ingénue* we begin to see exactly what it meant to the
women of this period – 'the age of Hollywood' – *not* to have a sexual
persona. Despite her husband's avowed distaste for feminine glamour, the
heroine continues to feel ashamed of her girlishness and is consequently
thrilled by the transformation wrought by the replica of Rebecca's dress
(see du Maurier 1992: 221). Whilst much has been made of the lesbian
subtext to this novel (that is, the supposition that both Mrs Danvers, the
housekeeper, and the heroine are secretly in love with Rebecca), I would
argue that this is indistinguishable from the heroine's quest for her own
spectacular (hetero)sexual self. Both her love for Maxim and her love for
Rebecca may be seen to serve that same end: in Maxim she sought the validation of the desiring lover; in Rebecca, a vicarious identification with the
sexual self.

In Margaret Mitchell's *Gone with the Wind*, meanwhile, Scarlett O'Hara
is given the means (that is, the looks, the flashing temperament) to determine her own sexual identity and is memorable chiefly (and in the film
version, especially) for the foolish cuckold she makes of the genteel Ashley
Wilkes. The extraordinary reception of this text (both the book and
the film) has led critics to speculate about the state of contemporary
marriage at the time: could that many thousands of readers really be
that discontented with their lives?[9] Was sexual self-fulfilment in danger

of becoming more important – or, at least, more alluring – than the notional security of 'love-and-marriage'? Had the Hollywood re-visioning of Cathy and Heathcliff as Scarlett and Rhett effectively dispensed with the grail of 'love *qua* love' for ever? Indeed, it could be argued that it was with *this* text that the exercise of female sexual power became a legitimate end in itself for the first time, and – most importantly – *despite* the fact that its heroine paid dearly for her indulgence. Helen Taylor has also pointed out that *Gone with the Wind* anticipates the 'family saga' of later decades inasmuch as Scarlett's marriage to Rhett *precedes* her sexual and emotional awakening (Taylor 1989: 138). This, in other words, is the first great twentieth-century women's 'blockbuster' in which 'good sex' becomes an objective distinct from romantic love and a happy marriage (see the discussion of Jackie Collins *et al.* in Chapter 7).

Other middle-brow writers from this period who appear to have been inclined to favour the sexual self over the socially respectable self include Rosamond Lehmann and Nancy Mitford. According to Beauman, indeed, Mitford's *The Pursuit of Love* (1970 [1945]) is 'the apotheosis of the woman's novel about love' (Beauman 1983: 198). What is especially significant about this text *vis-à-vis* my argument here is that the heroine, Linda, marries three times, but only on the third occasion is her sexual desire fulfilled and her sexual identity realized (Beauman 1983: 198–200). Such sentiment is not, of course, a million miles away from the pulp romance of Mills & Boon, though the tragic ending of *The Pursuit of Love* ('Fabrice dies fighting for the French Resistance at the same time Linda dies in childbirth' (Beauman 1983: 200)) further underlines the fact that their love was underwritten by passion rather than by social status. Rosamond Lehmann's *The Weather in the Streets* (1981 [1936]), meanwhile, is a wonderfully complex psychological drama of an upper-middle-class woman risking – and losing – everything on account of her passionate affair with a married man. As Beauman observes, what is especially impressive, and indeed modern, about this text is the fact that Olivia *expects* to be hurt and harbours no illusions of a happy ending. What we see here is thus another instance of women believing that romantic tragedy is a price worth paying for a validated sexual selfhood, albeit one that is cruelly transient. Where I differ from Beauman, however, is that I doubt whether love, understood specifically as *desire for an/other*, was ever the object of these affairs; it was always the heroine's own self that was pursued, captured, honoured and betrayed. As Friedan, writing from the perspective of 1963, observed: 'For the woman who lives according to the feminine mystique, there is no road to achievement, or status, or identity, except the sexual one: the achievement of sexual

conquest, status as a desirable sexual object, identity as a sexually successful wife and mother' (Friedan 1963: 232–3).

It would be wrong, however, to end this chapter with the impression
that the middle years of the twentieth century saw all the women of the
Western world (and the female authors who elected to represent them) so
fixated on the perfection of the sexual self that more positive correlations
of sex and love were entirely lost. We have already witnessed one text –
Jane Rule's *Desert of the Heart* – that makes a bold intellectual argument
for a different kind of 'modern love', whilst a black, feminist classic, Zora
Neale Hurston's *Their Eyes Were Watching God* (1986 [1937]), has the
remarkable love story of Janie Crawford and 'Tea Cake' embedded in a
narrative that is about so much more. Like Nancy Mitford's Linda, Janie is
married three times: first, by her grandmother, to an 'older, propertied
man' (Russell 1990: 41); next to Joe Starks, a political activist who is
involved in building a new town for 'coloured people' but who eventually
makes her feel 'muffled and marginalized' (Russell 1990: 41); and, finally,
to Tea Cake, with whom she has a fully reciprocal, loving relationship.
Despite the fact that their marriage ends in melodramatic tragedy when
Tea Cake contracts rabies and Janie is forced to shoot him in self-defence,
the text's extensive use of dialogue gives rich, verbal evidence of the emotional depth of their relationship, and the novel ends with a vision (Janie's
own) which ensures that – for all its earthy materiality – this, too, is a
romance that exceeds the self and will survive the grave:

> The day of the gun, and the bloody body, and the courthouse came and
> commenced to sing a sobbing sigh out of every corner of the room. . . .
> Then Tea Cake came prancing around her where she was and the song of
> the sigh flew out of the window and lit in the top of the pine trees. Tea
> Cake, with the sun for a shawl. Of course he wasn't dead. He could never
> be dead until she herself finished feeling and thinking. The kiss of
> his memory made pictures of love and light across the wall. (Hurston
> 1986: 286)

7

Postmodern Romance

The Gift of the Fourth Dimension

I

'This is Time, but not as we know it.' With apologies to *Star Trek* fans, I would suggest that this epigram sums up perfectly postmodernism's particular interest in the transformative power of romantic love. Viewed from the turbulent belly of a world in which 'grand narratives', foundational thinking and the 'old stable ego' have long been consigned to the dustbin of history, the de-centring of self and world wreaked by this most wayward of emotions may be seen as fully consonant with our post-Einsteinian vision of the universe.[1] The condition of being in love, in other words, submits us to the same measure of temporal relativity and disorientation that scientists have long suggested is needed to gain an (in)credible perspective on 'life, the universe and everything'.

In terms of the literary history I have been pursuing here, this special relationship between romantic love and 'the new science' would certainly help explain why, after the largely satirical and allegorical engagements of the 1950s and early 1960s, the period from 1968 onwards has witnessed a renewed enthusiasm for love as a transformative and enlightening experience.[2] Although it is but *one* of the ways in which the story of romantic love can be seen to have gone (of which more anon), it is noticeable just how many literary genres of the late twentieth century and the early twenty-first century express a fascination with the temporality of love and how it helps us rethink, more generally, the coordinates of human experience.[3] As I discuss below, metafiction, science fiction, magic realism and the noir thriller have all, on occasion, drawn parallels between the altered consciousness of the love state and the possibility of positively re-imagining our place, and time, in the world more generally. There is, moreover, a very specific aesthetic and cultural context for this vision inasmuch as – from the late 1960s onwards – the Western world began to experiment widely with recreational drugs, allowing individuals a new and liberating perspective on the artificial limitations of what Jeanette Winterson refers to as the life of 'the seasons and the clock' (Winterson 1989: 99). Placed alongside the popularization of quantum physics, the new perspectives on self/world enabled by these hallucinatory experiences contributed to a widely acknowledged time/space revolution, especially in the arena of rock music. The fact that the latter was, and continues to be, the artistic space where romantic love is most openly voiced, and explored, makes it a crucial point of reference for all those attempting to understand the contemporary world's fascination with the infinitely complex temporality of love. In the words of Rob, the protagonist of Nick Hornby's *High Fidelity* (1995) (discussed in Part III of this chapter):

> What came first, the music or the misery? Did I listen to the music because I was miserable? Or was I miserable because I listened to the music? Do all those records turn you into a melancholy person?
>
> People worry about their kids playing with guns, and teenagers watching violent videos; we are scared that some sort of culture of violence will take them over. Nobody worries about kids listening to thousands – literally thousands – of songs about broken hearts and rejection and pain and misery and loss. (Hornby 1995: 26–7)

Thus, although it is not the remit of this project to explore this other artistic avenue in any depth, I feel that we should at all times keep in mind the debts contemporary literature owes to popular music *vis-à-vis* the temporality of love, in both its mind/soul-expanding and entropic forms.

This last point – with its implication that love-time can be as painful and atrophying as it is joyful and expansive – also points to a further commitment of this chapter: that is – exponents of magic realism notwithstanding –, that we do not assume love's 'messing' with time to be necessarily benign. Despite the fact that the films and literature of the millennium abound with instances of 'alternative worlds' and 'parallel universes', a great many writers have focused instead on the terrible suffering of lovers who perceive themselves to be cheated by time as well as by love.[4] In certain genres – historiographic metafiction and the noir thriller, for instance – there are many instances of lovers betrayed either by various kinds of mistiming, or by the pitilessness of dull, plodding chronological time which divides, separates and ultimately extinguishes love 'not by inches, but by fractions of hair-breadths' (Heathcliff in Brontë 1995a: 291). The 'new science' may have endorsed the will of some writers and philosophers to defy, or transcend, the existing anthropocentric limits of time when thinking about human relationships, but many others have remained sadly sceptical or – more crucially – perceived its *dystopian* implications.

These two poles, utopian and dystopian, of how a broadly postmodern, post-Einsteinian model of time can help us rethink the condition of being in love are exemplified in the following extracts from Jeanette Winterson's *Sexing the Cherry* and Nick Cave's 'The Train Song':

> The inward life tells us that we are multiple not single, and that our existence is really countless existences holding hands like those cut-out paper dolls, but unlike the dolls never coming to an end. When we say, 'I have been here before,' perhaps we mean, 'I am here now,' but in another life, another time, doing something else. Our lives could be stacked like plates on a waiter's hand. Only the top one is showing, but the rest are there and by mistake we discover them. (Winterson 1989: 100)

> Tell me, how long the train's been gone?
> Tell me, how long the train's been gone?
> And was she there?
> And was she there?
> Tell me, how long the train's been gone?
> (Cave 2001 [1990]: 180)

In the Winterson extract the reader is instructed to believe that, once the chronological time of the clock is abandoned, there are *no* limits – literally – on love; as the narrator, Jordan, later smugly concludes: 'Either I have found Fortunata, or I will find her. Either I am remembering her or I am still imagining her. But she is somewhere in the grid of time, a co-ordinate, as I am' (Winterson 1989: 104). The reasoning here – once one accepts the notion of co-existent parallel worlds – is that Fortunata occupies a time/space which is always-already present and is hence always-already available. By the same, wonderfully redemptive, token, neither does love 'end' even if the lovers (moved to another space/time) no longer have sight of it.

How different, then, the view from Nick Cave's 'The Train Song': a searing dramatization of what one's apprehension of a 'parallel universe' amounts to when there is no access to it. In this scenario, Cave's protagonist can only *imagine* the time-space now occupied by his lover, and is tormented by the knowledge that others see her – share her chronotope – while he does not. The particularity of this pain is, moreover, marked by the acuteness with which he apprehends the temporal moment. The fact that this other time-space can be measured ('Tell me, how long the train's been gone?', 'When did the whistle blow?') attests both to its materiality and to his exemption from it: a real sting in the tale of Einstein's theory of special relativity ('there is no such thing as objective simultaneity between spatially separated events' (Price 1996: 14)). Although, like Winterson's

Jordan, Cave's protagonist knows that in another time-space his lover (still) exists, it is not on the other side of any temporal wall that can be easily collapsed. Her present is no longer his present, and their shared past ('What did she wear?', 'And did she dye her hair?') is already – like the train – pulling out of sight.

I shall return to some of the theories and philosophies that will better help explain the complex nexus of love and (postmodern) time at the beginning of Part II. First, however, I attempt a brief overview of the historical/cultural moment, the 1960s–90s and, in particular, the changing perception of the individual and the so-called 'project of the self' during this period.

The Culture(s) of Selfhood: 1960s–90s

As readers will appreciate, the huge tidal wave of social, political, cultural and technological change that has swept across the Western – and, indeed, non-Western – world during the past forty years is not easily encapsulated or narrativized, even when channelled through literary history. With respect to the cultural history of romance, a story of sorts can, nevertheless, be told: that is, the story of how the rolling (re)incarnations of individual selfhood have impacted upon interpersonal relationships and the values and traditions historically associated with romantic love.

The essential self

If we return, first, to the late 1950s and early 1960s, we are minded of a culture which – in its literary expression, at least – appears to have been swithering between a new agency and bravado, on the one hand, and an on-going post-war impotence and existential despair, on the other. One of the stories now commonly told about this period is that the booming American economy could not fail to engender a new sense of power and optimism amongst *its* citizens, but the consequences of this 'boom' for middle-class housewives and the family unit in general were, as we have already noted, mixed. Women, in particular, still struggled to find a meaningful sense of selfhood, and this led, according to proto-feminists like Betty Friedan, to a strained over-emphasis on femininity and sexuality. As both Bradbury (2001) and Waugh (1995) have observed, moreover, the social and cultural revolution we now associate with the 1960s is very much a phenomenon of the *late* 1960s and, even then, a revolution that was always restricted to certain social groups. In Britain, in particular, the writers and intellectuals of the early 1960s still tended towards the scepticism and angst of the post-war years, and this *zeitgeist* continued to cast its long shadow over what must be regarded as the best 'quality fiction' of the next three decades. In their often bleak and unflinching view of the world – including, especially, human relations –, writers of the 1970s and 1980s like Ian McEwan, Iain (M.) Banks and Martin Amis are inescapably the heirs of Auden, Larkin, Orton and Murdoch, and – before them – Beckett and the 'Angry Young Men' (Waugh 1995: 10). Moreover, in realist or post-realist texts, in particular, sex and sexual relations continued to be explored as dark expressions of a 'civilization' in crisis and rarely *vis-à-vis* the now problematically humanist concept of romantic love.

Even if we allow this bleakly despairing, manifestly dysfunctional, version of the self to figure as 'the dominant' in British post-war literature, however, there is no escaping the fact that the political revolutions and associated counter-culture(s) of the late 1960s *did* provide certain groups of citizens in the West with an alternative. If we conjure up that apocryphal 'Woodstock moment', it is impossible to deny that – for a short time, at least – an ideology of significant personal and social empowerment did emerge.[5] However empty the slogan 'Love and Peace' may seem in retrospect, it cannot be disputed that thousands – if not millions – of people (mostly young, mostly white, admittedly) *were* able to unite under its banner. Although it is now impossible to go beyond the myths and legends that surround it, the film and media images that have become the iconic record of the Woodstock festival – semi-naked, long-haired boys and girls holding hands, kissing, swimming and mud-wrestling – still convey a message of extraordinary anti-institutional defiance: what they announce to the world, then and now, is that there is nothing shameful in sex, nothing shameful about the naked body, and – most important for the story being told here – nothing more 'free' than love. Images of thousands of people 'making love' (that is, visibly engaged in demonstrations of affection as well as actual sex) out of doors ripped open the closed door on love-and/as-marriage with such force that one could imagine that things would never be the same again.

Before we move on to consider the demise of selfhood in the post-structuralist 1980s and 1990s, however, it is important to register the lingering importance of the 'essential self' to the literature(s) of romantic love during the earlier period. The notion that the human race constitutes a collective of repressed libidos awaiting sexual/political liberation remained a potent paradigm for a long time, and one writer whose early work is referred to repeatedly in this context is Doris Lessing. Although *The Golden Notebook* (1972 [1962]) was first published in 1962, the protagonist's search for an 'essential self' as well as its subsequent 'fragmentation' resonate with the views of both Herbert Marcuse (see *Eros and Civilization*

(1973 [1956]) and the poststructuralists. Bradbury deemed *The Golden Note-book* 'one of the most powerful of post-war novels' (Bradbury 2001: 381); a text which has at its heart '[Anna's] . . . desire for personal completeness and wholeness [which] seems to be dissolving under the pressures of modern life and her own expectations' (Bradbury 2001: 379). Equally important from the point of view of this volume is the fact that although (heterosexual) love and sexuality are repeatedly set up as the means to Anna's discovery of an authentic self, they fail (see Dollimore 1983: 71–2; Waugh 1989: 201–4). Yet it is also significant, in feminist terms especially, that the reflexive depth of Lessing's critique did nothing to deter subsequent generations of women writers (both literary and popular) continuing the search for the 'authentic self' and/through 'the real man' (or, indeed, woman). The number of texts from the seventies and eighties which are variants on this theme are too various to mention, but it would be fair to say that *most* of the feminist *Bildungsromanen* and lesbian 'coming out' novels published by the Women's Press during this period link sexual and gender identity and 'authenticity' in this way. It would be a mistake, moreover, to assume this to be a tendency of realist rather than fantasy and/or experimental fiction: plenty of formally experimental/postmodern texts by women still have the quest for selfhood at their core, as do, albeit in refracted form, the 'lifestyle' romances I shall be returning to in Part III of this chapter.

The de-centred self

Yet all the while this residual ideology of the authentic self was playing itself out, the emerging discourse(s) of poststructuralism were massing in continental Europe before finally, and a trifle belatedly, invading the anglophone consciousness. This said, there were plenty of novelists in Britain and America from the later 1960s onwards who did respond, and whose embrace of both poststructuralist and postmodernist principles changed the subjective (and romantic) landscape of the novel for ever. First among these were metafictional experimenters like John Fowles, whose *French Lieutenant's Woman* (1977 [1969]) is universally hailed as a landmark text. From the point of view of the history of romance, what is especially ground-breaking about this text is the way the dramatization of Charles's existential crisis (does he, or does he not, have control of his destiny?) is linked to his obsession with Sarah. To what extent does Sarah's flagrant 'performance' of a gendered/sexual self (see Bradbury 2001: 387) undermine (or not) the authenticity of Charles's own love? These are significant interventions in the theorization of love as well as the theorization of the self, and emphasize why – in a postmodern context – the two must both always be taken together.

The most important aspect of the debate *vis-à-vis* the notionally 'de-centred' *postmodern subject* for us to focus on here, however, is the tension that persists between those who pursue this de-centring in a radically anti-humanist direction and those (most notably feminist critics) who have embraced it as the door to a newly *relational* subjectivity. Foremost amongst the latter has been Patricia Waugh, whose *Feminine Fictions: Revisiting the Postmodern* (1989) was one of the first texts to re-engage with the (then) rather unfashionable 'object-relations' theories of Melanie Klein. In this ground-breaking text, Waugh reveals the preoccupations of 'male postmodernism' and – through her readings of a diverse range of texts – shows how women writers have responded very differently, and largely positively, to the perceived end of the 'old stable ego' (Waugh 1989: 8–10). Waugh's central gambit is that because women have never enjoyed an uncontested sense of selfhood, they have been largely untroubled by its notional loss and worked, instead, 'to discover a collective concept of sub-jectivity which foregrounds the construction of identity *in relationship*' (Waugh 1989: 10). Whilst some of the feminist criticism following Waugh has been inclined to interpret this notion of 'relationality' rather *too* benignly, her own readings focus more on the conflict at the heart of many classic authors and texts. There is certainly no easy assumption that because women enjoy a different relationship to the de-centred self they will necessarily be any better at romantic love relationships. In the 'post-realist' novels of Spark and Brookner, for example, Waugh identifies several characters whose relationships fail precisely because they cannot achieve the proper balance of 'separation' and 'connection' necessary (Waugh 1989: 142). The notion of the de-centred and/or 'relational' self has also been positively embraced by writers representing other oppressed and marginalized groups, such as the (post)colonial subjects of Salman Rushdie's fiction (see *Midnight's Children*, 1981; *Shame*, 1985). These are, indeed, texts which are not only thoroughly postmodern but also defiantly anti-humanist and, in this regard, contrast with those of writers like Jeanette Winterson who retain the paradigm of the quest, the desire for an essential self, *and* a belief in universal values such as romantic love.

The lifestyle self

Although they might approach the subject via different theorists, and with different political projects in mind, it would be fair to say that most liter-ary and cultural critics are agreed that the consumerist forces of late capitalism have fundamentally changed the way in which individuals view their responsibility to themselves and others. Anthony Giddens, in *The Transformation of Intimacy* (1992), coined the concept of 'the project of the self' to sum up this evolution: 'The self today is for everyone a reflexive project in a more or less continuous interrogation of past, present and future. It is a project carried out and a program of reflexive resources: therapy and self-help manuals of all kinds, television programmes and magazine articles' (Giddens 1992: 33). There is, moreover, a cogent political argument for how this new investment in the self (in the capitalist West, at least) came about. Reflecting on the social and cultural changes wrought by the 'Thatcher–Reagan' revolution, Waugh points to the way in which the rhetoric of individualism begun in the counter-cultural 1960s and 1970s was mobilized to new ends by the 'New Right' (Waugh 1995: 17). In other words, the 'residual ideology' of radical philosophers like Marcuse that had sent a generation of hippies and civil rights campaigners in search of their personal and collective 'essential selves' was now annexed by the 'emergent ideologies' of yuppiedom. However, it would be wrong to assume that all those who bought into this 'project of the self' were right-wing: far from it. Indeed, the 'self-help culture' to which Giddens refers is associated principally with the liberal Left, even though a persuasive case can clearly be made for why its practice is rooted in a profoundly bourgeois notion of personal *entitlement* (see Skeggs 2004: Chapters 3 and 8).

When we consider this latest incarnation of the self *vis-à-vis* the changing culture of interpersonal relationships, however, it is clear that intellectual disquiet is widespread. In their book *The Normal Chaos of Love* (1995), Ulrich Beck and Elisabeth Beck-Gernsheim caricature the new *zeitgeist* as a demand for 'Paradise now!' (Beck and Beck-Gernsheim 1995: 11) and observe that despite, or alongside, the various theoretical accounts of the 'death of the individual', from the 1980s onwards the Western world has been seized by a manic compulsion to do 'one's duty to oneself' (Beck and Beck-Gernsheim 1995: 43) even – or especially – within the realm of personal relationships. Love and marriage have become, for the privileged middle classes at least, things to be 'worked at' like never before, and a relationship which in any way impedes the wider 'project of the self' may have to be sacrificed: 'In the old days lovers ran up against institutional barriers, while nowadays they are wading through a swamp of ideology called happiness' (Beck and Beck-Gernsheim 1995: 100).

Zygmunt Bauman, meanwhile, writing from the perspective of what is clearly a 'former age', sees little hope for lasting, and meaningful, love-relationships in today's 'liquid modern society': 'In lasting commitments, liquid modern reason spies out oppression; in durable engagement, it sees incapacitating dependencies. That reason denies rights to bindings and bonds, spatial or temporal . . .' (Bauman 2003: 47). In arriving at this some-what despairing conclusion, Bauman was clearly deeply impressed by the way in which personal relationships have come to be treated in the media, and refers, in particular, to their packaging in the 'Lifestyle' sections of the Sunday newspapers (Bauman 2003: 35–7). Here is material evidence that personal relationships have become synonymous with 'lifestyle' choices and that – along with homes, gardens, holidays and soft furnishings – they are something to be worked on, traded up or abandoned.

Where Bauman sees heresy, Giddens (1992), however, sees hope. Despite the somewhat cynical cast of his organizing concept – 'the project of the self' –, his book focuses optimistically on the ways in which the contem-porary individual's desire to control and manage his or her life has trans-formed intimacy for the better. Central to his thesis is the belief that, once interpersonal relationships were freed from the exigencies of reproduction and inheritance, individuals could enter into them with significantly increased *expectations*. He has dubbed this 'the pure relationship':

> It refers to a situation where a social relation is entered into for its own sake, for what can be derived by each person from a sustained association with another; and which is continued only so far as it is thought by both parties to deliver enough satisfaction for each individual to stay within it . . . (Giddens 1992: 58)

For Giddens, moreover, this new form of relationship has entailed a major re-evaluation of romantic love. Whilst the latter may be seen, in its vari-ance from traditional reproductive / economic / institutional forces, to have sown the seeds for the 'pure relationship' in some respects, its privileging of 'projective identification' in the satisfaction of desire 'cuts across the development of a relationship whose continuation depends on intimacy' (Giddens 1992: 61). In other words, romantic love is so bound up with a projection / introjection of the other as an 'object-ideal' (Freud) that those bound by its values necessarily forfeit a deeper level of intimacy. Giddens continues:

> Opening oneself out to the other, the condition of what I shall call *conflu-ent love*, is in some ways the opposite of projective identification, even if such identification sometimes sets up a pathway to it. . . . Confluent love is active, contingent love, and therefore jars with the 'for-ever', 'one-and-only' qualities of the romantic love complex. The 'separating and divor-cing society' of today here appears as an effect of the emergence of confluent love rather than its cause. The more confluent love becomes

> consolidated as a real possibility, the more the finding of a 'special person' recedes and the more it is the 'special relationship' that counts. (Giddens 1992: 61–2)

On one level, this would seem to be a persuasive account of the ways in which romantic relationships have been re-evaluated in bourgeois Western culture since the late 1980s. Individuals within this group are now far less likely to stay in relationships that are not personally fulfilling than they used to be; in political terms, this has (according to Giddens) been of particular consequence for women who entered into romantic relationships and marriage on very unequal terms in the past, especially with respect to emotional/sexual satisfaction (Giddens 1992: 62–3). On another level, however, the self-interest that fuels Giddens's 'pure relationship' is necessarily at odds with the 'outward motion' that we have identified as one of the principal 'gifts', and defining characteristics, of romantic love.

The a-temporal self

This last point leads me back to the connection between postmodern time and romantic love with which I opened the chapter. Whilst Giddens's model might offer sensible advice on how individuals may improve their *relationships* by putting the articulated 'needs' of the self at their centre, it does so by marginalizing what – for want of a better word – I shall call the 'spiritual' gifts traditionally associated with romantic love. This bonus, or benefit, may be seen to derive *from* the relationship via some form of the $x + y \rightarrow x' + y' \ [= z]$ function, but its satisfactions manifestly *exceed* the relationship and are possibly best described as a refiguration of *self in relation to world*.

As I have already proposed, romantic love and postmodern time may be seen as correlatives of one another in their capacity to transport the subject to radically new worlds. Moreover, although it is easiest to entertain this transportation as a largely *subjective* experience, theorists working within the 'new science' have long argued that our everyday experience of the world is determined by our partial version of it. In other words, our alternative apprehension of the world through certain emotional/hallucinatory experiences (love/drugs) are not necessarily any less 'real' or valid than those we associate with the everyday. Our changed experience of time and/or space in these states is, moreover, agreed to be associated with a high degree of aesthetic and spiritual pleasure. Thus, whilst most contemporary theorizing on utopias has been concerned with their political project (that is, to envisage new *social* formations and ways of living), those associated specifically with altered emotional states must also be assessed in terms of their aesthetic/spiritual 'reward'.

According to the thesis I have been pursuing throughout this book, it is, moreover, possible to make a link between the 'outward motion' of romantic love and chronotopic displacement. As has already been observed, the moment of romantic rapture/desire (*ravissement*) is frequently seen to entail a spatial-temporal dislocation in which time either 'stands still' or proceeds according to different rules. There is an excellent illustration of this in Winterson's *The Passion*, which I discuss below, but it is worth also noting its prevalence in the philosophies of love. Niklas Luhmann, for example, cites Stendhal (*De L'Amour* 1822) on the peculiarity of love-time:

> Intimacy is the concept taken to describe the blending of the happiness of the two lovers. . . . This is only possible if love is brought to a standstill and each person takes his or her cue from that moment. . . . Immersing oneself in the infinite moment was now the condition of experiencing oneself in the self-referential reference to love . . . (Luhmann 1986: 141)

Love, then, transforms 'self', 'time' and 'world' in one fell swoop comparable to Barthes's description of the period immediately following the *ravissement* as a 'hypnosis' (Barthes 1990: 198).

In terms of subjectivity, it would be easy to dismiss this 'effect' of chronotopic displacement as simply another instance of the *sublimation* of the self long associated with romantic love. What I wish to hold on to vis-à-vis an expressly postmodern vision of the world, however, is the way in which it rethinks the self not in relation to the *other* (nor, indeed, to an 'evacuated' sense of *self*), but vis-à-vis a changed vision of *the world* (see also Nancy 1991: 103–5). As Luhmann has noted, since the days of German Romanticism, philosophers have realized the capacity of love to transform the 'self–other–world' modality:

> German Romanticism of the time, however, progressed from seeing the world only in relation *to* another person to a re-evaluation of the world *through* that other person. Having refined characters and how they were treated only in psychological terms, Romanticism now moved on to a kind of subjective conception of the world. The world of objects (i.e. nature) became the sounding board of love. (Luhmann 1986: 132)

He notes, moreover, that in the literature of the period, this epistemological shift was registered by a significant reduction in spoken dialogue and a new narrative focus on 'the enchantment of objects through which the lovers experience their love in relation to each other' (Luhmann 1986: 132) This is clearly a truly revolutionary moment, not only in the history of romantic love but in the history of human subjectivity. What Romanticism initiated, and what a good deal of postmodernist literature has clearly carried forward, is a reconfiguration of the self not only in the direction of the human other (as discussed in the previous section) but *vis-à-vis* the world and its 'enchanted objects'.

If this line of thought may be seen to reconfigure human subjectivity, via love, through a projection/introjection of *space*, other theorists may be seen to have made a similar claim with respect to *time*. The moment of *ravissement* may, in this instance, be compared to Deleuze and Guattari's proposition that personality is best understood as an *event* (or, indeed, as a series of events) for which they invoke the term *haecceity* ('a singularity that is the result of a connection between elements or a relation to the non-subjectified affects which come from the outside' (Gibson 2001: 201)). What this amounts to is a definition of the subject as a palimpsest of events, both human and *non-human*, which – when reflected back onto interpersonal relations – would place a new emphasis not only on the interanimation of personalities $(x + y)$ but, more radically, also on the *specific chronotopes associated with the other*.

My argument here, then, is that the radical displacement of time-space associated with romantic love (at least, in its first rapture) is consonant with a version of postmodern subjectivity that goes beyond egocentric self–other relations to envisage a new modality of *self-in-relation-to-world*. There are, of course, strong similarities between this 'outward motion' and that identified by de Rougemont (1983) as the mystic impulse of Courtly Love, even though the 'alternative worlds' sought by the postmodernists are versions of earth rather than heaven. Many theorists have, indeed, tended to see these postmodern worlds in terms of Foucault's *heterotopias* rather than more benign, or heaven-like, *utopias*. McHale (1987) surveys a wide range of 'alternative worlds' associated with postmodernism via various genres, but claims the most interesting to be those figured (post-Einstein) as the *'parallel* worlds' enabled by certain versions of quantum physics. Jorge Luis Borges is identified as the 'father' of this particular sub-genre, of whose story 'The Garden of Forking Paths' (1970 [1962]) McHale writes: 'He believed in an infinite series of times, in a dizzily growing, ever-spreading network of diverging, converging and parallel times. This web of time – the strands of which approach one another, bifurcate, intersect or ignore each other through the centuries – embraces *every* possibility' (McHale 1987: 61).

The particular debt that Winterson owes to Borges in this respect will quickly become evident in the next section. By way of conclusion, here, I would simply remind readers that such visions would not have been possible without the radical de-centring of the subject *away* from the 'cultures of the self' during an era that – in terms of the *dominant* discourse –

appears to be obsessed by it. My further gambit, as will, by now, be clear, is that romantic love – with its infatuated eyes still fixed firmly on 'the other' – can be seen to be an active agent in that resistance.

II

Jeanette Winterson's The Passion: *Agapic Love Revisited*

What distinguishes Jeanette Winterson from other postmodernist – and, specifically, magic-realist – writers is her unswerving commitment to romantic love. Although other exponents of the genre – Borges, Márquez, Allende, Rushdie, Carter – may weave numerous, colourful love stories into their fictions, none of them makes romance their *focus* in quite the way Winterson does. As a consequence, she most certainly deserves her reputation as queen of 'the postmodern romance', notwithstanding the fact that – at a philosophical level – the two terms do not sit easily together. Inasmuch as romantic love is regarded as a 'grand narrative' predicated upon an unreconstructed version of the humanist subject, one must observe that it is seriously at odds with the principles of postmodernism according to its widespread definition. Various romantically inclined post-structuralists, such as Roland Barthes, have, of course, found a way around this by vaunting the experiential 'truth' of love precisely on account of its power *as an ideology*; in his definitive study of the condition, *A Lover's Discourse* (1990), he signals the fact that the seemingly subjective/universal experience is, in fact, profoundly ideological by citing the names of various writers, artists, philosophers in the margins of his text. The message is clear: we may think this experience is unique to us – that love has somehow miraculously risen within us – but its true origins lie in the stories we have heard, the films we have watched, the books we have read. Other writers (for example, Atwood (1982a [1969], 1982b [1976]) and Weldon (1984 [1983])) have taken a more aggressively ironic and unsympathetic line, whilst the 'lad-lit' of the 1980s and 1990s (see discussions in Part III following) deploys self-deprecating first-person narration to signal that its protagonists are fully, and cynically, aware of their manipulation by this *grand récit*. In a world of such playful, ironic knowingness, Winterson's novels may appear – on this epistemological level – like testaments from a former time. For although *stylistically* experimental and wedded to the redemptive powers of story-telling, they retain a profoundly essentialist belief in the uniqueness of both the individual subject and love; as the narrator of *Oranges Are Not the Only Fruit* observes: 'somewhere it is still in the original, written in tablets of stone' (Winterson 1985: 170). However, the fact that *The Passion* – via the character of Henri – sheds doubt on the credibility of this postmodern paradox (that is, the claim that love can be both unique and infinitely scriptable) is why I have chosen to write about it here in preference to her other novels.

In addition to being the Winterson text to engage with the constraints, as well as the possibilities, of romantic love with the greatest complexity, *The Passion* is also the first to tackle the relativities of time and space in an extended way. While the later *Sexing the Cherry* (1989) may address the implications of the 'new science' more directly (see Waugh 1995: 192–7), *The Passion* initiates Winterson's fascination with the notion of the parallel universe at the level of both narratology and characterization. Borges, as we saw at the end of the previous section, is allegedly the first writer to experiment with the 'forking-path' theory of the world that Villanelle voices here ('The point at which my selves broke away and one married a fat man and the other stayed here . . .' (Winterson 1987: 144)) and the text, as a whole, supports the view of all those scientists and philosophers who have argued for the partiality of human perception (see Price 1996: 5–8). The text also deploys a typical array of magic-realist narrative techniques to illustrate the simultaneous existence of multiple chronotopes (see Pearce 1994: 177).

But although *The Passion* makes some classic, postmodernist points about the perspectival nature of time through its textual method, it is the principal characters – Henri and Villanelle – who bear its philosophical burden. Following on from this, we need also to acknowledge that neither of them *is* a character in the traditional classic-realist sense. Although the manner of their first-person address enables the reader to feel some sympathy for them, they are – to invoke the distinctions of literary history – 'types' rather than characters (see Watt 1987 [1957]: 19). It would be difficult, for instance, to submit their profiles to deep psychoanalysis or to suggest that they are in any way conflicted/deluded in their apprehension of themselves or the world. Like the majority of Winterson's protagonists, they are, indeed, closer to the heroes and heroines of fairy-tales inasmuch as their *symbolism* exceeds their *psychological* value. Villanelle, in particular, is defined almost entirely through her actions and it is her status as a prototypical 'hero of romance' that enables her to magically survive and conquer all the obstacles thrown in her way (including, most importantly, the temporary loss of her heart). It is, however, their role as the mouthpieces for a set of opposing views on the love/time nexus that most surely hi-jacks their identities; as I shall now proceed to show, Henri and

Villanelle are used by Winterson to test out the metaphysical consequences of a wide range of love/time calibrations.

Although there is no escaping the fact that, *vis-à-vis* the philosophies of love and time, Henri and Villanelle occupy the status of binary opposites, I would suggest that this polarity incorporates a range of temporal inflections. These can be summarized briefly as shown in Table 7.1. According to this schema, Villanelle is associated with those temporal modalities that may be seen to derive from a broadly post-Einsteinian view of the universe and bear explicit connotations of existential freedom. To take the conceit (*pace* Bakhtin) of 'adventure-time', first: I have already noted Villanelle's similarity to the heroes of romance in terms of her typology, but it is also clear that her whole life has been lived – in spatio-temporal terms – in that blessed state of suspended animation that Bakhtin believed characterizes literary adventure romance:

> In this kind of time, nothing changes: the world remains as it was, the biographical lives of the heroes do not change, their feelings do not change, people do not even age. This empty time leaves no traces anywhere, no indications of its passing. This, we repeat, is an extra temporal hiatus that appears between two moments of a real time sequence, in this case one that is biographical. (Bakhtin 1981: 91)

As I have noted elsewhere, this 'time-out-of-time' makes Bakhtin's 'adventure-time' consonant with a more broadly conceived 'chronotope of romantic love' (see Pearce 1994: 177), but what marks Villanelle out for particular identification with the former is the fact that her love for the lady with the elegant house and oval dining table takes place *alongside* a whole series of swashbuckling adventures. Indeed, when she returns to Venice after an eight years' absence, Villanelle has 'grown-up' (Winterson 1987: 143) rather than aged and – even more importantly – her 'essential self' remains unchanged. Even at the very end of the story, she is still seen to occupy the 'empty-time' of the mythic hero/heroine: as she rows past Henri's window, her hair is as red as ever. It is Henri, moreover, who

Table 7.1 *Chronotope and character in The Passion*

Villanelle	Henri
Adventure-time (cf. Bakhtin)	Nostalgia (including 'anticipatory retrospection')
Epiphany	Belatedness
Relativity (cf. parallel worlds)	(Traumatic) moment-in-time

indirectly observes the connection between Villanelle's adventuring and her freedom from nostalgia (his own particular curse). After she has told him and Patrick the story of her life to date, he observes: 'She seemed care-free and the shadows that crossed her face throughout her story had lifted, but I felt my own were just beginning' (Winterson 1987: 99). In crude therapy-speak, Villanelle is an exemplary patient: she has her adventures, tells their story – then moves on.

This capacity to exploit, and manage, time rather than become its victim is also manifest in Villanelle's approach to the two other temporal modalities I have associated her with: the epiphany and the notional existence of parallel worlds. Probably the most consummate illustration of the former is, not surprisingly, the moment she first meets her lover. Already granted its own special chronotope, Venice (a city which used to have its own calendar (Winterson 1987: 56)) becomes the spectacular backdrop to Villanelle's *ravissement* and, as can be seen, Winterson does not shy away from the clichés:

> She held the glass in a silent toast, perhaps at her own good fortune. The Queen of spades is a serious win and one we are usually careful to avoid. Still she did not speak, but watched me through the crystal and suddenly draining her glass stroked the side of my face. Only for a second she touched me and then she was gone and I was left with my heart smashing at my chest and three-quarters of a bottle of best champagne. I was careful to conceal both. . . . At midnight the gunpowder triggered and the sky above St Mark's broke into a million coloured pieces. The fireworks lasted perhaps half an hour . . . (Winterson 1987: 59–60)

As a consequence of this lightning-bright *coup de foudre*, Villanelle is seen to be thrown into the euphoric 'time-out' that is consequent upon *ravissement*. Although, as I have already suggested, her whole life may be seen to be lived outwith the constraints of chronological time due to her status as an 'adventure hero', here Winterson focuses more narrowly on the temporal dislocations of romantic love:

> Dawn breaks.
>
> I spent the weeks that followed in a hectic stupor.
>
> Is there such a thing? There is. It is the condition that most resembles a particular kind of nervous disorder. I have seen ones like me in San Servelo. It manifests itself as a compulsion to be forever doing something, however meaningless. The body must move but the mind is blank . . .
>
> I lost weight.
>
> I found myself staring into space, forgetting where I was going.
>
> I was cold. (Winterson 1987: 62)

This is, moreover, a temporal aberration that Winterson cannot resist philosophizing, making it clear that what has transformed Villanelle's apprehension of 'the present' is the fact that all her hopes and desires are now filtered through a *fantasy* of past and future:

> Without past and future, the present is partial. All time is eternally present, and so all time is ours. There is no sense in forgetting, and every sense in dreaming. Thus the present is made rich. Thus the present is made whole. On the lagoon this morning, with the past at my elbow, rowing beside me, I see the future glimmering on the water. (Winterson 1987: 62)

Elsewhere in the novel this view of time is contrasted not only with Henri's but also with Domino's (Henri's close friend and another foot-soldier in Napoleon's army), who espouses an overly simplistic 'belief' in the present ('There's only now' (Winterson 1987: 29)). The text's message in this regard may thus be summed up as a philosophical exhortation, in the manner of Ernst Bloch, to positively embrace active day-dreaming.[6] The further implication is that a healthy and fulfilling present is one that draws on past and future *in equal measure*; a present that is framed solely by the past will result in Henri's 'window' on the world.

Yet the most overtly postmodern articulation of time that Villanelle is associated with is, of course, that encapsulated in the notion of 'parallel worlds'. The scientific/philosophical and literary origins of the concept have already been discussed, but once we start exploring how these alter-realities are actually experienced/embodied by Villanelle we discover the lurking presence of postmodernism's gangster twins, *nostalgia* and *belatedness*. In the same way that the text as a whole does not permit the spirit of magic realism to totally redeem the tragic will of romantic love, so does it also resist the notion that Villanelle's lateral thinking is necessarily an emotional solution to all affairs of the heart. Whilst Henri might believe that Villanelle has 'imagined' herself out of her corner ('I'm not like Villanelle, I don't see hidden worlds in the palm of my hand nor a future in a clouded ball' (Winterson 1987: 153)), she herself is frequently tormented by her *exclusion* from the worlds she has seen but can no longer touch. The fact that 'the other life' goes on so palpably is anything but a consolation. By the end of the novel, moreover, Villanelle's feelings regarding these 'hidden worlds' appear to have hardened into fear and suspicion. Indeed, she now equates that way of thinking with disreality, madness and the more mundane double-consciousness of an affair: 'I don't dress up any more. No borrowed uniforms. Only occasionally do I feel the touch of that other life, the one in the shadows where I do not choose to live' (Winterson 1987: 150). Villanelle may not have given up her post-Einsteinian view of the universe entirely, but – equated as it is here with the shadow-life of a past love-affair – it is no longer how/where she wishes to 'choose to live'. Surprising? Disappointing? Or simply further evidence that this is, indeed, the one text in which Winterson has allowed the tragic, earth-bound, time-bound version of romantic love to triumph despite its early flaunting of the opposite?

The simplest way to figure Henri's relation to/embodiment of love-time is to present him as a character stuck tragically in the past (see Pearce 1995: 164). What he represents in terms of a thoroughgoing postmodern temporality is rather more complex than this, however; and especially when we consider that his proclivity to nostalgia pre-dated his love for Villanelle. The dominant modality with which he is associated in Part I of the novel is, indeed, that of *anticipatory retrospection*: a concept that describes a subject's tendency to imagine *present* events from a hypothetical future.[7] There are numerous instances of this, but here are just two:

> It is hard to remember that this day will never come again. That this time is now and the place is here and there are no second chances at a single moment. During the days that Bonaparte stayed in Boulogne there was a feeling of urgency and privilege . . . (Winterson 1987: 19)

> This year is gone, I told myself. This year is slipping away and it will never return. Domino's right, there's only now. Forget it. Forget it. You can't bring it back. You can't bring them back. (Winterson 1987: 42)

But Henri is cursed by his nature 'never to forget', and – as here – is acutely aware that his experience of being in a pleasurable present is undermined both by its transience and the fact that – in the future – it can only be imperfectly remembered. This, of course, is what causes him to start writing the diaries Domino mocks ('I don't care about the facts, Domino, I care about how I feel. How I feel will change, I want to remember that' (Winterson 1987: 29)). But the real curse, as he knows, is the way the future will subvert the past: the way in which intervening events, and memories, will spoil whatever image one attempts to preserve.

There are other moments in the text, however, when Henri is tormented less by how the treacherous future will rewrite the past and/or steal it than by its traumatic inescapability. I have written elsewhere about the links that may be drawn between the 'traumatic moment' (as conceived by psychologists) and the condition of being in love (see Pearce 2004: 527–31 and Chapter 1), and in many respects Henri's intense but unrequited love for Villanelle demonstrates the point. His account of the first time he makes love with Villanelle is, for example, stuck in his memory as an 'eternal present' that is both spectacularly vivid and 'ob/scene' (Winterson 1987:

103; see also note 5 to Chapter 1).Whilst the place in which Henri 'will always be' is, literally, the mad-house on San Servelo, the passage is clearly also meant as a window onto his traumatized mental state. Although he is doing the traditionally therapeutic thing of telling his story, he fails to make progress and is apparently stuck, for ever, in the illusory moment of hope that Villanelle might, after all, return his love.

The twist to Henri's story *vis-à-vis* the whirligig of time may, however, be read as an ironic mirror-opposite of Villanelle's. Whilst we see her faith in 'the path not taken and the forgotten angle' (Winterson 1989: 2) hit the brick wall of her unrealizable desire, *The Passion* ends with Henri becoming quietly reconciled to his tragic view of the world. In narrative terms, this is dramatized by his refusal to leave San Servelo; his past might be a tragic one, but he has learnt to live with it, as well as with his unalterable, irreversible love for Villanelle:

> Why would I want to get out? They're so preoccupied with getting out, they miss what's here . . .
>
> Where would I go? I have a room, a garden, company and time for myself. Aren't these the things people ask for?
>
> And love?
>
> I'm still in love with her. Not a day breaks but that I think of her, and when the dogwood turns red in winter I stretch out my hands and imagine her hair. (Winterson 1987: 157)

Unlike Villanelle, then, Henri is not interested in a 'reprieve' (Winterson 1997: 151) but has found an unexpected salvation in the *acceptance* of his love and his lot ('I know what I want and I can't have it' (Winterson 1987: 122)). This is a brave conclusion, both for him as a character and for the novel as a whole, and leads me on to some final thoughts on the way in which this text engages with a classically conceived agapic model of love. If we remind ourselves of the behaviour(s) typically associated with agapic love, we can see that, in most particulars, Henri and Villanelle are its faithful exponents. Both love instantly and with little regard for their beloved's 'properties', the key signature of erosic love ; one might even say they love blindly – *without seeing* – in an involuntary reflex that can only be explained as the working out of destiny (see Winterson 1987: 62, 88). And although Henri's moment of *ravissement* may conceivably be seen to have been inspired by an expression of Villanelle's personality through a linguistic act (she tells him that all snowflakes are different), it is, at most, a 'property' in the order of Barthes's 'fragment of behaviour' (Barthes 1990: 191). Thinking back to Chapter 3, readers will be minded just how far such 'fragments of behaviour' are from the socially and morally inflected 'properties' sought out by Jane Austen's heroes and heroines. In the case of Villanelle's rapture, moreover, cognition is further impeded by the fact that both she and her object-ideal are *in disguise* (Winterson 1987: 59); there is no question here, clearly, of individuals falling in love on account of the personality indicated by a 'nice smile' or 'good sense of humour'. Passion-love can be explained *only* as a quirk of the body (see Barthes) and/or a quirk of time: 'How is it that one day life is orderly and you are content, a little cynical perhaps but on the whole just so, and then without warning you find the solid floor is a trap door and you are now in another place whose geography is uncertain and whose customs are strange?' (Winterson 1987: 68).

As well as being involuntary and unlinked to 'personal properties' in any definitive sense, both Henri and Villanelle also make a good show of their loves being exclusive and unconditional. Where they do part company, however, is on the issue of love's (non-)repeatability. Villanelle's story, in fact, centres on her quest to 'win back her heart', whilst Henri knows his love to be irrevocable and unto death: 'Once more, what difference would it make to be near her again? Only this. That if I start to cry I will never stop' (Winterson 1987: 159). In terms of love-time, Henri's story ends where it begins (his heart has not faltered), whilst Villanelle – whose love for the woman with the elegant house and oval table appears to have been agapic in every other regard – has moved on ('I take my boat out on the lagoon and listen to the seagulls cry and wonder where I will be in eight years, say' (Winterson 1987: 150)).

But it is really as simple as that? We have already seen, in Chapter I, how exercised philosophers have been over the issue of whether longevity, up to and indeed *beyond* death, is the only 'real' test of agapic love. On this point, it would be fair to point out that – in true fairy-tale fashion – Villanelle only manages to revert to her original (and 'free') state through the help of a 'magical agent' (Henri: whose self-sacrificing love symbolically rescues her heart) and that, for all her bravado, there is no guarantee that she *will* fall in love again. Indeed, it could be that here, as in her initial enthusiasm for parallel worlds, she has been overly confident. However we look at it, love depends, for its meaning, on time:

$$\left(\frac{x+y \rightarrow x'+y'}{[\text{T}]} \right)$$

And while, in the first instance, there appears to be a logic in associating agapic love with what the Stoics called 'aionic time' (and, by extension, the proposition that travellers in that dimension will be rewarded by an experience of love not bound by chronological time), the literary history of romance militates against it.[8] 'Passion-love', as we have already seen through the example of *Wuthering Heights* (Chapter 4), often has to pay dearly on earth for the gift of immortality, and the 'time-out' associated with the first moment of *ravissement* is (according to Barthes) necessarily succeeded by a *sequel* in which love is put through new tests and trials, many of them associated with an unremitting chronological time (for example, the agony of 'Waiting' (see Barthes 1990: 37–40)). It would seem, then, that agapic, as well as erosic, love is bound by *chronos* even as it aspires to – and may yet achieve – *aion*. Henri, safe in his cell at San Servelo, appears to have, at last, realized this and prepared himself – in true mystical fashion – to wait patiently for the day when *chronos* will yield to *aion* and his dedication be rewarded. To quote one of Winterson's own favourite intertexts: 'Only through time time is conquered' (Eliot 1959 [1940]: 16).

III

Millennial Love

It will be remembered that I ended Part I of this chapter by suggesting that romantic love, with its centuries-long tradition of losing 'the self' in 'the other', may be figured as an antidote for the 'culture(s) of the self' that (according to one reading of the postmodern) appear to have consumed the contemporary Western world. In this final section, I shall pursue that proposition further via a selection of texts that look in both directions. As throughout its history, romantic love emerges as a discourse that is annexed by conservative and radical, mainstream and marginal, alike.

I thus start with those texts which, from the 1980s onwards, have attempted to accommodate romantic love within the culture(s) of the self. Foremost amongst these is, of course, the popular romance genre itself, whose story we left unfinished in Chapter 6. The first thing to observe here is that – contrary to popular perception – the 1980s was the all-time high-point of the Mills & Boon industry (see Dixon 1999 and Paizis 1998). Following the merger of Mills & Boon and Harlequin (its North American equivalent) in 1970, consumption rocketed from 27 million books in 1972 to 250 million by the mid-1980s (Dixon 1999: 20) This huge growth in sales can be partly attributed to a massive expansion in terms of the world market but also to a new targeting of readers in terms of interests and, indeed, *lifestyle*. It was during this period that the company expanded, and consolidated, the sub-genres for which it is now famous – 'Contemporary',

'Love Affair', 'Temptation', 'Masquerade' 'Medical', and so on (Dixon 1999: 23–4). Since their introduction, moreover, there has been a tendency for these niche markets to become ever more specialist (there are now series aimed at particular zodiac signs or focused on specific events like Christmas, for example) and the indication is that it is these lifestyle indicators, just as much as the degree of sexual explicitness involved in the stories, that attract readers to particular brands. It is obvious, moreover, that this re-packaging of the Mills & Boon product in market terms cannot be kept separate from the presentation of romantic love within the stories themselves. What all scholars working in this area are agreed upon, indeed, is that the heroine's needs and expectations *have* changed over time, although the positive interpretation usually offered (that the authors/texts have been responsive to feminism (see Dixon 1999: 195)) can certainly be countered with the argument that the change is better understood in the context of the changing culture(s) of the self. Inasmuch as the romantic love paradigm endorsed by Mills & Boon is one which puts the satisfaction/self-actualization of the heroine at its core and, as I suggested in Chapter 6, effectively dispenses with the hero once that has been achieved ($x + y \rightarrow x' - y$), it is all too easy to assume that what is really going on here is a *diversification* in the *self*-identities offered the heroine. Whilst in the 1950s–1970s this rarely went beyond an 'authentic' sexual self, post-1980s consumer/lifestyle culture has brought a wide range of matching accessories. Sometimes, for sure, these are presented in terms of career choices, but it is manifest that it is the glamour/kudos of these lifestyles that is being promoted rather than any meaningful observation on women's liberation.

A significant variant of popular romance that also significantly expanded its market share in the 1980s is the female 'block-buster'. Associated with the rise of Thatcherism/Reaganism, yuppiedom and increasingly sexually explicit lifestyle magazines such as *Cosmopolitan* (see Winship 1987), the novels of writers such as Jackie Collins and Judith Krantz quickly established themselves at the top of best-sellers lists and heralded a new era in 'women's fiction'. What was different about these texts was not only their raunchy sexuality and super-glamorous locations (this was also, after all, the era of *Dallas* and *Dynasty*) but the fact that in their celebration of fast-changing, episodic sexual relationships they may be seen to be radically *anti-romance*. As Ken Gelder has observed, Collins was one of the first 'sex and shopping' novelists, focusing on characters for whom 'celebrity-style fame, lots of money and good sex' are the *only* objectives (Gelder 2004: 129); whether this particular mode of *anti-romance* can be considered feminist in any meaningful sense or not is, of course, another question (see Robertson 1996). In terms of the history and evolution of the romance genre, such texts nevertheless represent a spectacular limit-point. With their formal origins in eighteenth-century picaresque, these block-buster anti-romances toss their heroines from one steamy board-room/bedroom to another with little thought of past or future. Both in their rejection of the classic 'narrative logic of romance' (Radway 1984) and their 'anti-love' philosophy, one might, indeed, be inclined to argue that these texts have scant affinity with romantic fiction *per se* were it not for their genealogical link to the next market category to be considered here: so-called 'chick-lit'.

Ten years after the first publication of Helen Fielding's *Bridget Jones's Diary* (2001 [1996]), the word coming through the media is that the concept that is 'Bridget' has had its day. Many women, feminist or otherwise, will doubtless greet this prediction with a sigh of relief, but there is no disputing the fact that during the past decade Fielding's novels – and the accompanying films – have seized the popular imagination in a powerful way. According to most commentators, the key to the success of the Bridget Jones phenomenon is that she is a latter-day 'Everywoman'; as the review in *The Times* (quoted on the back of the 2001 paperback edition) declares: 'any woman who has had a job, a relationship or indeed a mother will read it and roar' (Fielding 2001). Once again, then, we are back with the idea (regarded with horror by Zygmunt Bauman) that personal relationships have become but *one* in a list of lifestyle challenges. The form and presentation of Bridget's diary totally endorses this view via such comic effects as the heroine putting her weight and estimated calorie intake at the head of every diary entry. Here is a very visible indicator that – for Bridget – 'the project of the self' has engulfed all other objectives, including her quest for coupledom. Indeed, readers are left with the sneaking suspicion that – Mark Darcy's redemptive re-appearance notwithstanding – getting the man *without* the weight reduction (she is now a massive *9st 5lb!*) is a form of cheating. Bridget can never secure permanent happiness (as Fielding's sequel *Bridget Jones: The Edge of Reason* (2004 [2000]) attests) because happiness is, above all, a privilege to be *worked at*; the New Right ideology that gave rise to the unbounded sense of *entitlement* celebrated by Jackie Collins's heroines mutates – in the 1990s – into the anxious second cousin that is 'Bridget Jones'.

Shelved next to 'chick-lit' we have, of course, 'lad-lit', and it is worth reflecting briefly on the similarities and differences between the two genres. Although capturing the imagination of millions of readers (women and non-Arsenal fans as well as men) through the deployment of *partially* 'fucked-up' heroes who are often characterized as the male equivalent of Bridget Jones, Nick Hornby's 'lad-lit' classics *Fever Pitch* (1992) and *High Fidelity* (1995) inevitably articulate 'lifestyle' and 'romance' in significantly different ways. No matter how visible his vulnerabilities, the contemporary male ('new', unreconstructed or – as in these texts – a typically 'laddish' mixture of both) will never have to *work* at his lifestyle in the same way that Bridget does. As any examination of the explosion of men's magazines from the late 1980s and 1990s will attest, lifestyle might have become a *commodity* for men, but it is rarely presented as a 'project'.[9] Moreover, the vast majority of the lad's lifestyle effects (such as: knowledge of football, knowledge of music, 'GSOH', capacity to consume large amounts of alcohol and remain standing) do not require (much) money *or* effort; they are seen, rather, as the genealogical inheritance of the 'average lad'. What *has* to be worked at, of course, is romantic love. Lads need it, but they cannot admit to it; and when they get anywhere close to it, they either blow it or run. Although many laddish authors (for example, Martin Amis and Will Self) are often seen to revel in overtly misogynistic male characters, this is usually as the result of a visibly conflicted masculinity, especially as regards the pressures of heterosexual sex. Excusing themselves with large doses of self-deprecating humour, these literary lads explore the forces that have prevented them succeeding in long-term relationships, *vis-à-vis* which lifestyle activities such as football and music become mysterious totems. Fandom, it seems, is an easier and more reliable means of self-transformation and sublimation ($x \rightarrow x'$] than a girlfriend whose presence ever threatens to extinguish the thrill of the unknown (next Saturday's result, X's next album) in suffocating domesticity.

Having thus observed some of the limit-points of romantic love amongst the more popular genres, I now turn – in the final pages of this book – to a consideration of those textual spaces/places where the ['] lives on.

In terms of the philosophical tradition, it will be remembered that the ['] of love tends to have been identified with Agape rather than Eros. Within this paradigm, moreover, the ['] is associated with *a sudden moment of 'recognition'* (x spots something s/he has always known existed and has been waiting for); this, indeed, accounts for why x can fall in love with y without knowing anything about them or their 'properties'. Upon reflection, and having now worked my way through many hundreds of texts on, and about, romantic love, I have concluded that this element of *shock* or *surprise* is, indeed, a key constituent of love in its romantic form. Moreover, if we pause to consider what most commonly precipitates the *coup de foudre*, we (re)discover another factor long considered central in the instigation of both love and sexual desire: that is, *difference*. Articulated thus, it is possible to link the moment/manner of the lover's initial 'surprise' with the constitution of the other's difference: an equation that would help explain how – in the realm of specifically romantic love – *x* is 'seized' by *y*'s difference and singularity before s/he can even register them as 'properties'. Our further challenge here, however, must be to square this insight at the level of deep structure with the millennial transformation of intimacy considered earlier in the chapter. Does it help explain, for example, why romantic love *per se* might appear to be becoming increasingly mythical and/or defunct as a discourse? Why erosic love, or Giddens's 'confluent love', is taking its place as the more desirable/sensible lifestyle choice? Perhaps. For the white, middle-class heterosexual, certainly, the last century has seen a radical relaxation of those sorts of social controls – such as social/geographic mobility, parental approval, the prohibition of sex before marriage – that actually *facilitated* the 'sudden' arrival of a dangerous/desirable 'other' in one's life. Surprises, after all, most commonly occur when we are straying where we should not. Yet even if this is an experiential 'truth' for *some* social-cultural groups, and reflected in *some* literary genres, it can hardly be assumed to be the objective of us all. I therefore turn, in these last pages, to a brief overview of those texts and genres where romantic love – in its unreconstructed form – appears to have taken refuge and where, most importantly, the ['] has been sustained.

First amongst these genres are fantasy and historiographical metafiction (Hutcheon 1988: 5). To take the latter first, many readers will be aware that, with *Possession* (1990), A. S. Byatt produced the most successful *romantic* metafictional text since Fowles's *The French Lieutenant's Woman* (1977 [1969]). It is certainly *the* text to which all scholars interested in postmodern romance refer (see Morgan 2004: 502–20), and has become the model for a number of interesting variants, including the widely acclaimed *The Map of Love* by Adhaf Soueif (1999). What metafiction facilitates, in particular, is the simultaneous expression of foundationalist/essentialist thinking (that is, a belief in the truth-value of romantic love) and its relativization/questioning through a number of frame-narratives. Yet what strikes me about both *Possession* and *The Map of Love* is the fact that the Ur-historical romances to which both texts refer for inspiration singularly fail to convince; any ['] between the characters in the historical present depends less upon this inheritance (figured as a surprise/revelation) than upon contemporary circumstances. The fact that, in *The Map of Love*, Isabel's cross-cultural relationship with Rajeev Seth has been prefigured in the affair between her grandmother, Lady Anna Winterbourne, and the

Egyptian nationalist, Sharif, matters far less than the way in which Seth, himself, explodes upon Isabel's present-day, white, middle-class world (Soueif 1999: 48). Indeed, the texts of historiographical metafiction may be seen to play a risky game when it comes to the representation of romance, since the frame-breaks/meta-commentary will inevitably interrupt the reader's enjoyment of the *principal* love story. In this regard, indeed, metafiction formally, and flagrantly, breaks the rules of popular romance (no cynicism, no irony, no jokes, no sending oneself up) and frustrates the 'willing suspension of disbelief' considered a non-negotiable staple of the genre.

The fantasy worlds of science fiction, meanwhile, may be seen to facilitate the ['] of romance rather more successfully on account of their thoroughgoing dislocation of time, space and history. The most exciting aspect of SF romance is, indeed, its ability to enable relationships *across* both species and worlds that (superficially, at least) bear no relation to our own, and hence enable us to explore the role of 'difference' in romantic love/desire with fresh eyes. I have written elsewhere (see Pearce 1998: 98–111) on Marge Piercy's fantasy fiction in this regard, and, in particular, her splendid novel *Body of Glass* (1991), in which Shira's relationship with the cyborg Yod is a truly spectacular illustration of a new romantic love modality that is generated and, indeed, *sustained* by the lovers' exclusion from/opposition to historical/cultural events and affiliative norms. Assuming, as we have done, that couples – in the contemporary Western world – are likely to encounter far fewer obstacles of this kind than they used to (*vis-à-vis* the protocols of marriage and kinship), there is perhaps little surprise that we turn to the 'other worlds' of SF to pursue our lingering fascination with the *obstacles* that have traditionally precipitated romantic love. The relationship between Shira and Yod – like that between Deckard and the replicant Rachel, in the original version of Ridley Scott's film *Blade Runner* (Scott 1982) – is arresting, and affecting, precisely on account of the fact that it returns us to the differences that define, and sustain, love.[10] Yet what is significant in both these instances is that the cross-species difference between the lovers ultimately defines their love far less than the difference between them and the hostile world that they inhabit. Caught in a dark, dystopian future, their passion (to parody Winterson (1987)) is 'somewhere between defiance and fear';[11] thus whilst, in earlier chapters of this book, we have seen lovers realize the 'gift of love' in creative *manufacture* of some product (z), here it is figured as an external agent or threat (T) ($x + y$ vs $T \rightarrow x' + y'$); the all-important element of difference moves from *inside* to *outside* the relationship and is thus (in hostile worlds) infinitely sustainable. This is romance as 'you and me against the world' played out, quite literally, for ever.

Another genre to exploit this dynamic is the noir thriller, in both its literary and filmic forms (see Horsley 2001). Exactly how the 'doomed couple against the world' scenario is played out in these texts depends, as Lee Horsley has observed, on whether the director's overall objective is 'more' or 'less' noir;[12] while some canonical film noir texts give way to a Hollywood-style 'happy ending' (see Dawes, *Dark Passage*, 1947), the intensity of others such as *Out of the Past* (Tourneur 1947) depends upon the fact that *we know* that the relationship between the two lovers is ultimately bound to fail – and spectacularly. Also annexed to the noir thriller are the distinctive stable of film texts – from *Bonnie and Clyde* (Penn 1967) and *Butch Cassidy and the Sundance Kid* (Hill 1969) through to *Natural Born Killers* (Stone 1994), *True Romance* (T. Scott 1993) and *Sin City* (Rodriguez 2005) – in which the romantic/erotic charge between the lovers is created, and sustained, by their participation in (often violent) criminal acts. Whether these are to be regarded as 'true crimes' or acts of liberation will depend, of course, on both the moral status of the (purported) 'victim' and, once again, whether the film's objective is 'more' or 'less' noir. All the most successful noir texts are, however, characterized by an ambiguity of emotion and an indeterminacy of ending which lend a particular poignancy to the lovers' plight; exactly who, or what, constitutes *T* remains necessarily unclear.

Having played my theoretical trump card early, it seems that I am compelled to come back to earth – generically speaking – for my final few words. Having determined that difference, experienced first as shock, surprise or, indeed, trauma, is, and remains, one of the key defining features of a specifically *romantic* love, it makes sense to assume that the times/spaces in which it is likely to survive – notwithstanding the steady encroachment of individualist/lifestyle culture – are those in which 'difference' is most visibly marked and enabled. Whilst literary and other texts (most notably, film) have made SF a truly spectacular occasion for the exploration of such difference, it is clear that any writer whose interest is in worlds *where life is lived in opposition to T* is likely to keep his, or her, finger on the pulse of romantic love.

It is clearly for this reason that some of the most compelling late twentieth-century romance to be produced in the Western world has been that which focuses on the experience of diverse ethnic groups within a dominant white culture. A similar case can, of course, be made for homosexual romance, although the increasingly relaxed accommodation of gay relationships within the middle-class mainstream may be seen to have reduced the *T* factor *vis-à-vis* this category of texts. Indeed, as we move further into the twenty-first century, it would probably be fair to say that this particular incarnation of gay/lesbian romance has largely had its day, which is not to say that texts may yet be produced in which the specificity of homosexual romance is defined in this way (see Woods 1998: Chapter 31). Indeed, one particular category of contemporary fiction where notionally 'deviant' homosexuality is likely to remain a live concern is in the writings of non-white groups, where it exists in volatile relationship to a more explicitly ethnic/religious expression of *T*.

One British author who has worked at this particular interface for many years is Hanif Kureishi, whose texts/productions, from *Sammy and Rosie Get Laid* (Frears 1987) through *The Buddha of Suburbia* (1990) to *Intimacy* (1998), have included many memorable examples of romantic love flourishing in hostile circumstances. Like Carter and Winterson, Kureishi may also be thought of as a writer who was 'Queer' before his time: that is, he celebrated a wide range of highly mobile sexualities/sexual identifications before Sedgwick, Butler *et al.* theorized the possibility (see Oswell 1998 and Ilona 2003). Where his texts gain their particular edge, however, is in their insistence that these are not easy 'choices' for the subjects concerned. The film *My Beautiful Laundrette* (Frears 1985) is an excellent case in point in this regard: although the story ends with (white, working-class) Johnny (re)united with his (Asian, upwardly mobile) lover Omar, there is absolutely no chance that the hostile world outside the brightly lit launderette will fade away. Both characters are effectively 'marked for life' (see Magrs 1996) (Omar by his colour, Johnny by his National Front past), and their romance, even as it is sustained by *T*, remains precarious.

Within the broader context of postmodernism, what Kureishi's writing points to, above all, is that one cannot necessarily guarantee survival in the contemporary world by simply becoming a 'player' (Horsley 2001: 193).[13] Although this is now a popular, and useful, concept to explain the way in which postmodern individuals can wrest back a certain degree of agency in a world that is all spectacle and simulacra, it is clear that its exercise will be limited to certain groups (literary and otherwise). A redeeming twist to this particular exclusivity, however, is that it would appear to be those who are most thwarted in their actualization of the self (whether in this world, or in the simulacrum of some future noir fantasy) that are most likely to experience the beauty, *amidst the terror*, of romantic love. Those condemned, for whatever reason, to the social and cultural margins will never lack the opportunity to be *surprised* by the other, who, by some miracle, may also be 'the One'.

Notes

Chapter 1 Introduction: The Alchemy of Love

1 In his essay 'The Secret Life of the Love Song', Nick Cave cites W. H. Auden on 'the so-called traumatic moment' which lies in wait for each individual 'in order that its life become a serious matter' (Cave 2001: 6). For Cave, the trauma/sorrow of love and the creative process are inextricably linked: 'the desire, or more accurately, the need, to articulate the various feelings of loss and longing . . . have whistled through my bones and hummed in my blood all my life' (Cave 2001: 13).

2 Of the texts considered in this volume I would include: Barthes (1990 [1977]), Bauman (2003), de Rougemont (1983 [1940]), Giddens (1992), Nancy (1991), Paizis (1998), Soble (1990).

3 It is, of course, debatable whether love can, or should, be considered an 'emotion' or (as my colleague, Jackie Stacey, has observed) is better understood as a dynamic which is constituted by a range of emotions (for example, anxiety, fear, joy).

4 'Spectacular Spectacular': a reference to Baz Luhrmann's film *Moulin Rouge* (2001). Visually sumptuous, this postmodern and anachronistic treatment of a love story set in 1920s Paris has, as part of its central narrative thread, the production of a play called *Spectacular Spectacular*. This hyperbolic parody of the text's main action is a wonderfully shrewd comment on our desperate need for visibility, story and, indeed, cliché in the experience and understanding of romantic love.

5 I am indebted to my Ph.D. student Beth Johnson (2007) for alerting me to the powerful relay of the seen and the unseen ('ob/scene') in the production of sexual desire.

6 This is distinct from erotic love, and comprises 'the eros of Plato's *Symposium*, sexual love, courtly love, and romantic love' (Soble 1990: 2).

7 The extent to which romantic love entails a transformation of both x and y (and, indeed, of x in y) is also central to the work of Jean-Luc Nancy. See discussion following.

8 For a detailed discussion of 'Platonic love' (more properly, Aristophanic love), see Soble (1990: 78–81). For more on love as the 'oceanic merger' of two complementary halves in psychoanalytic theory, see Benjamin (1990) on 'inter-subjectivity'. Many readings of Freud, Lacan and Kristeva also characterize the early stages of ego development in these terms (see Wright 1992 on 'the semiotic' (195–6) and 'primary narcissism' (55–6)).

9 This part of Radway's analysis owes much to Nancy Chodorow's *Reproduction of Mothering* (1978), which offers a psychoanalytic explanation (via Melanie Klein) for why male and female children respond differently to the patterns of intimacy and dependence established in childhood (see Radway 1984: 135–40).

10 The conventions of Courtly Love (literary and otherwise) entailed a noblewoman 'favouring' a particular knight as her 'liege lord'; he, in turn, would demonstrate unerring devotion to her (through chastity and/or risking his life) in full knowledge that she could not return his 'gift' because of her already-married status.

11 Ragland-Sullivan, in her summary of Lacan's position on narcissism, emphasizes the fact that for him (unlike Freud) it was a normative and not a pathological function of the ego (see Wright 1992: 272).

12 See Lacan's Seminar VII, in which he affirms: 'There is no other good than that which may serve to pay the price for access to desire – given that desire is understood as the metonymy of our being' (Lacan 1992 [1959–60]: 321). By the same token, 'giving up on' desire (what Lacan himself refers to as 'giving ground relative to one's desire') must necessarily be revisited upon the subject in the form of guilt and (self-)betrayal. I am indebted to Scott Wilson for both this insight and its source in Lacan.

13 Nancy (1991: 91) also observed that it is *only* in the Occident that the wide range of figures and forms that 'we know as love' are brought together in one absolute and universal whole.

Chapter 2 Romance before the Eighteenth Century: The Gift of a Name

1 Margaret Cavendish, Duchess of Newcastle, was one of the most celebrated (indeed, notorious) noblewomen of her day, and not only for her writings, which were prolific in the extreme. The term generally associated with her was 'extravagance', be this in dress, conversation or behaviour, and it is clear that she held a strong fascination for women like Osborne, who secretly craved her visibility (see Osborne's Letter 17). See Graham *et al.* (1989: 87–9) for further biographical information. Cavendish's closet-drama *The Convent of Pleasure* will also be discussed in Part III of this chapter.

2 In understanding the differences between these texts, there is a crucial distinction to be made between *romantic* fictions, 'in which [the hero] is superior to other men', and *mimetic* fictions, 'in which he is superior neither to other men nor to the environment' (see Barron 2004: 67).

3 See, for example, Malory's extended treatment of Guinevere's psychological crisis in Book XX of Volume II of *Le Morte d'Arthur* (Malory 1969).

4 'Double-voiced discourse': a term derived from Bakhtin's work (see Bakhtin 1981 [1934–41], 1984 [1929]) and referring, broadly, to any discourse (spoken or written) which is oriented towards one or more interlocutors. For further discussion, see my *Reading Dialogics* (Pearce 1994: 43, 50–4, 85–6).

5 The Marxist critic Louis Althusser (1984 [1970]) draws an important distinction between the 'State Apparatus' (the police, army, judiciary) and the 'Ideological State Apparatus', consisting of education, the media, religion and discourses / value systems favoured by the state at an ideological level.

6 It is not altogether clear why Temple's letters to Osborne have not survived, but the common assumption is that she had to dispose of them immediately for security reasons. Moore Smith, however, suggests that Temple himself destroyed them after his wife's death (Osborne 1928: xliv).

7 For further discussion of the inclusion of gifts in letters, see Clay (2006: 68–9). Although it is possible to see these enclosures as a proxy for the absent-self (most obvious in the case of photographs), it would seem that other items (for example, dried flowers) are an attempt to include the other in a particular moment in time.

8 Sidney's sonnet sequence *Astrophil and Stella* is regarded as one of the great love poems of the sixteenth century, especially *vis-à-vis* its technical virtuosity and deployment of Petrarchan imagery (for example, fire and ice, sun and stars). See Sidney (1973) and Forster (1969). Gary Waller also makes a very interesting connection between the positioning of the lover in Sidney's poem and the positioning of the subject *vis-à-vis* Protestant cultural and religious practices (Waller 1984: 77).

9 'Companionate marriage': to be discussed in more detail in Chapter 3, companionate marriage is seen to have its origins in the new 'affective individualism' associated with the

English Revolution and show-cased in the domestic arrangements of Adam and Eve in Milton's *Paradise Lost* (1667).

Chapter 3 Courtship Fiction: The Gift of Companionship

1 'Symptomatic reading': a term first employed by Pierre Macherey in his *Theory of Literary Production* (1978) to describe a method of reading texts via their 'gaps' and 'silences'.

2 Some classic feminist 'appropriations' of Austen include: Spacks, *The Female Imagination* (1976); Showalter, *A Literature of Their Own* (1977); and Poovey, *The Proper Lady and the Woman Writer* (1984).

3 'Handfast': Before Hardwicke's Marriage Act of 1753, there were distinct stages involved in a marriage. These included: (1) the written legal consent between parents concerning the financial arrangements; (2) the spousals – that is, the formal exchange, usually before witnesses, of oral promises; (3) the public proclamation of the banns; (4) the wedding in church; and (5) the sexual consummation. Stone observes that, after 1753, the betrothal ceremony itself – the 'handfast' – continued to be treated by many (especially the poor) as sufficient for a binding union without the blessing in church (see Stone 1979: 30–1).

4 In *Distinction*, Bourdieu explores how 'taste' is (re)produced along class lines in which economic and 'cultural' capital are often at variance in the wrestle for social credibility and power (Bourdieu 1986 [1979]: 260–3).

5 Saussure was the first structuralist theorist to demonstrate that there is no necessary relationship between language (as an arbitrary system of sounds) and the things they describe. For an introduction to the basic principle, see Hawkes's *Structuralism and Semiotics* (1977: 19–28).

6 I am indebted to Eleanor Collins (2005) for introducing me to the debate about 'choice' in Austen's novels.

7 Delarivière Manley was one of the most infamous woman writers of the eighteenth century, whose texts were remarkable not only for their eroticism, but also for the fact that they were barely disguised satires of prominent Whig aristocrats, including the first Duke and Duchess of Marlborough. With the publication of the second volume of *The New Atalantis* in 1709, Manley was considered to have 'gone too far' and she was arrested, and imprisoned for a short time, accordingly. For more details, see Spencer (1986: 53–62) and Ros Ballater's introduction to *The New Atalantis* (1991).

8 See Barthes (1990: 197–8):

> It is by means of this *historical* hallucination that I sometimes make love into a romance, an adventure. This would seem to assume three stages (three acts): first comes the instantaneous capture (I am ravished by an image); then a series of encounters (dates, telephone calls, letters, brief trips), during which I ecstatically 'explore' the perfection of the loved being. . . . This happy period acquires its identity (its limits) from the opposition (at least in memory) to the 'sequel': the sequel is the long train of sufferings, wounds, anxieties, distresses, resentments, depairs and embarrassments, and deceptions to which I fall prey, ceaselessly living under the threat of a downfall which would envelop the other, myself, and the glamorous encounter that first revealed us to each other.

Chapter 4 Gothic Romance: The Gift of Immortality

1 Baldick's definition of the Gothic is especially resonant here: 'For the Gothic effect to be attained, a tale should combine a fearful sense of inheritance in time with a claustrophobic sense of enclosure in space, these two dimensions reinforcing one another to produce an impression of sickening descent into disintegration' (Baldick 1992: xix).

2 See Catherine Spooner's discussion of literary and other 'doubles', past and present, in *Fashioning Gothic Bodies* (2004: 128–58).

3 See Freud's 'Family Romances' (1977a [1909]) and Stephanie Lawler's discussion of the same (1995: 265–78).

4 The nineteenth century and the Victorian period are not, of course, interchangeable terms; in the course of this chapter I have attempted to use the two terms advisedly: that is, 'Victorian' denotes something specific to the *English* culture of the period.

5 Mark Musa, editor of the *Inferno*, writes: 'unlike Hell and Purgatory, Heaven in Dante's poem does not exist in a physical sense' but is characterized as a realm of 'light': 'God is light, and the Pilgrim's goal from the very start was to reach the light' (Dante 1984: 54).

6 Marsden presents a convincing argument which connects Emily Brontë's theology with that of the German Romantic Schleiermacher: '"Redemption" is the process which leaves behind the awareness of the self alone and becomes conscious of the totality that transcends the self' (Marsden 2000: 20).

7 In his essay 'On Narcissism' (1914) Freud distinguishes between 'sublimation' and 'idealization' thus:

> Sublimation in a process that concerns the object-libido and consists of the instinct's directing itself towards an aim other than, and remote from, the sexual satisfaction; in this process the accent falls upon the deflection from sexuality. Idealization is a process which concerns the *object*; but it, that object, without alteration in its nature, is aggrandized and exalted in the subject's mind. Idealization is possible in the sphere of the subject-libido as well as that of the object-libido. (Freud 1984a: 88)

8 A typical poetic example of this sort of fetishization of the landscape is Emily Brontë's poem 'The Bluebell' (18 December 1838) (Brontë 1995b: 71), in which the flower is clearly a site of projection/introjection *vis-à-vis* the absent lover.

9 In 'Three Essays on the Theory of Sexuality' (1905), Freud describes 'perversion' thus: 'Perversions are sexual activities which either (a) extend, in the anatomical sense, beyond the regions of the body that are designed for the sexual union, or (b) linger over the intermediate relations to the sexual object which should normally be traversed rapidly on the path toward the final sexual aim' (Freud 1990 [1905]: 98).

10 See Tanner (1979: 26–7) for a fascinating account of the role of *stranger-enemy* in the literary history of adultery.

11 See Bronfen (1992: 306), who sees the 'symbiotic imaginary duality' of Catherine and Heathcliff as a reflex 'where the beloved other is the same as the self', and Gilbert and Gubar (2000: 265) on the hugely important role Heathcliff plays in the aggrandizement of Catherine's ego.

12 'The foil': the foil is the male/female character who competes for the hero or heroine's affections and, most importantly, introduces the 'obstacle' of confusion and doubt into the love story. S/he is also often crucial in helping the hero/heroine recognize that they are in love by inciting jealousy. In popular romance, the female foil usually possesses a more glamorous (and hence 'artificial') femininity than the heroine (see Chapter 6).

13 Emily Brontë's 'Gondal' poems anticipate the relationship between Catherine and Heathcliff; see especially 'Remembrance' (Bronte 1995b: 8) and 'Light Up Thy Halls' (Brontë 1995b: 82–3).

14 See Rossetti's letter to T. Horner (11 March 1873): 'The Picture must of course be viewed not as a representation of the incident of the death of Beatrice but as an ideal of the subject, symbolized by a trance or a sudden spiritual transfiguration. Beatrice is rapt visibly into Heaven, seeing it as it were through shut lids' (in Pearce 1991: 52).

15 See Gaskell's *Mary Barton* (1987 [1848]) for discussion of the practice known as 'wishing' (that is, preventing a soul's departure from this world to the next).

Chapter 5 Wartime Romance: The Gift of Self-Sacrifice

1 The image of the skeleton with which I open this chapter was inspired by an extract from one of Leighton's letters (14 September 1915; Brittain 1981: 272) which focuses on the dehumanization of the rotting and dismembered corpses in the trenches in order to question the perceived gloriousness of war.

2 'Chronotopes': a term coined by the Russian theorist Mikhail Bakhtin to describe the way in which time and space combine in specific literary/cultural conceits and genres (for example, 'the adventure chronotope' or the 'chronotope of the road'). See Pearce (1994: 67–72) for a full discussion of the term.

3 Initially the butt of a good deal of lesbian/feminist anger for their apparent 'pathologization' of homosexual desire, recent commentators have engaged more positively with this group of men. See, for example, Ledger (1997) and Doan (2001).

4 Catherine Clay's *British Women Writers 1914–45* (2006) focuses on the complex and fascinating 'trade' of work, friendship and sexual desire in the lives and writings of this group of women (including, centrally, Vera Brittain and Winifred Holtby) but challenges whether 'sublimation' is the correct term to describe the relay of productivity and desire (Clay 2006: 39–40).

5 Although the Victorian era instigated some of the most repressive and iniquitous legislation ever directed at women, by the end of the nineteenth century small improvements began to be made *vis-à-vis* divorce and the (gradual) repeal of the (1860) Contagious Diseases Act. Another key piece of legislation for the *fin-de-siècle* was the 'Criminal Law Amendment Act' of 1885, which – via the 'Labouchere Amendment' – criminalized male homosexuality. See Ledger (1997: 112) and Showalter (1990: 14).

6 Ledger glosses the two terms thus: 'The "invert" was powerless to change her deviant sexuality, as her anomaly was genetic and so inborn. The "pervert", by contrast, exercised a degree of choice as far as her lesbianism was concerned. . . . For the "pervert" homosexuality was an acquired characteristic which could be both prevented and cured' (Ledger 1997: 130).

7 The amount of time given to the discussion of feminist matters in these diaries is impressive, especially for a woman of Brittain's age and background. *Vis-à-vis* her relationship with Leighton, it is seen in her reticence to first agree to, and then publicly declare, her engagement (see 21 and 23 August 1915; Brittain 1981: 261).

8 Catherine Clay has reminded me that this dynamic was also a key element in Brittain's relationship with her future husband, George Catlin.

9 Clay observes a similar discontinuity between textual and physical intimacy in the relationships between women considered in her book, including, especially, the relationship between Stella Benson and Naomi Mitchison (Clay 2006: 144).

10 By the time Brittain returned to Oxford in 1918 she was well on her way to becoming a pacifist: a conviction that assumed absolute form with her joining the Peace Pledge Union in the 1930s. See Shaw's biography of Winifred Holtby (1999: 227–9).

Chapter 6 Modern Romance: The Gift of Selfhood

1 For further discussion of these aspects of postmodernism, see Chapter 7 and note 1 to that chapter.

2 The desire of both women to do 'meaningful' work is encapsulated in Brittain's quotation from one of Holtby's letters in *Testament of Friendship*: 'I shall never quite make up my mind whether to be a reformer-sort-of-person or a writer-sort-of-person' (Brittain 1980: 130). The sense of 'mission' and the fight for social justice is, of course, implicit in both careers.

3 Numerous commentators have debated to what extent the relationship between Brittain and Holtby was a sexual one or not (see Clay 2006: 37–50; Faderman 1985 [1981]: 309–10; Shaw 1999: 289–90).

4 Miller and Mailer were both famously taken to task in the opening chapter of Millett's *Sexual Politics* (1977 [1969]), which quotes extensively from the more pornographic sections of their texts as instances of 'sexual politics' at work. See also my reading of Millett's text in *Feminist Readings / Feminists Reading* (Mills and Pearce 1996: 23–55).

5 Other texts which explore the mother–daughter dynamic in lesbian relationships include Adrienne Rich's essays (1977, 1981) and Patricia Highsmith's novel *Carol* (1990 [1952]). See also Thynne (1995) and my reading of *Carol* (Pearce 2006).

6 It is now commonly understood that the social and financial freedoms afforded to women during the Second World War (largely on account of their taking on work that had formerly been reserved for men) were reversed after the war through a mixture of ideology and state propaganda (see Hayes and Hill 1999; Sinfield 1983).

7 Although *Beebo Brinker* comes first in the sequence of five novels it was actually written last (see Hamer 1990 for further discussion).

8 The crucial importance of repetitive 'performance' to the production / endorsement of *all* sexual identities was first brought to critical attention in Judith Butler's work of the early 1990s (see Butler 1990, 1993).

9 Taylor's questionnaire revealed that the majority of female readers / viewers responded to / identified with Scarlett rather than the 'good heroine', Melanie (Taylor 1989: 78).

Chapter 7 Postmodern Romance: The Gift of the Fourth Dimension

1 Definitions of postmodernism, in both its cultural / historical and aesthetic sense, abound, but the following summation by Linda Hutcheon is especially germane to the types of texts and textuality discussed in this chapter:

> As Foucault and others have suggested, linked to this contesting of the coherent and unified subject is a more general questioning of *any* totalizing or homogenizing system. Provisionality and heterogeneity contaminate any neat attempts at unifying coherence (formal and thematic). Historical and narrative continuity and closure are contested, but again, from within. . . . The centre no longer completely holds. And, from the de-centred perspective, the 'marginal' and what I shall be calling the 'ex-centric' (be it in class, race, gender, sexual orientation or ethnicity) take on the new significance in the light of the implied recognition that our culture is not really the homogenous monolith . . . we might have assumed. (Hutcheon 1988: 11–12)

2 'The new science' is a phrase that has been adopted by cultural theorists to account for the way in which post-Einsteinian physics (and its implications for time, human subjectivity, etc.) has been popularized and disseminated by scientists like Stephen Hawking (1995) and Huw Price (1996). (See Waugh 1995: 196 for an overview of the concept and its adoption in contemporary literature.)

3 See also Diane Elam's *Romancing the Postmodern* and, in particular, her discussion of 'ironic temporality' *vis-à-vis* the discourse of romantic love (Elam 1992: 36–45).

4 The consequences of time-travel for romantic relationships is also given spectacular figuration in 'future noir' film texts such as *Total Recall* (Verhoeven 1990) and *Twelve Monkeys* (Gilliam 1995). The latter is an excellent example of a text which explores the darker side of the convention via a romance which is played out for ever courtesy of a time-loop that cannot be altered.

5 The fact that the Woodstock festival was also the subject of a documentary film (Wadleigh 1970) which continues to be enjoyed by successive generations means that its images of youth / drugs culture and permissive sexuality have become truly iconic. See also *Woodstock Remembered* (Bennett 2004).

6 See Ernst Bloch's *The Principle of Hope* (1986 [1959]) and my essay (Pearce 2004) which discusses how Bloch's work on daydreams and utopia may be used to rethink some of the processes of romantic love.

7 'Anticipatory retrospection': A term first introduced to me via the work of novelist Andrew Greig, and denoting the tendency, in certain individuals, to regard present and future events with the longing and nostalgia of hindsight.

8 Deleuze's conception of time as having two aspects is summarized by Gibson:

> The first aspect is measurable and relational. It is time as an order of movements and of their units. The second aspect is measureless, incommensurable. . . . They are the two forms of time according to the Stoics, *chronos* and *aion*. *Chronos* measures events and is inseparable from matter. It is the temporal dimension of causation. *Aion* by contrast is the unlimited past and future of the incorporeal. It is the dimension of surface effects. It is the time of pure becoming . . . [the] continuum of time out of which the present ceaselessly emerges. (Gibson 1996: 179–80)

9 For further discussion of this aspect of 'lad-lit', see Gunnell (2002).

10 On this point it is important to note that *Blade Runner* exists in two versions: the original film (1982) and the Director's Cut (1993), in which it is revealed that Deckard is also a replicant and which (despite the removal of this particular obstacle to his relationship with Rachel) has a much less upbeat, more ambiguous, ending.

11 'Somewhere between fear and sex passion is' (Winterson 1987: 62).

12 Special thanks to Lee Horsley, for her invaluable insights (and examples of relevant film texts) in these last pages. I am also indebted to her for notes 4 and 10.

13 'The player': In *The Noir Thriller* Horsley notes how 'acting as a player has become a prime metaphor for many, moving from the status of victim to that of an active agent of domination and change' (Horsley 2001: 193), and the concept is clearly crucial in an understanding of how a new kind of existential agency has been achieved by the subject in the contemporary, postmodern world.

References

Abbott, M. 1993: *Family Ties: English Families 1540–1920*. London and New York: Routledge.

Althusser, L. 1984 [1970]: Ideology and the Ideological State Apparatus. In *Louis Althusser: Essays on Ideology*. London and New York: Verso, 1–60.

Anderson, R. 1974: *The Purple Heart Throbs: The Sub-literature of Love*. London: Hodder and Stoughton.

Atwood, M. 1982a [1969]: *The Edible Woman*. London: Virago.

Atwood, M. 1982b [1976]: *Lady Oracle*. London: Virago.

Austen, J. 1972 [1813]: *Pride and Prejudice*. Harmondsworth: Penguin English Library.

Austen, J. 1985 [1818]: *Persuasion*. Harmondsworth: Penguin Classics.

Austen, J. 1990 [1811]: *Sense and Sensibility*. New York and Oxford: Oxford University Press.

Austen, J. 1996 [1816]: *Emma*. Harmondsworth: Penguin Classics.

Bakhtin, M. 1981 [1934–41]: *The Dialogic Imagination: Four Essays by M. M. Bakhtin*. Trans. C. Emerson and M. Holquist. Austin, TX: University of Texas Press.

Bakhtin, M. 1984 [1929]: *Problems of Dostoevsky's Poetics*. Trans. C. Emerson. Minneapolis, MN: University of Minnesota Press.

Baldick, C. 1990: *The Oxford Dictionary of Literary Terms*. Oxford: Oxford University Press.

Baldick, C. (ed.) 1992: *The Oxford Book of Gothic Tales*. Oxford: Oxford University Press.

Bannon, A. 1962: *Beebo Brinker*. San Francisco, CA: Cleis Press.

Barron, W. R. J. 2004: Arthurian Romance. In C. Saunders (ed.), *A Companion to Romance: From Classical to Contemporary*, Oxford: Blackwell, 65–84.

Barthes, R. 1990 [1977]: *A Lover's Discourse: Fragments*. Trans. R. Howard. Harmondsworth: Penguin.

Bauman, Z. 2003: *Liquid Love: On the Frailty of Human Bonds*. Cambridge: Polity.

Bayley, J. 1963: *The Character of Love*. New York: Collier Books.

Beauman, N. 1983: *A Very Great Profession: The Women's Novel 1914–39*. London: Vintage.

Beck, U. and E. Beck-Gernsheim 1995: *The Normal Chaos of Love*. Trans. M. Ritter and J. Wiehal. Cambridge: Polity.

Belsey, C. 1988: *John Milton: Language, Gender, Power.* Oxford: Blackwell.

Belsey, C. 1994: *Desire: Love Stories in Western Culture.* Oxford: Blackwell.

Benjamin, J. 1990: *The Bonds of Love: Psychoanalysis, Feminism and the Problem of Domination.* London: Virago.

Bennett, A. 2004: *Remembering Woodstock.* London: Ashgate.

Bloch, E. 1986 [1959]: *The Principle of Hope.* Trans. N. Plaice, S. Plaice and P. Knight. Oxford: Blackwell.

Borges, J. L. 1970 [1962]: The Garden of Forking Paths. In *Labyrinths.* Trans. D. A. Yates. Harmondsworth: Penguin, 44–54.

Bourdieu, P. 1986 [1979]: *Distinction: A Social Critique of the Judgement of Taste.* Trans. R. Nice. London: Routledge.

Bradbury, M. 2001: *The Modern British Novel.* Revised edn. Harmondsworth: Penguin.

Brewer, D. 2004: The Popular English Metrical Romances. In C. Saunders (ed.), *A Companion to Romance: From Classical to Contemporary.* Oxford: Blackwell, 45–64.

Brittain, V. 1979a [1933]: *Testament of Youth.* London: Fontana Paperbacks in association with Virago.

Brittain, V. 1979b [1957]: *Testament of Experience.* London: Fontana Paperbacks in association with Virago.

Brittain, V. 1980 [1940]: *Testament of Friendship.* London: Virago.

Brittain, V. 1981: *Chronicle of Youth: Vera Brittain's War Diary 1913–17.* Ed. A. Bishop. London: Victor Gollancz Ltd.

Bronfen, E. 1993: *Over Her Dead Body: Death, Femininity and the Aesthetic.* Cambridge: Cambridge University Press.

Brontë, C. 2000 [1847]: *Jane Eyre.* Harmondsworth: Penguin Classics.

Brontë, E. 1995a [1847]: *Wuthering Heights.* Harmondsworth: Penguin Classics.

Brontë, E. 1995b: *The Poems of Emily Brontë.* Ed. D. Roper with E. Chittam. Oxford: Clarendon Press.

Brown, R. 1987: *Analysing Love.* Cambridge: Cambridge University Press.

Butler, J. 1990: *Gender Trouble: Feminism and the Subversion of Identity.* London and New York: Routledge.

Butler, J. 1993: *Bodies That Matter: On the Discursive Limits of 'Sex'.* London and New York: Routledge.

Butler, M. 1975: *Jane Austen and the War of Ideas.* Oxford: Clarendon University Press.

Byatt, A. S. 1990: *Possession: A Romance.* London: Chatto and Windus.

Byron, Lord 1996: *Selected Poems.* Harmondsworth: Penguin Classics.

Carter, A. 1979: *The Bloody Chamber and Other Stories.* Harmondsworth: Penguin.

Cave, N. 2001: *The Complete Lyrics 1978–2001.* Harmondsworth: Penguin.

Cavendish, M. [Duchess of Newcastle] 1989 [1656]: *A True Relation of My Birth, Breeding and Life* from *Nature's Pictures Drawn From Fancy's Pencil to the Life.* In E. Graham, H. Hinds, E. Hobby and H. Wilcox (eds), *Her Own Life:*

Autobiographical Writings by Seventeenth-Century Englishwomen. London and New York: Routledge, 87–100.

Cavendish, M. [Duchess of Newcastle] 2002 [1688]: *The Convent of Pleasure.* In S. Hodgson-Wright (ed.), *Women's Writing of the Early Modern Period 1588–1688: An Anthology.* Edinburgh: Edinburgh University Press, 257–87.

Chodorow, N. 1978: *The Reproduction of Mothering: Psychoanalysis and the Sociology of Gender.* Berkeley: University of California Press.

Clay, C. 2006: *British Women Writers 1914–1945: Professional Work and Friendship.* London: Ashgate.

Collins, E. 2005: Reading Gender, Choice and Austen Narrative. Unpublished D.Phil., Oxford University.

Collins, W. 1973 [1860]: *The Woman in White.* Oxford: Oxford University Press.

Cooper, H. 2004: Malory and the Early English Prose Romances. In C. Saunders (ed.), *A Companion to Romance: From Classical to Contemporary.* Oxford: Blackwell, 104–20.

Coward, B. 1994: *The Stuart Age 1603–1714.* 2nd edn. London: Longman.

Craft, C. 1988: 'Descend, Touch and Enter': Tennyson's Strange Manner of Address. *Genders*, 1, 83–101.

Dante 1984 [c. 1308–14]: *The Divine Comedy 1 (Inferno).* Trans. M. Musa. Harmondsworth: Penguin Books.

Dante 2004 [c. 1308–14]: *The Divine Comedy: 3 (Paradise).* Trans. D. L. Sayers and B. Reynolds. Harmondsworth: Penguin Classics.

Darce Frenier, M. 1988: *Good-Bye Heathcliff: Changing Heroes, Heroines, Roles and Values in Women's Category Romances.* Westport, CT: Greenwood Press.

Davies, T. 1996: 'The Meaning, not the Name': Milton and Gender. In W. Zunder and S. Trill (eds), *Writing and the English Renaissance.* London: Longman, 193–212.

Dawes, D. (dir.) 1947: *Dark Passage.* US: Warner.

de Beauvoir, S. 1984 [1943]: *She Came to Stay.* Trans. Y. Moyse and R. Seahouse. London: Flamingo.

de Rougemont, D. 1983 [1940]: *Love in the Western World.* Trans. M. Belgion. Princeton, NJ: Princeton University Press.

Derrida, J. 1992: *Given Time: Counterfeit Money.* Trans. P. Kamuf. Chicago and London: University of Chicago Press.

Derrida, J. 1995: *The Gift of Death.* Trans. D. Wills. Chicago and London: University of Chicago Press.

Dixon, j. 1999: *The Romance of Mills & Boon 1909–1990s.* London and New York: Routledge.

Doan, L. 2001: *Fashioning Sapphisms: The Origins of a Modern English Lesbian Culture.* New York: Columbia University Press.

Dollimore, J. 1983: The Challenge of Sexuality. In A. Sinfield (ed.), *Society and Literature 1945–1970.* London: Methuen & Co, 51–85.

du Maurier, D. 1992 [1938]: *Rebecca.* London: Arrow Books (Random House).

Eagleton, T. 1975: *Myths of Power: A Marxist Study of the Brontës*. London: Macmillan Press.

Elam, D. 1992: *Romancing the Postmodern*. London and New York: Routledge.

Eliot, G. 1973 [1871]: *Middlemarch*. London: Pan Books.

Eliot, T. S. 1959 [1940]: *The Four Quartets*. London: Faber and Faber.

Eliot, T. S. 1961 [1922]: *The Waste Land*. In *Selected Poems*. London: Faber and Faber, 51–74.

Ellis, S. 1983: *Dante and English Poetry: Shelley to T. S. Eliot*. Cambridge: Cambridge University Press.

Faderman, L. 1985 [1981]: *Surpassing the Love of Men: Romantic Friendship and Love between Women from the Renaissance to the Present*. London: Women's Press.

Faderman, L. 1991: *Odd Girls and Twilight Lovers: A History of Lesbian Life in Twentieth-Century America*. Harmondsworth: Penguin.

Fairer, D. 2004: *The Fairie Queene* and Eighteenth-Century Spenserianism. In C. Saunders (ed.), *A Companion to Romance: From Classical to Contemporary*. Oxford: Blackwell, 197–215.

Farwell, M. 1990: Heterosexual Plots and Lesbian Subtexts: Toward a Theory of Lesbian Narrative Space. In K. Jay and E. Glasgow (eds), *Lesbian Texts and Contexts: Radical Revisions*. New York and London: New York University Press, 91–103.

Felman, S. and D. Laub (eds) 1992: *Testimony: Crises of Witnessing in Literature, Psychoanalysis and History*. London and New York: Routledge.

Fernando, L. 1977: *'New Women' in the Late Victorian Novel*. University Park, PA and London: Pennsylvania State University Press.

Fielding, H. 2001 [1996]: *Bridget Jones's Diary*. London: Picador.

Fielding, H. 2004 [2000]: *Bridget Jones: The Edge of Reason*. London: Picador.

Forbes, J. 1995: Anti-Romantic Discourse as Resistance: Women's Fiction 1775–1820. In L. Pearce and J. Stacey (eds), *Romance Revisited*, London: Lawrence and Wishart, 293–305.

Forster, L. W. 1969: *The Icy Fire*. London: Cambridge University Press.

Foucault, M. 1988 [1984]: *The Care of the Self: The History of Sexuality Volume 3*. Trans. R. Hurley. London: Penguin.

Fowles, J. 1977 [1969]: *The French Lieutenant's Woman*. London: Triad/Granada.

Frears, S. (dir.) 1985: *My Beautiful Laundrette*. UK: SAF/Channel 4.

Frears, S. (dir.) 1987: *Sammy and Rosie Get Laid*. US: Cinecom/Film 4.

Freud, S. 1977a [1909]: Family Romance. In *On Sexuality*. Trans. J. Strachey. Penguin Freud Library, Vol. 7. Harmondsworth: Penguin, 217–26.

Freud, S. 1977b [1912]: On the Universal Tendency to Debasement in the Sphere of Love. In *On Sexuality*. Trans. J. Strachey. Penguin Freud Library, Vol. 7. Harmondsworth: Penguin, 243–60.

Freud, S. 1984a [1914]: On Narcissism. In *On Metapsychology*. Trans. J. Strachey. Penguin Freud Library, Vol. 11. Harmondsworth: Penguin, 65–97.

Freud, S. 1984b [1915]. Mourning and Melancholia. In *On Metapsychology*. Trans. J. Strachey. Penguin Freud Library, Vol. 11. Harmondsworth: Penguin, 247–68.

Freud, S. 1984c [1920]: Beyond the Pleasure Principle. In *On Metapsychology*. Trans. J. Strachey. Penguin Freud Library, Vol. 11. Harmondsworth: Penguin, 269–338.

Freud, S. 1986 [1905–33]: *The Essentials of Psycho-Analysis*. Trans. J. Strachey. Harmondsworth: Penguin.

Freud, S. 1990 [1905]: Three Essays on Sexuality. In E. Young-Bruehl (ed.), *Freud on Women: A Reader*. London: Hogarth Press, 89–145.

Friedan, B. 1963: *The Feminine Mystique*. Harmondsworth: Penguin.

Fromm, E. 1974: *The Art of Loving*. New York: Harper and Row.

Frye, N. 1976: *A Secular Scripture: A Study of the Structure of Romance*. Cambridge, MA and London: Harvard University Press.

Gaskell, E. 1987 [1848]. *Mary Barton*. Oxford and New York: Oxford University Press.

Gelder, K. 2004: *Popular Fiction: The Logics and Practices of a Literary Field*. London and New York: Routledge.

Gibson, A. 1996: *Towards a Postmodern Theory of Narrative*. Edinburgh: Edinburgh University Press.

Giddens, A. 1992: *The Transformation of Intimacy: Sexuality, Love and Eroticism*. Cambridge: Polity.

Gilbert, S. and S. Gubar 1989: *No Man's Land: The Place of the Woman Writer in the Twentieth Century. Vol. 2: Sexchanges*. New Haven and London: Yale University Press.

Gilbert, S. and S. Gubar 2000 [1979]: *The Madwoman in the Attic: The Woman Writer and the Nineteenth-Century Literary Imagination*. New Haven and London: Yale University Press.

Gilliam, T. (dir.) 1995: *Twelve Monkeys*. US: Polygram / Universal.

Graham, E., H. Hinds, E. Hobby and H. Wilcox (eds) 1989: *Her Own Life: Autobiographical Writings by Seventeenth-Century Englishwomen*. London: Routledge.

Greene, G. 2001 [1951]: *The End of the Affair*. London: Vintage Classics.

Greer, G. 1993 [1971]: *The Female Eunuch*. London: Flamingo.

Gunnell, R. 2002: Playgirls and Puritans: Gender and Policing in the Literatures of the Nineteenth and Twentieth Century. Unpublished Ph.D. thesis, Lancaster University.

Hall, R. 1994 [1928]: *The Well of Loneliness*. London: Virago.

Hall, R. 1995 [1934]: Miss Ogilvy Finds Herself. In T. Tate (ed.), *Women, Men and the Great War: An Anthology of Stories*. Manchester: Manchester University Press, 125–40.

Hamer, D. 1990: 'I am a Woman': Ann Bannon and the Writing of Lesbian Identity in the 1950s. In M. Lilly (ed.), *Lesbian and Gay Writing: An Anthology of Critical Essays*. London: Macmillan, 47–75.

Hardy, T. 1975 [1895]: *Jude the Obscure*. London: Macmillan (The New Wessex Edition).

Hawkes, T. 1977: *Structuralism and Semiotics*. London: Methuen.

Hawking, S. 1995: *A Brief History of Time*. London: Bantam.

Hayes, N. and J. Hill (eds) 1999: *Millions Like Us? British Culture and the Second World War*. Liverpool: Liverpool University Press.

Highsmith, P. 1990 [1952]: *Carol*. London: Bloomsbury.

Hill, C. 2001 [1961]: *The Century of Revolution 1603–1714*. London and New York: Routledge.

Hill, G. R. (dir.) 1969: *Butch Cassidy and the Sundance Kid*. US: CF/ Campanile.

Hoeveler, D. L. 1998: *Gothic Feminism: The Professionalization of Gender from Charlotte Smith to the Brontës*. University Park, PA: Pennsylvania State University Press.

Hogle, J. E. 2004: Gothic Romance: Its Origins and Cultural Functions. In C. Saunders (ed.), *A Companion to Romance: From Classical to Contemporary*. Oxford: Blackwell, 216–32.

Holtby, W. 1995 [1934]: So Handy for the Fun Fair. In T. Tate (ed.), *Women, Men and the Great War: An Anthology of Stories*. Manchester: Manchester University Press, 52–67.

Hornby, N. 1995: *High Fidelity*. London: Indigo.

Hornby, N. 1992: *Fever Pitch*. Harmondsworth: Penguin.

Horsley, L. 2001: *The Noir Thriller*. Basingstoke: Palgrave.

Hurston, Z. N. 1986 [1937]: *Their Eyes Were Watching God*. London: Virago Press.

Hutcheon, L. 1988: *A Poetics of Postmodernism: History, Theory, Fiction*. London and New York: Routledge.

Hutcheon, L. 1994: *Irony's Edge: The Theory and Politics of Irony*. London and New York: Routledge.

Ilona, A. 2003: Hanif Kureishi's *Buddha of Suburbia*. In R. J. Lane, R. Mengham and P. Tew (eds), *Contemporary British Fiction*. Cambridge: Polity, 87–105.

James, H. 2004 [1902]: *The Wings of the Dove*. New York: Random House.

Johnson, B. 2007: Ocularcentric Revision. Unpublished Ph.D. thesis, Lancaster University (forthcoming).

Jones, S. 2004: Into the Twentieth Century: Imperial Romance from Haggard to Buchan. In C. Saunders (ed.), *A Companion to Romance: From Classical to Contemporary*. Oxford: Blackwell, 406–23.

King, A. 2004: Sidney and Spenser. In C. Saunders (ed.) *A Companion to Romance: From Classical to Contemporary*. Oxford: Blackwell, 140–59.

Kipling, R. 1995 [1926]: Mary Postgate. In T. Tate (ed.), *Women, Men and the Great War: An Anthology of Stories*. Manchester: Manchester University Press, 255–67.

Kureishi, H. (1986): *My Beautiful Laundrette and The Rainbow Sign*. London: Faber and Faber.

Kureishi, H. (1990): *The Buddha of Suburbia*. London: Faber and Faber.

Kureishi, H. (1998): *Intimacy*. London: Faber and Faber.

Lacan, J. 1988 [1975]: *The Seminar. Book 1: Freud's Papers on Technique (1953–4)*. Trans. J. Forrester. New York: Norton.

Lacan, J. 1992 [1959–60]: *The Seminar of Jacques Lacan. Book 7: The Ethics of Psychoanalysis 1959–60*. Trans. D. Porter. London and New York: Routledge.

Langford, W. 2002: *Revolutions of the Heart: Gender, Power and the Delusions of Love*. London and New York: Routledge.

Laurence, A. 1994: *Women in England 1500–1700: A Social History*. London: Weidenfeld and Nicolson.

Lawler, S. 1995: 'I Never Felt As Though I Fitted': Family Romances and the Mother–Daughter Relationship. In L. Pearce and J. Stacey (eds), *Romance Revisited*. London: Lawrence and Wishart, 265–78.

Ledger, S. 1997: *The New Woman: Fiction and Feminism at the Fin-de-Siècle*. Manchester and New York: Manchester University Press.

Lehmann, R. 1981 [1936]: *The Weather in the Streets*. London: Virago.

Lennox, C. 1970 [1752]: *The Female Quixote or The Adventures of Isabella*. Oxford and New York: Oxford University Press.

Lessing, D. 1972 [1962]: *The Golden Notebook*. London: Michael Joseph.

Levinas, E. 1969 [1961]: *Totality and Infinity: An Essay on Exteriority*. Trans. A. Lingis. Pittsburgh, PA: Duquesne University Press.

Luhmann, N. 1986: *Love as Passion: The Codification of Intimacy*. Trans. J. Gaines and D. L. Jones. Cambridge: Polity.

Luhrmann, B. (dir.) 2001: *Moulin Rouge*. US: Twentieth-Century Fox/Bazmark Productions.

Lumley, J. 1993: *Forces Sweethearts: Wartime Romance from the First World War to the Gulf*. London: Bloomsbury.

McHale, B. 1987: *Postmodern Fiction*. London and New York: Routledge.

Macherey, P. 1978: *A Theory of Literary Production*. London: Routledge and Kegan Paul.

McMaster, J. 1996: *Jane Austen the Novelist: Essays Past and Present*. London: Macmillan.

Magrs, P. 1996: *Marked For Life*. London: Vintage.

Manley, D. 1991 [1709]: *The New Atalantis*. London: Pickering and Chatto.

Marcuse, H. 1973 [1956]: *Eros and Civilization: A Philosophical Inquiry into Freud*. Aylesbury: Sphere Books.

Marsden, S. 2000: *Wuthering Heights* and the Theology of Fiction. MA thesis, Lancaster University.

Mauss, M. 1990 [1950]: *The Gift: The Form and Reason for Exchange in Archaic Societies*. Trans. W. D. Halls. London: Routledge.

Millett, K. 1977 [1969]: *Sexual Politics*. London: Virago.

Mills, S. and L. Pearce 1996 [1989]: *Feminist Readings/Feminists Reading*. Brighton: Harvester-Wheatsheaf.

Mitchell, J. 1974: *Psychoanalysis and Feminism*. Harmondsworth: Penguin.

Mitchell, M. 1974 [1936]: *Gone with the Wind*. London: Pan.

Mitford, N. 1970 [1945]: *The Pursuit of Love*. Harmondsworth: Penguin.

Modleski, T. 1982: *Loving with a Vengeance: Mass-Produced Fantasies for Women.* London and New York: Routledge.

Morgan, C. 2004: Between Worlds: Iris Murdoch, A. S. Byatt and Romance. In C. Saunders (ed.), *A Companion to Romance: From Classical to Contemporary.* Oxford: Blackwell, 502–20.

Moulsworth, M. 2004 [1632]: The Memorandum of Martha Moulsworth, Widdowe. In H. Ostovich and E. Sauer (eds), *Reading Early Modern Women: An Anthology of Texts in Manuscript and Print, 1550–1700.* London and New York: Routledge, 258–61.

Nancy, J.-L. 1991: Shattered Love. In *The Inoperative Community.* Minneapolis and London: University of Minnesota Press, 82–109.

Nancy, J.-L. 2001: Love and Community: A round-table discussion with Jean-Luc Nancy, Avital Ronell and Wolfgang Schirmacher, August 2001. *www.egs.edu/faculty/nancy/nancy-roundtable-discussion2001.html* (accessed 6 June 2006).

Newcomb, L. H. 2002: *Reading Popular Romance in Early Modern England.* New York: Columbia University Press.

Newcomb, L. H. 2004: Gendering Prose Romances in Renaissance England. In C. Saunders (ed.), *A Companion to Romance: From Classical to Contemporary.* Oxford: Blackwell, 121–39.

Osborne, D. 1928: *The Letters of Dorothy Osborne to William Temple.* Ed. G. C. Moore Smith. Oxford: Clarendon Press.

Oswell, D. 1998: True Love in Queer Times: Romance, Suburbia and Masculinity. In L. Pearce and G. Wisker (eds), *Fatal Attractions: The Representation of Romance in Contemporary Literature and Film.* London: Pluto, 157–73.

Paizis, G. 1998: *Love and the Novel: The Poetics and Politics of Popular Romance.* Basingstoke: Macmillan.

Panter-Downes, M. P. 2003 [1941]: Goodbye, My Love. In A. Boston and J. Hartley (eds), *Wave Me Goodbye: Stories of the Second World War* and *Hearts Undefeated: Writings of the Second World War.* London: Virago, 45–51.

Parker, D. 2003 [1943]: The Lovely Leave. In A. Boston and J. Hartley (eds), *Wave Me Goodbye: Stories of the Second World War* and *Hearts Undefeated: Writings of the Second World War.* London: Virago, 134–47.

Pearce, L. 1991: *Woman/Image/Text: Readings in Pre-Raphaelite Art and Literature.* Hemel Hempstead: Harvester-Wheatsheaf.

Pearce, L. 1994: *Reading Dialogics.* London: Edward Arnold.

Pearce, L. 1995: 'Written on Tablets of Stone': Roland Barthes, Jeanette Winterson and the Discourse of Romantic Love. In S. Raitt (ed.), *Volcanoes and Pearl Divers: Essays in Lesbian Feminist Studies.* London: Onlywomen Press, 147–68.

Pearce, L. 1996: Sexual Politics. In L. Pearce and S. Mills (eds), *Feminist Readings/Feminists Reading.* Hemel Hempstead: Harvester-Wheatsheaf, 23–55.

Pearce, L. 1998: Romantic Love in Contemporary Feminist Fiction. In L. Pearce and G. Wisker (eds), *Fatal Attractions: The Representation of Romance in Contemporary Literature and Film*. London: Pluto, 98–111.

Pearce, L. 2004: Popular Romance and Its Readers. In C. Saunders (ed.), *A Companion to Romance: From Classical to Contemporary*. Oxford: Blackwell, 521–38.

Pearce, L. 2007. After the Twilight: Intimacy and Its Demise in Late Twentieth Century Lesbian Romance. In K. Leydecker and N. White (eds), *After Intimacy: The Culture of Divorce in the West since 1789*. London: Peter Lang.

Pearce, L. and G. Wisker (eds.) 1998: *Fatal Attractions: The Representation of Romance in Contemporary Literature and Film*. London: Pluto.

Penn, A. (dir.) 1967: *Bonnie and Clyde*. US: Warner/Seven Arts.

Piercy, M. 1991: *Body of Glass*. Harmondsworth: Penguin. [Also published in the USA as *He, She and It*. New York and Toronto: Ballantine Books/Random House.]

Poe, E. A. 2003 [1845]: Ligeia. In *Tales of Mystery and Imagination*. London: Collector's Library, 368–88.

Poovey, M. 1984: *The Proper Lady and the Woman Writer: Ideology as Style in the Works of Mary Wollstonecraft, Mary Shelley and Jane Austen*. Chicago: University of Chicago Press.

Porter, R. 2001: *Enlightenment: Britain and the Creation of the Modern World*. London: Penguin.

Price, F. 2004: 'Inconsistent Rhapsodies': Samuel Richardson and the Politics of Romance. In C. Saunders (ed.), *A Companion to Romance: From Classical to Contemporary*. Oxford: Blackwell, 269–86.

Price, H. 1996: *Time's Arrow and Archimedes' Point*. Oxford: Oxford University Press.

Probyn, C. 2004: Paradise and Cotton-Mill: Re-reading Eighteenth-Century Romance. In C. Saunders (ed.), *A Companion to Romance: From Classical to Contemporary*. Oxford: Blackwell, 251–68.

Propp, V. 1968 [1928]: *Morphology of the Folktale*. Trans. L. Scott. Austin, TX and London: University of Texas Press.

Radway, J. 1984: *Reading the Romance: Women, Patriarchy and Popular Literature*. Chapel Hill, NC and London: University of North Carolina Press.

Rich, A. 1977: *Of Woman Born: Motherhood and the Experience of the Institution*. London: Virago.

Rich, A. 1981: *Compulsory Heterosexuality and Lesbian Existence*. London: Onlywomen Press.

Richter, D. H. 1996: *The Progress of Romance: Literary Historiography and the Gothic Novel*. Columbus, OH: Ohio State University Press.

Robertson, P. 1996: *Guilty Pleasures: Feminist Camp from Mae West to Madonna*. London: Tauris.

Rodriguez, R. (dir.) 2005: *Sin City*. US: Dimension Films.

Rose, J. 1986: *Sexuality in the Field of Vision*. London: Verso.

Rousset, J. 1981: *Leurs yeux se rencontrèrent*. Paris: José Corti.

Rule, J. 1992 [1964]: *Desert of the Heart*. Tallahassee, FL: Naiad Press Inc.

Russell, S. 1990: *Render Me My Song: African-American Women Writers from Slavery to the Present*. London: Pandora.

Sartre, J.-P. 1956 [1943]: *Being and Nothingness*. Trans. H. E. Barnes. New York: Philosophical Library.

Saunders, C. 2004a: Introduction. In C. Saunders (ed.), *A Companion to Romance: From Classic to Contemporary*. Oxford: Blackwell, 1–9.

Saunders, C. 2004b: Chaucer's Romances. In C. Saunders (ed.), *A Companion to Romance: From Classical to Contemporary*. Oxford: Blackwell, 85–103.

Schreiner, O. 1911: *Woman and Labour*. London: T. Fisher Unwin.

Schreiner, O. 1924: *The Letters of Olive Schreiner 1876–1920*. Ed. C. Cronwright-Schreiner. London: T. Fisher Unwin.

Schreiner, O. 1971 [1883]: *The Story of an African Farm*. Harmondsworth: Penguin English Library.

Scott, R. (dir.) 1982: *Blade Runner*. US: Warner.

Scott, R. (1993). *Blade Runner: The Director's Cut*. US: Warner/Lad/Bladerunner.

Scott, T. (dir.) 1993: *True Romance*. US: Warner.

Sedgwick, E. 1985: *Between Men: English Literature and Male Homosocial Desire*. New York: Columbia University Press.

Sedgwick, E. 1994: *Tendencies*. Durham, NC: Duke University Press.

Sedgwick, E. 1997: *Novel Gazing: Queer Readings in Fiction*. Durham, NC: Duke University Press.

Shaw, M. 1999: *The Clear Stream: A Life of Winifred Holtby*. London: Virago Press.

Showalter, E. 1977: *A Literature of Their Own: British Women Novelists from Brontë to Lessing*. Princeton, NJ: Princeton University Press.

Showalter, E. 1990: *Sexual Anarchy: Gender and Culture at the Fin de Siècle*. Harmondsworth: Penguin.

Sidney, Sir Philip 1973 [1581–2]: *Astrophil and Stella*. In K. Duncan-Jones (ed.), *Sir Philip Sidney: Selected Poems*. Oxford: Oxford University Press, 117–88.

Simons, J. 2004: Chapbooks and Penny Histories. In C. Saunders (ed.), *A Companion to Romance: From Classical to Contemporary*. Oxford: Blackwell, 177–96.

Sinfield, A. (ed.) 1983: *Society and Literature: 1945–1970*. London: Methuen & Co Ltd.

Singer, I. 1984–7: *The Nature of Love*. 3 vols. Chicago: University of Chicago Press.

Skeggs, B. 2004: *Self, Class, Culture*. London and New York: Routledge.

Soble, A. 1990: *The Structure of Love*. New Haven and London: Yale University Press.

Soueif, A. 1999: *The Map of Love*. London: Bloomsbury.

Spacks, P. M. 1976: *The Female Imagination: A Literary and Psychological Investigation of Women's Writing*. London: Allen and Unwin.

Spencer, J. 1986: *The Rise of the Woman Novelist: From Aphra Behn to Jane Austen*. Oxford: Basil Blackwell.

Spender, D. 1976: *Mothers of the Novel: One Hundred Good Women Writers before Jane Austen*. London: Pandora.

Spooner, C. 2004: *Fashioning Gothic Bodies*. Manchester: Manchester University Press.

Stacey, J. and L. Pearce 1995: The Heart of the Matter: Feminists Revisit Romance. In L. Pearce and J. Stacey (eds), *Romance Revisited*. London: Lawrence and Wishart, 11–45.

Stone, L. 1979: *The Family, Sex and Marriage in England 1500–1800*. Abridged version. Harmondsworth: Penguin Books.

Stone, O. (dir.) 1994: *Natural Born Killers*. US: Warner/Regency.

Stubbs, P. 1981: *Women and Fiction: Feminism and the Novel 1880–1920*. London: Methuen.

Sweet, M. 2002: *Inventing the Victorians*. London: Faber and Faber.

Tanner, T. 1979: *Adultery in the Novel: Contract and Transgression*. Baltimore and London: Johns Hopkins University Press.

Tate, T. 1998: *Modernism, History and the First World War*. Manchester: Manchester University Press.

Taylor, H. 1989: *Scarlett's Women: Gone with the Wind and the Female Fans*. New Brunswick, NJ: Rutgers University Press.

Tennyson, A. 1974 [1850]: *In Memoriam*. In *Tennyson, In Memoriam, Maud and Other Poems*. Ed. J. Jump. London: J. M. Dent, 75–153.

Thornton, A. 1989 [1668]: *A Book of Remembrances*. In E. Graham, H. Hinds, E. Hobby and H. Wilcox (eds), *Her Own Life: Autobiographical Writings by Seventeenth-Century Englishwomen*. London: Routledge, 147–64.

Thynne, L. 1995: The Space between: Daughters and Lovers in *Anne Trister*. In L. Pearce and J. Stacey (eds), *Romance Revisited*. London: Lawrence and Wishart, 103–16.

Tourneur, J. (dir.) 1947: *Out of the Past*. US: RKO.

Verhoeven, P. (dir.) 1990: *Total Recall*. US: Guild/Carolco.

Wadleigh, M. (dir.) 1970: *Woodstock*. US: Warner/Wadleigh-Maurice.

Waller, G. 1984: The Rewriting of Petrarch: Sidney and the Languages of Sixteenth-Century Poetry. In G. Waller and M. D. Moore (eds), *Sir Philip Sidney and the Interpretation of Renaissance Culture*. London: Croom Helm, 69–83.

Watt, I. 1987 [1957]: *The Rise of the Novel*. London: Hogarth Press.

Waugh, P. 1989: *Feminine Fictions: Revisiting the Postmodern*. London: Routledge.

Waugh, P. 1995: *Harvest of the Sixties*. Oxford: Oxford University Press (Opus Books).

Weldon, F. 1984 [1983]: *Lives and Loves of a She-Devil*. London: Coronet Books.

Wheeler, M. 1990: *Death and the Future Life in Victorian Literature and Theology*. Cambridge: Cambridge University Press.

Wheeler, M. 1994: *Heaven, Hell and the Victorians*. Cambridge: Cambridge University Press.

Williamson, J. 1978: *Decoding Advertisements: Ideology and Meaning in Advertising*. London: Marion Boyars.

Winnifrith, T. 1973: *The Brontës and Their Background: Romance and Reality*. London: Macmillan.

Winship, J. 1987: *Inside Women's Magazines*. London: Pandora.

Winterson, J. 1985: *Oranges Are Not the Only Fruit*. London: Pandora.

Winterson, J. 1987: *The Passion*. Harmondsworth: Penguin.

Winterson, J. 1989: *Sexing the Cherry*. London: Bloomsbury.

Wollstonecraft, M. 1976 [1788 and 1798]: *Mary, and The Wrongs of Woman*. Oxford: Oxford University Press.

Woods, G. 1998: *A History of Gay Literature: The Male Tradition*. New Haven and London: Yale University Press.

Wright, E. 1984: *Psychoanalytic Criticism: Theory and Practice*. London: Methuen.

Wright, E. 1992: *Feminism and Psychoanalysis: A Critical Dictionary*. Oxford: Blackwell.

Wrightson, K. 1982: *English Society 1580–1680*. London: Hutchinson.

Wroth, Lady Mary 2002 [1621]: *Pamphilia to Amphilanthus*. In S. Hodgson-Wright (ed.), *Women's Writing of the Early Modern Period, 1588–1688: An Anthology*. Edinburgh: Edinburgh University Press, 143–99.

Young-Bruehl, E. (ed.) 1990: *Freud on Women: A Reader*. London: Hogarth Press.

Index